ALVAR AALTO

Göran Schildt

ALVAR AALTO
The Mature Years

First published in the United States of America in 1991 by
RIZZOLI INTERNATIONAL PUBLICATIONS, INC.
300 Park Avenue South, New York, NY 10010

This book was originally published in Finland by
Otava Publishing Company Ltd under the title:
Inhimillinen tekijä – Alvar Aalto 1939–1976

Library of Congress Cataloging-in-Publication Data

Schildt, Göran, 1917–
   [Mänskliga faktorn. English]
   Alvar Aalto, the mature years / by Göran Schildt.
   p. cm.
   Translation of: Den mänskliga faktorn.

1. Aalto, Alvar, 1898–1976. 2. Architects–Finland–Biography. I. Title.

NA1455.F53A23725 1991 720'.92–dc20 [B] 90-53591

ISBN 0-8478-1329-0

Printed and bound by
Kustannusosakeyhtiö Otavan painolaitokset
Keuruu 1991 Finland

I am skeptical of all verbal reform programmes – they have never led to new ideal societies. However, by advancing from one work to the next we can find the elements for building a new, more harmonious society.

Alvar Aalto, 1956

Contents

Preface

This is part three of the biography of Alvar Aalto that I began working on in 1978. The first volume, *The Early Years*, covered the period from 1898 to 1927: Aalto's family and youth, his cultural background and professional activity up to 1927, when he moved from Jyväskylä to Turku and joined the Rationalist movement in architecture. Part II, *The Decisive Years*, dealt with his life and work up to the outbreak of war in 1939, describing how he came to terms with the Rationalist ideology and achieved an architectural language of his own. The present volume describes Aalto's life and work until his death in 1976.

In contrast with the preceding volumes, Part III, *The Mature Years*, contains no list of works and generally devotes relatively little space to individual architectural projects or problems of form. The main emphasis is on Aalto's personal history and the political, social, and economic circumstances of his life. The reason for this omission is that I hope to publish a fourth and final volume shortly, providing as complete and systematic a description of Aalto's entire body of work in architecture, design, and other fields as can be established with the available material. The cultural and historical emphasis of the present volume will thus receive the architectural complement necessary to provide an overview of Aalto's career.

I am keenly aware that for all its three volumes, my biography can give but a summary of the vast material. At best it will provide a reasonably factual background for specialized studies of individual works and various aspects of Aalto's activity; other scholars have already produced such studies and, more important, will produce more when the sources become available to them. I was fortunate enough to be the first to examine the very extensive documentary material preserved in Aalto's home and architects' office. This material comprises some 200,000 sketches and drawings from his 55-year architectural career as well as perhaps 20,000 incoming and outgoing private and professional letters gathered by secretaries into more than 100 files, which no one had studied systematically before me. The Aalto office also has a large though by no means comprehensive collection of newspaper cuttings from the 1920s on concerning his work and various public appearances. Of special interest were the draft speeches and lectures, shorthand statements and published articles of Aalto which turned up among the papers in his files and drawers or which I tracked down in obscure publications and archives. I have made a dossier of them comprising some 150 texts by Aalto. To fill in the picture, I delved into archives abroad, mainly in the United States and Sweden, and examined drawings owned by clients in Finland and abroad.

Aalto was not interested in his own past, and was not cooperative with anyone who wished to document his work and place it in its historical context. Narcissism or the wish to enshrine himself had nothing to do with why he had such an astonishing wealth of documentary material preserved. He simply needed to keep drawings of previous projects at hand in case enlargements or repairs became necessary or he needed support from old ideas for new designs. He kept his letters as reference material for later correspondence. As for cuttings, they provided hints on how to defend his designs and on who were his allies and adversaries. His consistent and obstinate concentration on the future, on new challenges and projects, thus inadvertently made him his future biographers' best assistant. Moreover, because he made contacts so easily and had such an unforgettable personality, his contemporaries retained vivid memories of him.

The people who surrounded Aalto were in fact among my best sources. In retrospect, now that almost all of his contemporaries are dead and the circle of younger friends is dwindling rapidly, I regret not having recorded more interviews with people who knew him. The list of missed opportunities is long, but so is the list of people I did talk to: both his siblings, now dead; his colleagues Väinö Tuukkanen, Ragnar Ypyä, Harald Wildhagen, Erling Bjertnaes, Hakon Ahlberg, and Hilding Ekelund, all likewise beyond recall. Other friends I have interviewed include Maire Gullichsen, Carola Giedion, James Sweeney, Harmon Goldstone, Betty Church, Vernon de Mars, and a vast number of younger friends and colleagues. The information and views of Aalto's two children, Hanni Alanen and Hamilkar Aalto, were invaluable. I shall not include among my sources the twenty or so surreptitiously recorded conversations between Aalto and myself in the office 'taverna', at my house, or in Muuratsalo, which I discussed in the first volume of this biography. The reason is that I have been unable to bring myself to listen to them. These tapes hardly contain any facts that I do not remember from innumerable unrecorded conversations with Aalto, but all the more of the friendly confidence and intimacy which his death irrevocably cut off. I find it hard to revive this intimacy artificially. Shall I ever dare to listen to those tapes?

In view of my own timidity concerning my painful loss, I fully understand the reserve Elissa Aalto, with so much more reason, has shown towards my work. She has not thwarted it; she has loyally permitted me to examine all of the existing material, but she has not wished to share any confidences or memories

10

with me. In fact she has been opposed to the whole biography from the start, especially its more personal passages. Obviously she could have supplemented the section that deals with the years she shared with Alvar. However, I made Aalto's acquaintance at about the same time that Elissa appeared in his life, so my own insight should partly make up for the gap.

This volume, like the preceding ones, is based on two principal elements: first, facts provided by written records and interviews, and second, my personal relationship with Alvar Aalto the man. His scintillating personality overwhelmed me during our long acquaintance so completely that I could no longer see him objectively, but thought of him rather as an all too close father figure. My work on this biography has greatly enriched me in that it has enabled me to distance myself from Aalto and to achieve greater independence in our relationship without diminishing my affection for him.

Leros, November 14, 1989
Göran Schildt

The Absent Warrior

Alvar Aalto's architectural career began just as Finland was emerging with independence from the turmoil of the First World War. When World War II broke out in 1939, threatening to obliterate that hard-won independence, Aalto was already a famous architect and a respected citizen in his home country. His love for Finland was not just a conscious basic attitude, as it was for most of his countrymen: it also suffused his architecture, turning his World's Fair pavilions in Paris and New York into manifestos of a specific "Finnishness". In 1939 Aalto had plans to publish an arts magazine called *The Human Side,* which was discussed in the second volume of this biography. This journal was to have taken a clear political stand on the Soviet threat to Finland at the time.

One might therefore reasonably have expected Aalto to respond with the same patriotism and self-sacrifice that most Finns showed at the outbreak of the Winter War. He did not. This psychological paradox once again reveals the split or tension in his personality between a deep trauma of hypersensitivity, reserve, and fear of death and an apparent self-confidence, openness, and bravado. Painful memories of the Finnish Civil War in his youth may have contributed to his horror of violence and death. His brother Einar must have borne a similar burden, to judge by his tragic fate that autumn. As we saw in Part I, Einar, the youngest of the Aalto brothers, had bowed to his father's wish that one of his sons should choose an army officer's career. Einar Aalto was a sensitive man with a gift for music and a genuine liking for people: he was ill-suited for the army even in peacetime. He committed suicide shortly after the war broke out, before being ordered to the front. In those militantly patriotic days, the tragedy was of course particularly painful for his family. Their rather far-fetched explanation was that Einar's desperate act was caused by his impatience with not having been sent out to fight soon enough.

Bear in mind that Finland on the threshold of the Winter War was not peopled solely with heroes and battle-hungry warriors. Quite the contrary: most of us hoped for a peaceful solution to the conflict that arose from a Russian ultimatum demanding sizable territorial concessions and military bases within Finland for the Red Army. The moral support of our Scandinavian neighbours and, in fact, the whole western world (with the exception of Germany, bound by its pact with the Russians), kept up our hopes of peace to the very last. However, Finland's resolve to defend herself was strengthened by events in the Baltic states, where concessions to similar demands, coupled with internal Communist agitation, had led to national disasters. Would smaller concessions perhaps suffice? Could foreign pressure persuade Stalin to change his mind? Could we hope for foreign military aid if the worst came to the worst? Meanwhile, those who were prudent began to prepare for an escape to safety in Sweden in the event that the Russians should actually occupy Finland. They started sounding out transport alternatives and escape routes. Some even decided to leave while it was still permitted and easy to do. And that is exactly what Alvar Aalto and his family did.

As we remember from Part I, Aalto had been trained as a reserve officer in 1922. Like any able-bodied man, he was expected to do his duty when the time came. His military passport said he should report to headquarters in Kuopio to receive arms in the event of mobilization. But here he was in a hotel in Stockholm, panic-stricken. The Aalto archives contain an undated letter from Maire Gullichsen to Aalto in Stockholm; it captures the atmosphere in Finland in those days very vividly.

Dear Aino and Alvar,

It is now too late for us to come to Sweden. Harry has been called up and we are expecting general mobilization any day. The atmosphere is terribly serious, yet calm, collected, and firmly resolute. Evacuation of the cities has led to a touch of panic here and there, but everything is going surprisingly well overall. I am staying here (at the Villa Mairea) *for the time being with all the women and children of the family. If things turn out really badly, the Ilmatar* (a passenger ferry plying between Finland and Sweden) *is in Mäntyluoto, and will start regular service to Sundsvall if war breaks out. If so, I am planning to take the children to Sweden and then return to Finland. I will stay home as long as possible – beyond that, all is uncertain. We are still very hopeful that things will turn out all right. But we must prepare for the worst. I love you both and my thoughts follow you at all times. Maire.*

1. Aalto designed one of the most harrowing war memorials in Finland, twenty years after the war. It was erected in 1959 on the battleground at Suomussalmi, where Finnish troops annihilated an invading Soviet corps of 20,000 men which was trying to cut Finland in half. Photo: Göran Schildt.

Aalto's dilemma was compounded by his inability to admit his trauma either to himself or to others. In everything he did, and thus also as an officer and a defender of his country, he had to be a he-man and top dog. When the mobilization order finally came, he had no alternative but to return to Finland and go to Kuopio, where he was handed a second lieutenant's uniform. We do not know why he was not sent to the front from Kuopio. Whatever the reason, he reacted differently from most of us who were called up. We put on our uniform unwillingly, and were all aware of the disadvantage we were at against the powerful Soviet Union, but the Russian attack on November 30 left us no

14

choice. When Stalin installed a Communist puppet government of Finland in
the border village of Terijoki, even the most credulous among us understood
that the Russians were looking for something more than an honourable
settlement. Our resistance was desperate, and therefore unexpectedly successful. International support, embodied in the League of Nations' condemnation
of the invasion, and the flow of volunteers from many countries aroused the
desperate hope that all was not lost yet. The World War was not yet in full swing
in Europe; Hitler and Stalin, in accordance with their pact, had merely divided
up the countries that stood between them, and in the west the opposing armies

15

2. Pencil study for the Suomussalmi Memorial. Wilderness pine devastated by artillery fire, with snow-clad, roadless fells in the background.

stood guard on either side of the Maginot line. The world's attention was thus free to focus on the poignant struggle between David and Goliath, between Finland's brave defenders and the Red Army, which was suffering unexpected setbacks in the snowy wilderness. Before the world's admiring eyes, the Finnish soldiers were transformed, to their own surprise, into something they had never expected to be.

Aalto, though a born actor, was not swept along by the tide, which shows the strength of the psychosis he suffered from. Instead of acquiescing with the

3. Pencil study for Suomussalmi Memorial. The bronze column, twenty-five feet high and weighing nearly 4,000 pounds, evokes both blown-up pine trees and wisps of smoke driven by the wind.

transfer to the front he could expect, he used his connections to get himself transferred to a safe job with the Government Information Centre in Helsinki. His own version of the transfer was naturally more heroic. It started with the assertion that he had been assigned to sort out army boots in Kuopio, but had considered this task insufficiently patriotic, and had therefore cabled his friend Lawrence Rockefeller in New York: SEND LAFAYETTE FIGHTER PLANE CORPS TO HELP US AALTO. A few days later, so the story went, a letter addressed to the Government of Finland arrived, containing a check for a million dollars and the request "say hello to Aalto", which prompted someone high up to recommend the miraculous intermediary for special service in the capital.

There can of course be no doubt that Aalto did his country a greater service by working to obtain material and moral support for Finland from abroad through his influential contacts in the United States, Britain, Switzerland, and Scandinavia than he could have done by risking his life as an officer at the front. This was not, however, easy for all his friends to accept at a time when courage and self-sacrifice were expected from all. Aalto's apparent egotism, culminating in March 1940, with the war at its height, in his using every concervable connection to arrange to be ordered to the United States, aroused misgivings in many people.

The ostensible reason for his flight was a series of propaganda talks that his American friends had promised to arrange at various universities. The urgent telegrams sent to Helsinki on the subject by Rockefeller, Harrison, Sweeney,

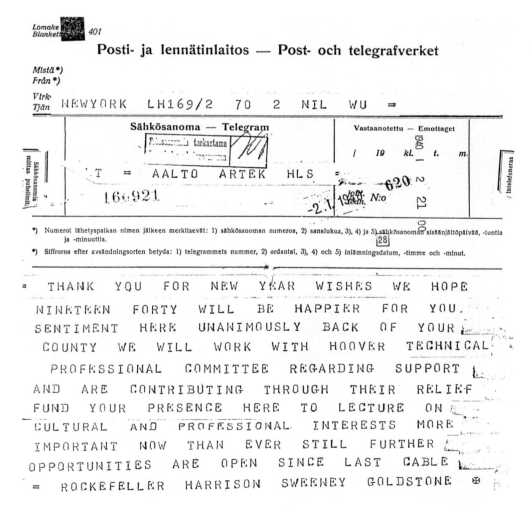

4. A telegram that Aalto received during the Winter War from his American friends.

and Goldstone suggest an unspoken desire to save Aalto from Finland's sinking ship as much as sympathy for the threatened country. Taking Aino and both children with him, Aalto left for Sweden on March 4, and embarked on the *Drottningholm* passenger liner in Gothenburg. The harsh yet nonetheless honourable peace treaty between Finland and the Soviet Union, to which Stalin agreed rather than risk having a British army unit land in Scandinavia to fight for Finland, was signed while Aalto was in the middle of the Atlantic.

Aalto's order called for a six-week stay in the United States. With peace, demobilization, and the reconstruction problems involved in returning to civilian life, it was both hoped and expected that he would soon return to Finland. Instead he made a determined effort to obtain a professorship at the Massachusetts Institute of Technology (MIT) in Boston, neglecting one opportunity after the other to return to Finland on one of the freighters that still regularly plied between Petsamo, Finland's port on the Arctic Ocean, and the U.S. In several letters to Aalto in the United States, his loyal friend Maire Gullichsen again tried to persuade him to do the right thing. On August 6, 1940 she wrote:

Yes, dear Alvar, we hope that you will come home some day, at any rate. Many think that you are going to stay there, but it would be too sad to believe . . .

On August 26, 1940 she made another appeal:

Dear Aino and Alvar,

We cannot help feeling a little disappointed about the new postponement of your journey and do not quite understand the reason. Are there particular rumours about a danger factor? (MG is referring particularly to the ever-present threat of a Soviet occupation.) *Or is it the danger of the voyage, which is of course full of risk? But all the Finnish ships have reached harbour and the* Mathilda Thordén, *which we thought you would be on, is expected home any day . . . Frankly I must say that I believe it would be very important for you to come home to get a clear idea of the situation for yourself. You remember we spoke last winter of the important western front for which you left. Now the home front is the most important one, and the question of how to keep it under control.* (MG is referring to the delicate balance between the need to fulfil the terms of the armistice with the Russians and efforts to avert the threat of a Russian occupation with the help of a German presence in the country.) *This could be a great task for you, Alvar. We need your wisdom and your initiative more than ever. I may sound a little bitter in saying all this, but it is not so good to fight alone here. We are living under constant pressure, sometimes stronger, sometimes weaker. But if we are to resist it in the long run, we shall need all our constructive forces . . . Home at Mairea for a few days for the first time in a long time. The house is lying still and purring like a large luxury cat in the silence. Harry is at a fair in Leipzig; we are tending increasingly towards German cooking. Dear Alvar, there is much that I wanted to say to you, but I no longer know if I have the right to do so . . . I will stop now in the meagre hope that this letter will no longer reach you, and that you are on your way home on the next Thordén boat. Maire.*

Aalto refused to be moved, but on October 8 he received the following cable from his military superiors through the Finnish Embassy: RES. 2ND LIEUTENANT

AALTO ORDERED TO RETURN TO HIS POST. Just over a month later, on November 11, 1940, the Aalto family landed in Petsamo in Finnish territory. On hearing the news, Aalto's Swedish friends jokingly said that the signal "Danger over" had really sounded for Finland (interview with Hakon Ahlberg, September 6, 1978).

Unfortunately, however, this was not the case. The "Continuation War" broke out in June 1941. During it the Finnish Army, together with the Germans, reconquered the lost territory in Karelia and occupied Russian Karelia all the way to Lake Onega. Once again Aalto found more important things to do than fighting at the front with most other able-bodied Finnish architects.

I shall try to show later how useful Aalto's peaceful activity during the war was both for himself and for his country, and what a fascinating chapter these years constituted in his life, but as a contrast I shall also recount the tragic consequences of his behaviour for one of his closest associates, Nils-Gustav Hahl. Perhaps I should add here that my own course of action during the war differed so much from Aalto's that I am inclined to sympathize with Hahl in this matter.

As we saw in the second volume of this biography, Hahl was the initiator and titular head of the Artek company, and managed the sales of Aalto furniture. Hahl's own conception of his role appears from a letter (dated April 24, 1936) to Maire Gullichsen, in which he said "Aalto will be the soul, Artek the body, and I the hand" in the venture they were about to embark upon. In practice it turned out that Artek had two directors, Hahl and Aino Aalto, who had her own views and plans on all matters. Hahl had started out as one of Aalto's blind admirers who always smoothed the master's path and unselfishly worked on his behalf, but over the years he became increasingly critical of Aalto the human being. Hahl's view was that Artek should act as a public relations centre for a modern social ideal and for the design of the public and private environment that went with it. He admired Aalto's contribution to this ideal, but thought that Artek should not exist solely to promote Aalto's interests. He felt that Artek should cover the whole modern design movement of which Aalto was only one part. As Pekka Suhonen writes in his 50th anniversary book on Artek, Hahl pleaded in 1941 for closer contact with the popular movements, and furniture production that would be more acceptable to the rural population than that Artek had offered during the prewar years. In other words, he hoped to offset Aalto's elitism, centred on his own creative work, with a more conventional counterbalance aimed at ordinary people.

The growing tension between Aalto and his managing director resulted, among other things, in Aino categorically refusing to grant Hahl a three months' paid leave he requested in order to complete his doctoral thesis on the painter Magnus Enckell. Hahl's attitude in the days of the Winter War, when Aalto sat in Helsinki restaurants talking about how his cultural journal *The Human Side* would save Finland, appears from a letter (January 1, 1940) he sent to Maire Gullichsen:

The changed circumstances (that is, the outbreak of war) *do not seem to have changed his bad habits. He was perhaps a little tipsy, but most optimistic. Of course I believe in the importance of his idea* (The Human Side), *although I turned down all his proposals for collaboration. Think he should for once carry something through by himself. To be honest, there was another reason for my refusal: all of his plans involve a certain measure of fantasy – "artistic" ditto if you will – and his working habits have kept that Bohemian aspect which can be so charming but is dubious right now. For these reasons I find that he does not have the self-discipline and level-headedness that I absolutely require of my working environment for as long as this war goes on. Besides, according to many witnesses he is nervous about the unease in the air, and I feel that is improper.* (This last comment was confirmed by others: at the first indication of enemy overflight Aalto precipitately headed for the nearest air-raid shelter.)

Hahl was released from active duty for reasons of health, but he volunteered during the Winter War for service at the front as an interpreter and orderly with an ambulance sent by English Quakers. We may guess how he felt about Aalto's trip to the United States. When war broke out again in the summer of 1941, he reenlisted for service as a medical orderly in Hanko. This had nothing to do with the enthusiasm for fighting side by side with the Germans which was spreading throughout Finland at the time, as is shown by a letter he wrote to Maire Gullichsen on July 7, just before he set out. The letter begins with practical worries concerning Artek's operations, then continues:

Discussed these concerns with Puhakka (head of the furniture factory). *He is, however, filled with a happiness that transcends all ordinary joys and sorrows, the spirit of a great righting of wrongs. As you know, I look on the matter as you do; I have given up trying to find our position on the great chessboard. When the task at hand is done* (that is, when Finland has regained its lost territory and safeguarded its existence), *another question, at least as thorny, will follow concerning the future of our country* (in relation to a victorious Germany). *Today we must bite into a sour, green apple in the hope that it will ripen and taste sweet before we have swallowed the last morsel. And that we shall be able to spit out the core itself, so that it does not take root at home and grow out of our control.*

There were surely many reasons for Hahl's eagerness to volunteer for service, but one of them seems to have been the urge to protest against Aalto's merely verbal patriotism. Two pieces of evidence suggest this. The last words of his last field message to Maire Gullichsen, before he took part in a bloody landing on an island off Hanko, were: "Heard nothing from the Aaltos. Is Alvar not at the front? Misinformed." When it became known soon after that Hahl had not returned, his widow Gunnel received a visit from a very distressed Aino Aalto, who said: "Have I sent him to his death?" (Quote from a letter dated January 10, 1986, from Gunnel Gummerus to the author).

A few comments are in order after this unflattering account of Aalto's actions. First, Hahl felt that Artek was focusing too much on Aalto's work. Obviously Giedion's Zurich company Wohnbedarf, with its broadly Modernist orientation and its ideal of promoting a progressive mentality rather than individual designers, corresponded with Hahl's own goals as well as Artek's explicit

5. In spring 1941, a 'marching match' was arranged between Finland and Sweden. The winner was to be the country that could call up a greater number of civilians to walk a marathon under controlled conditions. Finland won overwhelmingly. The picture shows Aalto's office at the time of the competition. Left to right: Alvar Aalto, Trygve Ahlström (killed in the Continuation War), Diedrich Dahlberg, Otto Murtomaa, Paul Bernoulli, Poul Hansen (killed in the Continuation War).

programme. Artek's practical focus on Aalto design, however, had less to do with manipulation by the Aaltos than with the fact that Aalto's designs were so unique and in such high demand that they were the very reason Artek was set up in the first place, and for fifty years they have continued to be the company's raison d'être.

My other comment concerns Hahl's complaint "all of his plans involve a certain measure of fantasy – 'artistic' ditto if you will." This is literally true, not only in various projects such as *The Human Side,* the construction of *An American Town in Finland,* and Aalto's wartime proposal of an 'Architectural Training Institute' that I will later discuss in detail. The same goes for Aalto's architectural projects, both those which never got off the drawing-board and those that were built. He always transcended the obvious realities to a magnificent vision of fundamental significance that others could not see until he gave it form. In the first volume, I told the story of how Aalto learned from his childhood idol August Nyberg to elevate the merest boyish prank to the heroic level of the Trojan War, and how he was likewise able to infuse even the most unpromising architectural projects with enhanced significance. This quality, which made social contact with him so stimulating and gave his creations their special lustre, could naturally be irritating in the urgency and total antipathy to playfulness of the war years, as Hahl's reaction shows. With the advantage of fifty years' hindsight and a more relaxed atmosphere for examining Aalto's wartime actions, we are more apt to be amused and impressed by the "artistic fantasies" of an unusually resourceful, basically positive genius.

After this overview of Aalto's wartime activities, I should like to go into greater detail concerning his actual contribution to the war effort.

The Founding of Office A

Aalto seems to have been released from military duty in Kuopio in early December 1939 and designated a propaganda agent under Minister of Social Affairs K.A. Fagerholm by special order. He was assigned to an air raid shelter in Meilahti, just outside Helsinki. On December 20, his position was 'normalized': he was placed formally under the Government Information Centre, but given an independent unit of his own, *Office A*, to direct. Probably no one in the Finnish Army achieved greater personal freedom in those days of heavy duties. He lived at home, looked after by the family housekeeper. Aino and the children had been evacuated to Bogaskär island near Pori, where they lived in a building belonging to the Ahlström family. The architects' office functioned as best it could, run by the remaining female employees, and *Office A*'s affairs were managed from there as much as from the government's air raid shelter.

Aalto also became a member of an unofficial committee that called itself the *Kolkhoz Brothers* and included trade union leaders such as Eero Wuori and K.A. Fagerholm as well as leading industrialists like Harry Gullichsen, Åke Gartz, and William Lehtinen. They promoted national solidarity and labour-management consensus across party lines, both necessary for a concerted war effort. The group continued to meet for twenty years after the war.

The important, perhaps crucial service for the future of his country that Aalto had persuaded his superiors he could perform consisted first of turning his newly conceived international journal, *The Human Side,* into a propaganda vehicle for Finland. His reasoning was that Finland was not fighting just for her own interests but on behalf of all western civilization. This was therefore a common struggle in which all freedom-loving nations must unite to ward off the Bolshevist threat to the world in what Aalto did not hesitate to call "a war of religion" (for a more detailed discussion, see pp. 182–186 in *The Decisive Years*). As we already know, The Human Side remained a beautiful but unrealized dream.

Another aspect of *Office A*'s work consisted of Aalto sending letters and cables

6. A chief of staff studying his maps? No, Alvar and Aino Aalto preparing for peacetime reconstruction while the war still rages.

to his many influential friends abroad, pleading for active help for Finland. A memorandum prepared by Aalto for his superiors contains an impressive list of members of the international cultural and financial elite he contacted. On it are the Museum of Modern Art circle including the Rockefellers, Frank Lloyd Wright, Lewis Mumford, and Buckminster Fuller in the United States; Giedion and Hélène de Mandrot in Switzerland; Le Corbusier and Léger in France; Morton Shand in Britain; and innumerable friends of friends such as Edsel Ford, Conger Goodyear, Eugene O'Neill, Sinclair Lewis, Ernest Hemingway, John Steinbeck, Bernard Shaw, and perhaps a hundred ordinary mortals.

The gist of the message to these addressees was summed up almost surrealistically by the New Year's telegram Aalto sent Lawrence Rockefeller in New York:

DEAR FRIEND BEST WISHES FOR A HAPPY NEW YEAR TO YOU AND MRS ROCKEFELLER I TRUST OUR NEWYEAR WILL BE MORE SATISFACTORY THAN ONE MIGHT THINK OWING TO THE UNITY OF WILL ALL CLASSES AND NATURAL MAGINOT LINE OF OUR 100,000 LAKES BETTER THAN ANY ARTIFICIAL ONE I BELIEVE THIS TO BE AMERICAS AND NORTHERN EUROPES COMMON STRUGGLE FOR BALANCED SOCIAL EVOLUTION WHERE INDIVIDUALS AND MASSES TAKE RIGHT PROPORTIONS TO EACH OTHER AGAINST A POLICETERROR WHICH LONG AGO HAS LOST IDEOLOGICAL SOCIAL AIM AND PRACTICALLY FOR MANY YEARS HAS GONE BACKWARDS LEAVING THE PEOPLE TO A SUFFERENCE WHICH THEY NOW WANT TO BESTOW UPON US I HOPE ESPECIALLY YOU CAN HELP US FIND PLAN SAVE MY COUNTRY AND ALL OTHERS FROM THIS UNACCEPTABLE FUTURE YOURS AALTO.

This propagandist's name would not have been Aalto if he had not come up with a most original idea for how the assistance to Finland should best be arranged. He called it "a new kind of active Red Cross". His reasoning went thus: During the early weeks of the Winter War, Russian aircraft had laid waste to Finnish towns and villages far behind the frontlines, as Finland had virtually no antiaircraft capability. The enemy was able to bomb the civilian population unhindered, and, worse still, shoot from a low altitude. Such terror was not yet commonplace at this early stage of the war – as is well known, the German bombardment of England was the first to break the old, unwritten law of sparing women and children. Aalto knew that neutral countries, such as the United States and Switzerland, balked at giving Finland anything beyond "humanitarian" aid, and therefore suggested that if these countries raised funds to send Finland interceptors and fighter aircraft with a view to protecting the civilian population, guarantees would be given that these planes would not be used at the front or for offensive purposes, but would serve only to protect the civilian population.

7. A corner of the Artek Pascoe sales outlet on Madison Avenue, New York, 1940.

Here again, Aalto was overshooting the mark somewhat, as Lawrence Rockefeller's cabled reply of January 24 suggests:

AIRPLANES MEN MUNITIONS OUT OF OUR PROVINCE STOP HAND YOUR CABLES TO HOOVER COMMITTEE TO PUT IN PROPER HANDS TO EFFECT SOMETHING IF POSSIBLE ALONG LINES SUGGESTED STOP PERSONALLY WE ARE GLAD TO DO ANYTHING IN OUR SCOPE FOR CULTURAL RELATIONS.

In Sweden, however, Gunnar Asplund succeeded in raising a considerable sum for the purpose from building professionals, and Norwegian architects also contributed to fighter planes for Finland without having to appeal to the concept of a "humanitarian", fighting, airborne Red Cross.

On the whole it is clear that all of Aalto's efforts during the Winter War led to very few concrete results. As far as the United States was concerned, this was partly because the Rockefellers' financial aid was channelled through the Hoover Committee for Finland, which was active throughout the country. But it also had to do with American hesitation to make commitments to Finland. The 20,000 members of the Hoover Committee managed to scrape together a mere two million dollars despite almost daily reports in the newspapers of the brave struggle put up by a small country; the more aggressive Fighting Fund for Finland raised only 300,000 dollars. It is symptomatic that when the Boston Society of Architects started a subscription among its membership, the grand total came to $25, which was solemnly presented to the Finnish Embassy.

In his 1941 book *Kontakt med Amerika* (Contacts with America), Gunnar Myrdal explains the reasons for this cold-blooded attitude. On the one hand, U.S. neutrality laws had just come into effect, and Finland was the first test case. Isolationism was still firmly rooted, and Roosevelt could keep up deliveries to Finland only by the fiction of declaring Finland a "non-belligerent". Herbert Hoover, who headed the fundraising effort, was not a popular figure, and the public suspected that his humanitarian activities were only aimed at a presidential comeback. What is more, the Americans were not sure how democratic Finland really was: memories of the 1918 Civil War still lingered at the back of their minds.

The Finnish lobby thus struggled against a strong headwind in the United States until Finland reentered the war at Germany's side in the summer of 1941, which led to a complete freeze in relations. We should note, however, that the United States, unlike Great Britain, did not break off diplomatic relations with our country during the Continuation War; the PR campaign of the Winter War had achieved something after all.

An American Town in Finland

In the previously mentioned memorandum by Aalto concerning his activities during the Winter War, he emphasized in various ways that letters are not as effective as personal meetings, and overall that it would be extremely useful for "someone" from Finland to travel to the United States to lecture at universities about Finland's harmonious social conditions, and generally to bring the right kind of pressure to bear on influential American circles. This would also provide a suitable opportunity for taking the housing exhibition that had opened in Helsinki in autumn 1939 (cf. *The Decisive Years,* pp. 181–182) to the United States, where it could be called "What Finland Is Fighting For". The Finnish pavilion at the New York World's Fair would also remain open for another summer, and could be furnished with new informative material. What could be more appropriate under these circumstances than for *Office A*'s intrepid chief, familiar as he was with American ways, to be sent to the United States? And what could be more natural than his unwillingness to leave his wife and children in Finland, struggling as it was at the brink of collapse?

Aalto's knack for adapting rapidly to new situations was phenomenal throughout his life. Even as he was leaving, he told Maire Gullichsen that she need not bother with *The Human Side* any more (though she had recently been talked into investing large sums of money in it). Other projects would take precedence. And of course Aalto came out with a whole slew of projects as soon as he had found his bearings in the United States.

His first, basically private project involved the sale of his furniture and glassware in the United States by (as it would soon turn out) the rather too smart businessman Clifford Pascoe. The company *Artek Pascoe Inc. Contemporary Furniture,* with Pascoe as CEO, was set up in New York City at 640 Madison Avenue. Co-owners with Pascoe were Artek and Maire Gullichsen in Helsinki. The first consignment left Finland March 23, and sales were most promising. At this time it was still possible to export a limited amount of

8. James Sweeney and Alvar Aalto at Cape Cod in the 1940s. Photo: Aino Aalto.

goods from Finland's Arctic seaport, Petsamo; production of Aalto furniture also began at the Eggers works in Wisconsin. The American Aalto furniture, however, was of very uneven quality. San Francisco architect Thomas Church, who retailed the furniture, wrote in a letter in 1941 that the last genuine Aalto furniture from Finland had been snapped up at high prices as veritable museum pieces.

Business, however, was not Aalto's strong suit, nor did he take a particular interest in it. His stay in the United States was marked from the start by occupations that were both more pleasant and more high-flown. Foremost were the social contacts with influential people that Aalto always maintained with gusto and which provided the seed bed from which his creative ideas could spring up towards the sky. Aino Aalto's brief calendar notes give some idea of the events of their visit to the United States in 1940.

Apparently they managed to meet their best friends in the United States on March 19, the very day they landed in New York. They had lunch with James and

9. At Wallace and Ellen Harrison's on Long Island. Aalto's daughter Hanni on the seesaw.

10. At the Kaufmanns' House in Bear Run. Photo: Aino Aalto.

11. The Rockefellers' bathing area in Tarrytown. Photo: Aino Aalto.

12. Nelson Rockefeller's guesthouse. Photo: Aino Aalto.

Laura Sweeney* and dinner with Sandy Calder. Other friends who appeared very soon to welcome Aalto included Eliel Saarinen and his entire family, Sigfried Giedion, Buckminster Fuller, William Lescaze, Lewis Mumford, Harmon Goldstone, and John McAndrew, to cite some of the people named previously in this biography.

The Aaltos spent most of their weekends that spring and summer in the country with various friends. In April they visited Howard Myers in Bronxville, in May they stayed with a Mr. Pomerance on Cape Cod, with Wallace and Ellen Harrison on Long Island, and with Edward Kaufmann Jr. at Fallingwater, the house designed by Frank Lloyd Wright in Bear Run, Pennsylvania. In June they stayed with the Fordyces in Leicester, and had the experience of meeting a large part of the Rockefeller family at their country estate in Tarrytown. During a very hot July, they visited the Lescazes in New Jersey, the Storonow family's Broadwater Farm in Phoenixville, Pennsylvania, and the Gropiuses in Lincoln. From August 3 to 22 they had the Kaufmann guesthouse in Bear Run at their disposal. They then spent a weekend with the Saarinens in Cranbrook, followed by visits to Buffalo and Niagara Falls.

It could not have been easy for Aalto, who was living on a shoestring budget, to associate with all these millionaires and highly paid professionals, especially as Alvar always wished to appear as a gentleman of the first rank. In New York they stayed at the small but reputable Wyndham Hotel, just a stone's throw from the Plaza Hotel. His honoraria for lectures at various universities were between 150 and 250 dollars. The Finnish government also paid him $500 through the Finnish Embassy.

These weekend excursions may give the impression of just so many pleasant, idle holidays. In fact Aalto had an astonishingly intense and varied programme. Reorganization of the Finnish pavilion at the New York World's Fair, which reopened on May 11, his PR speeches in Brooklyn Church on May 12, at a Finnish Folk Festival in Central Park on June 16, and at a Finland Day in the World's Fair exhibition area on Midsummer Day with Mrs. Roosevelt in the seat of honour: these were mere trifles. More important were his university lectures. His tour began at MIT and proceeded via Yale, Princeton, the Pratt Institute, Dartmouth, the Summer Art School in Somerset, and the Cranbrook School back to MIT in October. The theme of most of these lectures was the

*James Sweeney, who was head of the department of painting and sculpture at the Museum of Modern Art for many years, and later became director of the Guggenheim Museum, came from a wealthy Irish-American family. His magnificent home with a rooftop garden at 120 East End Avenue, New York City, was a second home for Alvar and Aino Aalto during all their visits to the United States. When the present author visited the house in 1981, it was filled with paintings by Picasso, Mondrian, and other painter friends. Sweeney had suffered a stroke and was very depressed by his wife's death. He could dig up little in the way of concrete information about his long friendship with Aalto, but an astonishing circumstance bore witness to how close they had been more eloquently than all words: Sweeney's way of telling stories with assumed innocence, understatement, well-timed emphasis, and a very special sense of humour were so uncannily reminiscent of his Finnish friend that one could almost think one was listening to Aalto. I still wonder which of them imitated the other.

reconstruction of Finland, a subject that Aalto gradually developed until he made it a course he taught during his professorship at MIT. Now is the time to recount how this transformation came about.

You will recall that the Winter War was at its height when Aalto left Finland. By the time that he landed in New York, Finland had signed a peace treaty with the Soviet Union, and Aalto's plan to seek help for the defensive war had lost its point. Instead, Finland faced hard times in recovering from the devastation of the war and in looking after the evacuees from the territory ceded to the Russians. When Aalto met Lawrence Rockefeller a few days after his arrival, he no longer wanted financing for "humanitarian fighter planes" from the Rockefeller Foundation, which had been founded by Lawrence's grandfather. Instead, Aalto took up a project he thought should appeal to the technology-minded Americans. He suggested that the Helsinki Institute of Technology, an institution dear to his heart that had been virtually levelled by bombs, should be rebuilt with Rockefeller money.

Professor John Burchard of MIT wrote an amazingly frank report (in the MIT archives in Cambridge, Mass.) of Aalto's negotiations with the Rockefeller Foundation. The report begins with this remark: "Aalto has had excellent connections with the Rockefellers ever since he first came over here, first through Wallace Harrison (Lawrence Rockefeller's brother-in-law) and subsequently through his own personality." Burchard goes on to say that the directors of the Foundation turned down reconstruction of the Helsinki Institute of Technology because the purpose was not sufficiently humanitarian. Aalto then came up with another proposal: the Foundation should pay for the construction of a small new town in Finland for Karelian refugees. This suggestion, too, was found unacceptable, as it had no link with either the United States or with subjects of general interest, such as science or art. Aalto's next move was truly ingenious: the Foundation should defray the expenses of a scientific research laboratory for housing construction at a U.S. university, at the same time allowing this laboratory to test its theories in full scale in various parts of the world. Finland would provide an ideal location for the first experimental town, having been the very first country to suffer large-scale destruction during the continuing war. Now that it had concluded peace, Finland had complex reconstruction problems to solve. The experience obtained from building an experimental town in Finland and the methods that could be tested there would be invaluable for other countries when the day dawned for rebuilding their war-torn areas.

This time the gentlemen at the Foundation listened with pronounced interest, especially when Aalto embellished his proposal with concrete details, such as that the Finnish government would make land available for the experiment, answer for the basic costs of road construction, water supply, etc., and grant loans of up to 50 % for the buildings, which would ultimately be sold to the inhabitants, freeing up funds to build another experimental town somewhere else. The main profit would consist of scientific experience, which could then be passed on to the American construction industry.

Aalto elaborated on this idea in a lecture he gave at MIT on April 25. John Burchard, head of the MIT-affiliated Albert Farwell Bemis Foundation for Low Cost Housing, had invited his Finnish colleague to speak. Aalto made his pitch in his usual extravagant style. Not only did he introduce himself to an interviewer from the leading Boston newspaper as "Finland's leading architect and most outstanding non-political figure"; he also claimed that the Finnish government had appointed him to head the whole reconstruction effort.

In his lecture at MIT, he said that 500,000 Finns were homeless, that "from 8 to 12 completely new towns must be built in new locations", and that "20 new hospitals and 200 school buildings were needed for the evacuated population". The Finnish Embassy in Washington had provided Aalto with the basic facts concerning the extent of the destruction. The most pressing need, however,

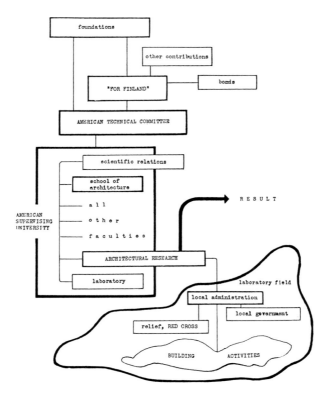

13. Organizational schema for the combined research centre and experimental building site suggested by Aalto to MIT.

was for an unprecedented quantity of housing to be built without delay. The crucial problem was to avoid repeating the mistake made in continental Europe after World War I, where temporary tenement housing was erected initially and torn down when the worst distress was over. This was replaced with housing that was somewhat better but still unsatisfactory, and again had to be replaced. This stagewise construction proved both uneconomical and directly harmful, as it resulted in disease, social tensions, and what Aalto called "psychological slums". He continued:

These problems can be solved by setting up an Institute for Architectural Research, where we can experiment with flexible standardization, permitting variation in spite, or rather because of the fact that the building components are mass-produced. This kind of construction system can also be developed by starting with the construction of the simplest type of housing, 'a roof over one's head', subsequently providing it with 'warmth and light', and then with amenities and generally better materials, finally giving rise to a fully-equipped modern home without having to demolish anything previously built.

Aalto pointed out that Finland primarily needed single-family houses built of wood, but that it should be possible to develop similar methods for apartment houses using building materials such as concrete and steel.

It is not clear whether Aalto was already hoping to carry out his idea of a laboratory at MIT when he gave this lecture. Be that as it may, when the Rockefeller Foundation's interest in the project became known two months later, John Burchard sent a letter to his school's board of directors, suggesting that Aalto should be appointed professor at MIT. Burchard wrote:

While it is obviously not possible to say that if we appoint Aalto the Rockefeller grant will follow, it is true that they seem very interested in this general proposal and I think it is safe to say that this work will not be undertaken at the MIT without Aalto, because I believe he represents the key to the Foundation in this connection.

Aalto's idea of linking an experimental town with a scientific institution had obvious advantages from his own point of view. For one thing, it opened up the possibility of substantial U.S. aid to Finland. Hjalmar J. Procopé, who was Ambassador of Finland to Washington, called the idea "quite simply brilliant" in a letter to Maire Gullichsen, and was happy to accept an honorary membership, together with Eliel Saarinen, on the American Architects Committee for an American Town in Finland, which was set up in July. It turned out that the gentlemen of the Rockefeller Foundation continued to hesitate, but by then Aalto had already been appointed professor at MIT, with his own experimental department to direct. The project for an American town in Finland had received the official stamp of approval in Finland, and the city of Tampere had designated an ideal land area for the purpose on its outskirts. If the Rockefeller Foundation did not appropriate the money, it would be raised in some other way in the United States. In the first telegram Aalto sent to Finland on the subject, he spoke of "an experimental town for 1000 families" and announced that "the Rockefeller Foundation is sending observers to Finland". A later cable dated May 31 speaks of only 40 families. The Continuation War, fought by Finland on Germany's side, eventually took the wind from the project's sails, but this was no fault of Aalto's. However fanciful the project may have seemed at the outset, it might have been feasible under different circumstances. In an article dated May 31, Aalto outlined the philosophy on which he based the plan. This turned out to be an elaboration of the programme he had set out for his colleagues in San Francisco the preceding year (cf. *The Decisive Years*, p. 178). The key passages deserve to be quoted in full, as they explain an attitude that was fundamental to him throughout his life:

In all architectural training, the student's contact with the living realities of construction is of the utmost importance. There can be no doubt that students today have far too little of such contact, even though practice in various branches of the construction industry and at architects' offices is compulsory in training. It should in fact be organized in such a way that the student would first be trained in rational thinking and then be allowed to put into practice the ideas that primary thinking has led him to adopt.

Conventional architectural activity also needs to have a broader emphasis on research to achieve results of value. Architects must concentrate more on scientific methods for finding the correct solutions. Both the training of architects and practical construction thus have the same need for organized research.

In architectural training, construction with the emphasis on research can be done only to a limited extent by schools. The reason is that architectural research calls for a simultaneous consideration of all constituent parts, from the town plan, the grouping of buildings, and traffic issues to the building itself, with its construction details, industrial design, and interior decoration, to which we must add the study of human psychological and physiological reactions to all of the above. RESEARCH AS A COMPONENT OF INSTRUCTION IS POSSIBLE ONLY IN DIRECT CONTACT WITH REAL BUILDING.

Such building, however, is of no use to research without the support of a central institution, in which the results are evaluated and combined, and methods for new research are devised.

14. Schematic sketch of "An American Town in Finland": b) indicates an administrative and commercial centre; a) single-family homes, rowhouses, and apartment houses; c) schools and sports fields. After these are built, the type houses are to be further developed in areas d), e), and f). The houses are related to those already built in Sunila and Kauttua, i.e., single-family homes, 'slope houses' of the ROT type, and terrace houses.

If we could conceive of a technical institution that existed not merely to provide instruction but equally to act as a centre for general progress, it would be clear that centralization of all kinds of research performed in conjunction with real construction could be achieved best by a technical institution already having an active architecture department.

I know of no other technical academy in the world better suited to such an activity than MIT. The institute has all the tradition needed for the purpose, and the fact that it has various forms of technological research and laboratories working closely together with a school of architecture makes conditions there particularly propitious.

If MIT could organize research at various locations and even in various parts of the world, and if the results of this research could be assembled, compared, and combined at MIT, to be used as teaching material at the school, we would have every reason to expect excellent results.

Financially this could be done without burdening the school with extra expenses: research could be based on a system I have used in building in my home country. This system is based on the principle of designating ten per cent of every building project as a research experiment. For the client – whether a government institution or an individual person – these experiments take the form of expert consultation. When at a later stage the experiment leads to practical results, the organizers – in this case MIT – will receive some kind of return to cover the previous additional expenditure. Another factor that could facilitate such research is that certain foundations which take an interest in specific sectors of building will support the work.

As for practical implementation, it would call for some of the work to be done outside the Institute and some – say three months a year – within it. A fixed number of students interested in research should be assigned to the project. Methods similar to those suggested have been used in other fields with good results. The system should resemble that of a university which performs archeological research in various parts of the world and publishes reports which are used in instruction. But the programme should not serve just the training of architects; it should also make a significant contribution to practical construction.

The same ideas, with more detailed arguments and a comprehensive plan for coordinating research into the American town in Finland, were laid out by Aalto that summer in a handsome, illustrated 24-page booklet, printed in New York and distributed by the American committee for the project. The title of the booklet was *Post-war reconstruction, rehousing research in Finland, by Alvar Aalto.*

The interesting aspect of the Aalto programme is the way it blends a purely scientific quest for 'architectural inventions', or rational solutions to various problems of detail, with an equally strong determination to see to the whole, always pragmatically evaluating the results on the scales of practicality and general quality of life. The assumption was that reason should not serve merely limited goals and short-sighted ambition, but something that Aalto called "general progress", and which we might call quality of life or a genuine interest in society.

It is equally obvious that Aalto's text was superbly crafted to proffer a bait that the technocrats who headed MIT could not resist. Results were not slow in coming: only a few weeks later Aalto received an offer to become "research professor" at MIT. He accepted on July 22. His contract stipulated that he should be on duty in the United States three months a year for a remuneration of $2500 plus $500 in travel expenses. He would give seminars for the more advanced students and lecture once a week to the entire student body; his main task, however, would be to direct a new research institute of the kind projected in his writings. For the remainder of the year, he was to devote himself to the Institute's first practical building project, which – not surprisingly – turned out to be *An American Town in Finland*.

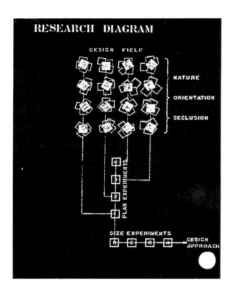

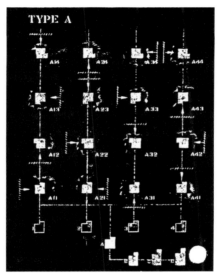

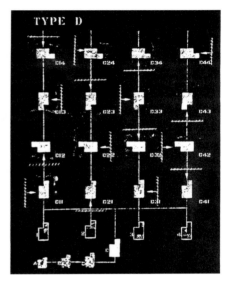

15. Some of Aalto's tables for the MIT research institute. Local conditions on building sites and families' needs for space give rise to an extremely wide range of combinations.

In early September, Aalto submitted the programme of his research institute for the autumn term. It consisted of three separate projects. The first involved the relationship between mechanical standardization and good architecture, that is, his old theme of flexible standardization. His plan was to determine systematically the variants that should be available for wooden single-family homes, with all due consideration to variation called for by family size and environmental conditions. Diagrams were prepared showing all relevant factors, whether positive, such as view, sunlight, and accessibility, or negative, such as exposure to neighbours, traffic disturbance, and unfavourable terrain. Every conceivable combination of these was considered, including the family size variable, in an effort to determine which standard components were needed in order to manufacture all desirable variants. Each of the nine participating students was to design his own specific variants within the overall system.

The second research project involved "the quality of artificial light in a room", based on both physiological and psychological criteria. A number of variables were to be considered, including the size and expected use of the room, the intensity of light, focus, and the need for shaded areas to make objects appear real. MIT's department of lighting and a lighting specialist from the Rockefeller Institute were expected to take part.

The third project dealt with the relationship of the facing materials and surface structure of buildings to durability, heat absorption, direct sunlight, aesthetic qualities, and other factors which could justify the use of different facing materials for the same building.

A comparison of this research programme with Aalto's own architecture in the following years invites itself. The first MIT project was closely related to his efforts in Finland to introduce the 'AA House' in collaboration with the Ahlström house factory in Varkaus. After all, the problem of lighting had been one of his principal concerns since he designed the Viipuri Library. This was also true of his later work, as we see from designs such as the Aalborg Museum, where he sought to use shaded areas as part of the lighting. As for the study of various materials for external walls, it had obvious offshoots in the varied wall surfaces of the MIT dormitory and in the durability tests of various kinds of brick and tile that he performed in his 'Experimental House' at Muuratsalo.

Aalto's professorship at MIT began on October 8, but lasted only just over a week. In a letter to MIT principal Carl T. Compton, he expressed his regret that "the difficulties in Atlantic traffic have compelled me to leave almost two weeks earlier than planned", but said he expected to return in March 1941. As it turned out, he would not resume his work in the United States until November 1945.

Despite Aalto's more than meagre contribution, work in his laboratory continued under the direction of his assistant, Arnold W. Tucker. In a letter to Aalto, Tucker referred to I.M. Pei, later famous, as "a clever graduate student of MIT", and reported that Pei wished to work with Aalto and had brought the Chinese ambassador and Burchard together to set in motion an American Town project in China, modelled on the Finnish one.

This letter also provides evidence that Aalto had succeeded in arousing the interest of a very influential organization, the American Red Cross. During a visit to Washington, he had called on this institution and, with his usual hypnotic powers, had immediately received a response for his cooperation plans. Interest in Aalto's ideas within the Red Cross was sparked by the hope of solving some of the problems the organization faced in aiding victims of natural disasters.

Albert Evans, head of the Red Cross Disaster Services, wrote an internal memorandum to the directors of the Red Cross after his meeting with Aalto:

Mr Aalto has a very practical understanding of the problems . . . His thinking on rehousing activity on a large scale is towards a system which would give full play to individual effort and variety and yet takes full advantage of mass production and standardization . . . His discussion of post war reconstruction is a very suggestive and promising approach to the whole problem.

16. Three examples from Aalto's American type register for emergency housing that can be converted into permanent homes.

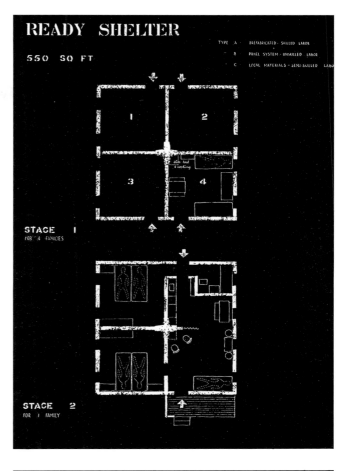

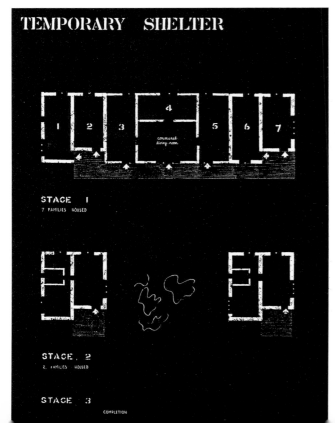

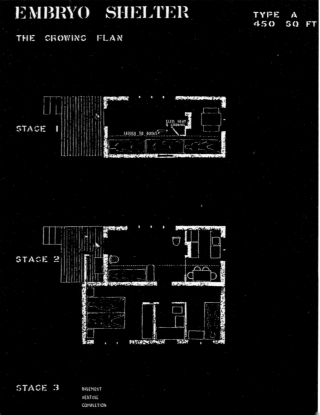

The Red Cross immediately entered into negotiations with MIT on cooperation with and economic support to the research institute. In the end, the project petered out when Aalto's dynamic contribution ceased. Burchard was quite clear from the start about how important Aalto had been to the whole enterprise. He wrote to an acquaintance who was curious to know what this much-touted research institute at MIT really was:

There is no institute of architectural research at all. What we have is Aalto appointed as a research professor in architecture and he will study, as announced, fundamental problems of low cost housing.

The story of Aalto's architectural 'laboratory' and the system for flexible standardization of housing, developed in innumerable diagrams, can be wound up appropriately with the observation that in 1951 the head of MIT's Bemis Foundation published a 466-page book on the problems of prefabricated housing and on the activities of the Foundation. In it he did not once mention either Aalto or his laboratory. (Burnham Kelly: *The Prefabrication of Houses*, a study by the Albert Farwell Bemis Foundation of the Prefabrication Industry in the United States, MIT 1951).

Obviously the project had too large a measure of utopianism and "artistic fantasy" to find a place in a refractory reality.

Aalto's Swiss Sermon on the Mount

On October 20, 1940, Alvar and Aino Aalto and their children Heikki and Hanna Maija embarked on their long and, in prevailing conditions, risky return voyage from New York to Finland. They sailed on the Bore X, a freighter of the Finland-America Line, which also had a handful of passenger cabins. Among their fellow passengers were Marshal Mannerheim's sister Eva and her husband, the Swedish artist Count Louis Sparre, with whom the Aaltos forged a lasting friendship. Aino's pocket almanac contains the following notes on the voyage:

October 10:	Saturday. Ship left New York for oil harbour on NJ side.
October 20:	Ship sailed for Petsamo. Captain Pettersson.
October 28:	Mid-Atlantic. Props and oil on surface. Sunken ship.
October 31:	In Kirkwall. Ship admired. Cameras confiscated.
November 1:	Captain went ashore.
November 3:	Sir Palmer takes command aboard.
November 5:	Left Kirkwall. Shetland loomed in distance.
November 7:	Calm on Arctic Ocean.
November 12:	Wednesday. Arrived in Petsamo.

The contrast between the peaceful, bright, vital America they left behind and their home country, brooding in the polar darkness, must have been a shock. At this time Finland had barely started to recover from the stranglehold of the Winter War. Abandoned, at the victor's mercy, and depressed by the distress of the evacuated population resettled throughout the country, Finland was still licking her wounds. Eight months, virtually to the day, had passed since the Aaltos left. Their time in the United States had been filled with positive human contact, success, and optimism on many levels. Would Aalto be able to bring some of this glory home with him? His bold plan for "an American town", which appeared to have the wholehearted support of the Rockefeller Foundation, the American Red Cross, and a special committee established by influential American architects in July, was not the only issue. His ambition to apply his

17. Aalto at the drawing board in the early 1940s. Photo: Kolmio.

marvellous reconstruction theories to Finnish reality was also at stake. Now he faced the 500,000 homeless people he had spoken of in his lectures; it was no longer enough for him to have named himself head of the reconstruction effort. Finland's true powers that be, the bureaucracy and the budget process, the limited resources, the incurable inertia, and the jealous rivals – in short, the painful realities – lay ahead like some untraversable morass. He did bring something of lasting value back from his stay in the United States, however: the title of professor, so important to Finns, which lent greater authority to the initiatives and ideas he immediately started disseminating with his dauntless vitality.

And yet Aalto's record for the remaining war years until his next visit to America shows a series of failures. This was partly because the portion of "artistic fantasy" Hahl had talked about cropped up again. The defeats he suffered were not ignominious ones, however, since his vitality and his ability to show the way had significant consequences in stimulating the people he came into contact with as well as in leading up to the tangible results he gradually began to achieve later.

The first task for Aalto at home was to tidy up in the practical sense. The office was in disarray, the tax authorities were after him; the construction projects for the Ahlström and Tampella companies, which had been started before the war, had been handled in his absence by his assistants, who had been able to do only the bare minimum. Moreover, he wished to enter a competition for high-rise housing announced by the HAKA building society. This meant that he had to hurry, as the deadline for entry was only 18 days after his return. On top of all this, he was still on the army rolls as a civil servant at the Information Centre.

It was an impressive feat in itself that for all the stress he was under, he did not for a moment lose sight of his principal goals. Aalto always lived on two levels: he was a realist and a tactician who solved practical problems with astonishing inventiveness and unfailing diplomacy; but he was also an intuitive, often utopian interpreter of the long perspective, and he always related individual phenomena to the totality. The stages of his life therefore leave us with a mixture of amused wonder at his canniness and genuine admiration for his broad-mindedness. We shall have ample opportunity to adopt both approaches in following him on the trip he made to Switzerland in April 1941.

Once again, persistent and skilfully elicited letters of invitation from abroad persuaded the directors of the Information Centre to send the no. 1 man at *Office A* on a diplomatic mission. Sigfried Giedion, Alfred Roth, and other Swiss friends of Aalto's had set up lectures for him at universities in Zurich, Basle, Berne and Geneva. For Finland, recently extricated from the war and now neutral, Switzerland provided an ideal platform for reminding the world that the small country still existed and for talking with the European intellectual élite.

Aalto's lecture bore the title *The Reconstruction of Europe is the Key Problem for the Architecture of Our Time*. His main thesis was the same as in his speeches in the United States: Finland, the first country to have been devastated and then to have got out of the war, should serve as a test case for the imminent reconstruction of all Europe. He also played on the compassion and admiration the dramatic Winter War had won for Finland. But the real theme of his lecture was much more general; so much so that it still remains topical today, almost a half century later. Aalto spoke of the crucial problems of modern architecture in words that still capture our attention. This was something of a Sermon on the Mount on the dangers of the blind worship of technology and on nature as the great teacher and foundation of all things.

The lecture – or rather, the essay that Aalto later developed it into – is much too long to be reprinted in its entirety here, but the brilliance, clarity, and depth of the presentation appear clearly enough from just a few key excerpts:

I have here a series of photographs which illustrate man's building instinct when confronted with war. First we see the inhabitants of a destroyed village returning to their now ruined former homes in a military vehicle. They are struck by amazement at first, a concentrated will to rebuild their homes, but mixed with uncertainty about how to go about it. First of all, the instinct to tidy up appears. A touching example of life starting anew

18. Some of the slides Aalto
showed his Swiss audience
in spring 1941. Here is the
peasant woman baking bread
in the oven of her destroyed
home. The next step is the
reconstruction of "roof and
walls", using the remnants
of the old building. The
children also take part in
building. The forms of the
house gradually become
more solid, but the hearth
must still be left outside.

is the peasant woman who has found her oven intact among the ruins of her home and is now baking her first loaves of bread there. This is a home without walls or roof, its damaged but still-beating heart.

The next picture shows the first primitive cottage rising up, its 'walls and roof' built with the remnants of the old house. We could think of this as the first, hesitantly raised structure that gives the family shelter from the rains. And so life goes on. Despite its primitive character, it slowly and touchingly takes on ever richer forms. The shelter put together from sheets of roofing and fragments of board has already become a kind of house. A smile plays on the builders' faces, the builders here being the entire family, from the eldest to the last-born. It reminds us of the building games children play in backyards, with everyone finding a task of his own. We see that no artificial system of leisure is needed to offset their work, but that work, joy, satisfaction, and rest merge into a harmonious unity. The forms of the buildings become increasingly solid; already we can trace the influence of Classical architectural forms, based on the ridgepole system and columns: all very humble, but a house anyway. Never mind that 'fire control' has turned out to be such a difficult technical problem that the hearth has still been left outside the house.

But then the propitious development is suddenly interrupted. Individual 'creative work' is replaced by the manufactured house, the super-standardized hut or the ready-made block. Which it will be depends on which of the two systems prevalent in our reconstruction is used. This turning point marks the end to the work of individual, harmoniously assembled groups, replacing it with paid factory labour. The primitive shack and the original, destroyed homes were all different from one another, because of differences in local conditions and materials and individual preferences. They were adapted to the surroundings and terrain just as an animal's nest in the forest is. Instead we are now getting housing areas made up of identical buildings. The individual house no longer grows out of its site and for the people who live in it; it is a product of civilization, trade, technology, etc., but unadapted and with no instinct for assimilation.

To be sure, people get technologically better housing, a comfortable life in a restricted form, but something is missing: the price paid for comfort is a certain disharmony. At the root of this disharmony is the break with the individual's genuine psychological needs, and in the forces, unknown in some respects, which account for the striving for inner balance and the unification of work and leisure in society and in the way people form groups. It is worth trying to find out to what extent the break in development is real or merely the result of an excessively rapid process. We need to establish whether this phenomenon is inevitable when laying the foundation for future development.

At the outset, standardized manufactured housing is probably all to the good. Nor could it be otherwise: the need is obvious; our society tends naturally towards civilization, and our production machinery follows suit. The means of production based on spontaneous individual contributions are infinitesimal in comparison. For man - that adaptable animal – it is obviously much easier to adapt to a technology that only partly takes him into account than for technology to accommodate man's complex needs.

When I gave a lecture at Yale University in 1938, I perceived from my discussions with graduate students a lively enthusiasm for standardized housing. The students still dreamed of housing production based on the principles applied in the automobile industry.

19. Gift house from Sweden erected in the Pirkkola single-family housing district in 1941. "To be sure, people get technologically better housing, but ..."

They thought the housing problem could be solved in this way, "first in the United States, of course, then in the rest of the world". It was really difficult for me to dispel this Ford dream from their heads. The standardization of automobiles appears to be closely related to the standardization of buildings, and to be an exemplary success. A closer comparison reveals, however, that its methods cannot be reconciled with the distinctive character of architecture.

Let us begin by comparing the relationship of the car and the house to nature and people. How does the car relate to nature? Briefly defined, every car has virtually the same relationship with nature and the same purpose in nature. It stands in the road on four rubber tyres, and its purpose is to move in a certain direction. Its function is thus simple: to move and to transport. Its relationship with people is also the most primitive one could imagine, restricted as it is to some demands on space and comfort, with due consideration for the fact that one will use it only occasionally and temporarily. It is thus natural that the best solution to the function of the automobile consists of developing the most advanced and most simplified type product possible. That is why standardization has yielded such excellent results in this case, the ideal being to crystallize the world of the car into a handful of general types. This process could be called standardization with a centralizing tendency. The same applies to most purely technical objects or instruments which have a relationship to nature that is primitive in the scientific sense of the word, and which exist solely to perform a single technical task.

This is not the case for a building. As opposed to a car, a building has a fixed relationship with nature: it belongs inseparably on a specific plot of land, and is affected by the specific natural conditions that result from the site's distinctive character. We can confidently assert and at least theoretically prove that no two building sites in this world are alike.

We may define the ideal goals of architecture by saying that the purpose of a building is to act as an instrument that collects all the positive influences in nature for man's benefit, while also sheltering him from all the unfavourable influences that appear in nature and the building's specific environment. If we accept this, we must also understand that a building cannot fulfil its purpose if it does not itself possess a wealth of nuances equal to that of the natural environment to which it will belong as a permanent ingredient. In the name of common sense, any standardization that can come into consideration here must be of the decentralizing type.

The most remarkable standardization institute of all is nature. Nowhere else does one find such thorough and effective standardization. Let us take a plant or a tree. We find that every blossom on a spring-flowering fruit tree differs from all the others. If we investigate further, we realize that this difference is not fortuitous. The blossoms face in different directions; they are shaded by different branches, leaves, and adjacent blossoms. This determines the variety of forms. Each blossom has a different position, a different relationship with the stem, a different orientation, and so on. To fulfil its purpose, the blossom itself must adapt to this scale of variation. And yet this immense variety of function and form, this total dissimilarity, has arisen within an extremely strict 'system of standardization'. Every blossom is made up of innumerable apparently uniform proto-cells, but these cells have a quality that permits the most extraordinary variety in the linkage of cells. This leads to a tremendous wealth of forms in the final product; yet all these forms are based on a specific system.

Standardization borrowed from the domain of pure technology, which has recently invaded architecture, is of an entirely different nature. This invasion springs from the fatal misconception that architecture is a form of technology. It is not. In fact, the problems of architecture cannot be solved at all with the methods of modern technology. Of course, architecture uses technology, but it does so by applying various technologies simultaneously, and its principal goal is to bring these technologies into harmony. Architecture is thus a kind of super-technical creation, and the harmonization of many disparate forms of activity is central to it.

Our century, and even the preceding one, is full of examples of attempts to treat architecture as a specialized form of technology. The result has not been limited to failure in each individual case. It has also led to malignant social complications with devastating effects on large groups of people. Even such a notable man as Thomas Alva Edison wasted years of his life trying to solve the problems of the standardized house using technological methods. In this protracted effort, he suffered his life's only real defeat. A building is not in the least a technological problem; it is an architechnological problem.

After this pronouncement, Aalto went on to describe 'flexible standardization' and 'the growing house', both familiar to us from his MIT project. His tendency to confuse his own wishes with reality reappeared in this section of the lecture, as he embarked on a highly detailed description of the fruitful results the MIT project had allegedly achieved. He stated that "research in the technical laboratories" had made it possible to work out a complete assembly system for flexible wooden single-family homes. He claimed that "a special miniature factory at the Institute" had produced all parts of the building in miniature. During the subsequent "first work phase", the architects and students working at the institute had combined these miniature components into a great variety of houses, adapted to different variables. "During each three-month term, the institute produces between 25 and 50 of these test units." The nine students Aalto had just left behind at the MIT 'architectural laboratory' after ten days together certainly would have been astonished to hear this Swiss tale.

Giedion was impressed, however, and he wrote a panegyric on the lecturer in the journal *Die Weltwoche:*

The Finn Alvar Aalto travels to Switzerland to speak about reconstruction. The mistake made in the reconstruction of France and Belgium after the last war is revealed. Aalto comes to warn us against an unmethodical procedure dictated by chance. He seeks a painstaking, scientific, systematic approach, a grasp of the problem as a whole, from the individual cell all the way to regional planning. The destruction of the present war is on a scale that surpasses anything hitherto perpetrated by man. For Finland, the ordeal is over, but others still face it or are in its midst. This difference between Finland and the rest of Europe conceals a searing tragedy. While bombs are falling left and right, here is someone already speaking of and working on a judicious plan for future regeneration.

Aalto grew up in Finland, a peripheral country far from Paris, far from Berlin. As a student, he sat in jail during the Czarist period. He was arrested at a white-tie dinner. He carries Finland with him wherever he goes. Finland is his source of inner strength, and keeps reappearing in his work, like Spain for Picasso or Ireland for James Joyce. Part of the nature of modern art is that its proponents have their roots in something firmly delimited, not in empty space. But it is also in its nature to break down the boundaries between countries, and to boldly seek contact with its own time, with the world, and with history. Perhaps a later age will hold it in our favour that we tried to reunite technological development and primal force. In all the arts, we find the same phenomenon: the primitive man inside us is drawn into the light from a forgotten layer of consciousness; and at the same time a unity with modern-day progress is sought.

Alfred Roth was equally impressed. In a letter to the present author (September 2, 1977), he mentioned that Aalto's lecture gave him the idea of starting a series of publications under the title *CIVITAS – Sammelwerk. Die Menschliche Siedlung* (CIVITAS – An Anthology. The Human Housing District). One volume was to include Aalto's lecture, *Der Wiederaufbau Europas* (The Reconstruction of Europe), but the publisher lost interest after the first two volumes and Aalto's book was never published.

Aalto's stay in Switzerland proved very inspiring to him. He met many of his closest personal friends and some architects who had worked at his office previously. Probably these contacts induced him to initiate a project that should have appeared utopian from the beginning. With his customary persuasiveness, however, he managed to talk a number of sensible people into taking it seriously. The idea was that younger Swiss architects did not have enough work at home under prevailing conditions, whereas Finland had a shortage of architects for the recently launched reconstruction effort. Why not invite Swiss banks to invest in the Finnish rental market?

Aalto's friends introduced him to people in financial circles, and he presented them with concrete and apparently realistic figures on building costs in Finland and on the profits to be made by a Finnish-Swiss joint venture in construction. He also guaranteed that investments in Finland "were just as secure as in any other European country", an opinion that was not shared by the other party. When Finland was drawn into the Continuation War a few months later, the whole idea was buried quietly.

The Swiss friend who supported Aalto most wholeheartedly in this, and indeed in all of his projects, was Hélène de Mandrot, his friend from the earliest CIAM years, the legendary patroness of modern architecture and a surviving representative of ancient feudal tradition. Aalto had kept in touch with her through the years, and she had retained the romantic infatuation that shines through in her letter of May 8, 1940 to Aalto in New York:

My dearest Aalto. I can't tell how wonderful you appear to me, wonderful in every thing. I have never met a man with such a brain and such activity, always up to date, and always ready to help in life, and face it, always in the right way . . .

Sometimes she complained that he did not answer her letters and he excused himself chivalrously with "the impossibility of writing from heart to heart in telegrams and war time letters". One of the few letters Aalto sent her was written in the summer of 1941 after their meeting in Switzerland:

Dear, dear Madame. Many thanks for your kind telegram. It is always nice to hear from you. I can imagine how the conference in La Sarraz (Madame de Mandrot's castle) was going on, with you as the spiritual rector, hammering the other ones ahead, according to your personal philosophy of "never stop the human activity and constructive intellectual work". You know I like your philosophy, it is like a motor for my work here and just now I think your attitude is the most beautiful one, because there are so few thinking this way.

Here are now happening the things I spoke about: more war and again a war which destroys practically every roof and shelter for human beings. There are very few houses left on the Karelian territories, and that means that the big problem of "the war against houses" now again is increasing here. I see that this autumn the problem will be at least twice as big as after the last war. There is exceptional hurry to speed up the housing aid to the people. But more than this I think people psychologically need security, that there will be a great constructive period right after the destruction. That's why I am so extremely glad of your telegram. I think now should be the right time to start even the formal organization we spoke about with Roth . . . According to that I think the first step should be a committee for Swiss-Finnish co-operation in reconstruction. It would be very interesting for me to hear if you have discussed this according to the old plan of sending Swiss architects and ingenieurs here, together with Swiss bank-capital, or have you found out some other forms?

I am soon going to the east to see destroyed areas and I think I can send Roth very helpful informations for his magazine. But the best should be to get you and Roth here. I should like to show the ground of the drama and our future work to you. And you with your enormous sensitivity would probably find out what are the real problems of the human soul in this Europe of smoking ruins. I kiss your beautiful eyes and hands. Yours Alvar Aalto.

20. Madame de Mandrot always refused to be photographed. Alfred Roth managed to take this picture unnoticed in the early 1940s.

The tone of this letter, particularly its conclusion, could lead one to suspect that Aalto was playing a cynical game with the enamoured lady. She was in her seventies at the time, and seriously ill*, but this did not prevent her from accepting Aalto's invitation and going to Finland in the summer of 1942, defying all the hardships of war to "renew and rejuvenate myself" with "my best friend", as she herself put it. "You are so bracing – in Switzerland all is slow, it does not fit me at all", she wrote after her return. Aalto's relationship with the lady of the castle, however, was not dictated by cold calculation. His attitude was partly due to his natural propensity to adopt a flirtatious tone with women; more important, however, was that Madame de Mandrot, with her visionary character and dynamism, was his true kindred spirit.

* Madame de Mandrot died December 25, 1948 at Le Pradet, her house in southern France designed by Le Corbusier.

Hélène de Mandrot's ability to get excited about new ideas extended equally to the secrets of earth magnetism, the study of which she generously supported, as to the CIAM architects' aspirations. Aalto had no reason to complain about this propensity, however, for at his urging she arranged and largely paid for an ambulance to be sent from Switzerland to Finland during the Winter War, and with the same generosity she donated pistols to Finnish officers and chocolate to Finnish children. She also eagerly embraced the plan for a Swiss contribution to the reconstruction of Finland, and ultimately became so involved in Aalto's ideas on standardization that in a 1943 letter he called the newly established Finnish Standardization Institute "this our mutual baby".

Hélène de Mandrot surely ranks as one of Aalto's most faithful disciples.

Refractory Reality

Among the letters Aalto received from the home country during his visit to the United States, one was from his faithful assistant at the office, Otto Murtomaa, who reported in May 1940: "Large-scale standard housing manufacture starting in Varkaus." In August, Maire Gullichsen wrote: "The Varkaus house factory has many orders, we are building one house and one hut a day. Sent 25 C2s last week to Mätäsvaara, the Grönblom mine in Nurmes. Now starting a C3 series. The factory enlargement will be finished by autumn. Now we just want you home so we can have more types."

The writers thought that the beginning of mass production of the Aalto type houses, designed before the war for low-rise areas in Varkaus, Inkeroinen, and other industrial towns, would be good news to him. After all, he had been a pioneer of the type principle in Finland, and the numbered house variants he had designed were intended for mass production. Before the war, they had been erected individually on site, using only certain prefabricated standard components such as windows, doors, and sized timber. During the reconstruction of 1940, fully industrialized house production began in Finland for the first time.

The Ahlström company, which owned the rights to Aalto's type designs, was quick to start up its own house factory. Sweden's assistance to Finland included 2,000 houses prefabricated in Sweden, where the sector was already flourishing, but designed by unprepared Finnish architects under great time pressure. The results of this donation were unsatisfactory. The houses were bare minimum units, and wherever large quantities of them were erected, the result was oppressive.

Aalto understood this without even having seen the new housing areas. In fact this was exactly what he had cautioned against in his American lectures on the failure of emergency construction after World War I. Aalto's reaction to the drawbacks of Rationalism had led him even before the war to design such polemically irrational and complex buildings as the Viipuri Library, the World's Fair pavilions, and the Villa Mairea. The intentional differences in the "type" forms of his single-family home designs in the late 1930s were aimed at both variation and adaptation to site. Only in the United States, however, did he hit upon the logical solution to the need for adaptation and variation:

21. Type house C 2, made by the Varkaus house factory in 1940. Elevations and plan.

22. Tampere village of comrades in arms, with rows of two-family type houses, did not correspond to Aalto's ideal of flexible standardization.

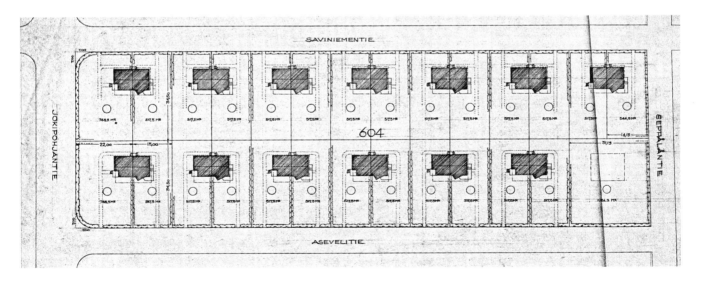

instead of serial houses, or types, one should build only series of units that could be combined in any number of ways to produce truly individual variants. In his 'Swiss Sermon on the Mount', we find this idea in fully developed and ideologically reasoned form.

Aalto could not stop the production of his own type houses at the Varkaus factory when he was made responsible for its development at the beginning of

53

23. View of the "village for comrades in arms" outside Tampere. Photo: Göran Schildt.

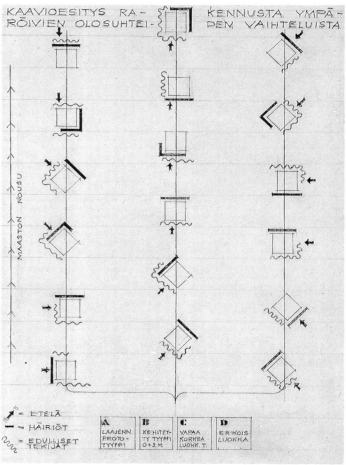

24. Scheme of the external variables of a building site to which the house must be adapted. From a description of the Ahlström house factory.

1941. He was not even able to loosen up the rigidity of its type system when invited to build "a village for comrades in arms" outside Tampere. Kalle Kaihari, the project's initiator, had managed to collect donations from various sources to build homes for a few dozen families of war invalids. The Varkaus factory did not have enough capacity at the time to experiment with different solutions, so thirteen semidetached houses, pleasant enough in themselves but all identical, were built in two straight rows, with a separate sauna building. This was the first large-scale complex of small houses designed by Aalto to be built, but it was a very poor reflection of the designer's true intentions. The impression of monotony is relieved today only by the vegetation that has transformed the emergency village into a tree-shaded, flowering idyll.

The concessions of the moment did not, however, mean that he had abandoned his goal. He understood that he must prepare for the long term by building up a production system for manufacturing the units for more flexible housing. He set out his programme for a complete reorganization of the house factory in a 19-page memorandum to the Ahlström management. He started with the now familiar argument concerning the difference between the standardization of motor cars and houses, then went on to explain the system of flexible housing he had developed at MIT. He claimed that 96 different model houses had been developed there using prefabricated units. "In our Finnish conditions, however, I suggest that we follow a much simpler scheme, by concentrating on just three size variants, i.e. houses with one, two, or three bedrooms, and the external variables of 1) orientation; 2) positive factors, such as view, sheltered yard, etc.; and 3) negative factors, such as traffic, disturbance from neighbours, etc.; to this we should add the slope of the terrain."

This gave a total of 69 models for which Aalto made drawings. He also provided guidelines for further improvements.

A basic prerequisite for developing the whole system and achieving satisfactory sales was that the company build an experimental village in which the largest possible number of variants could be tested in practice, and the public would have the opportunity to compare various alternatives and decide which of them best suited their needs. Aalto had a specific location in mind: Savonmäki, a Varkaus suburb for which he had designed an area of single-family homes for Ahlström employees before the war. This area would simultaneously meet the company's practical needs for housing and serve as a testing ground and showcase for the house factory.

The suggestion seemed both sensible and economical. It had the enthusias-

25. Scheme of some AA system variables.

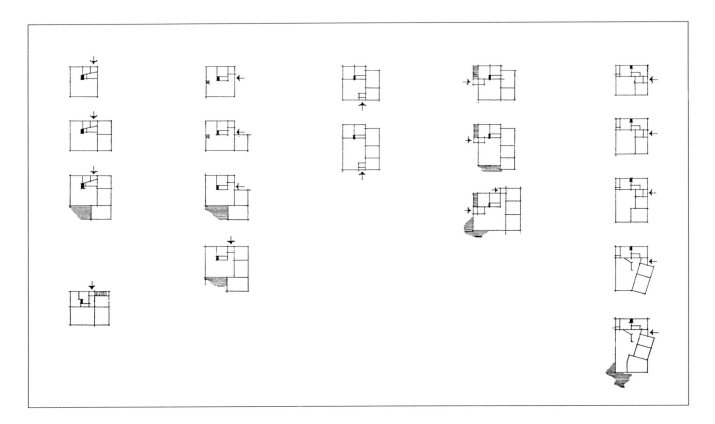

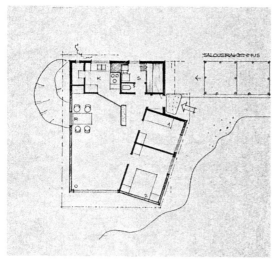

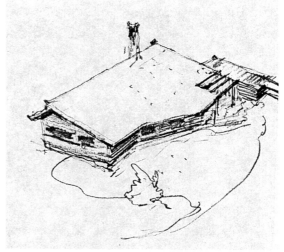

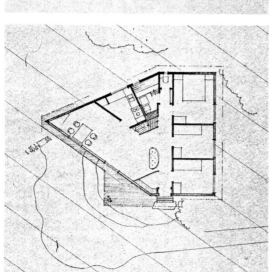

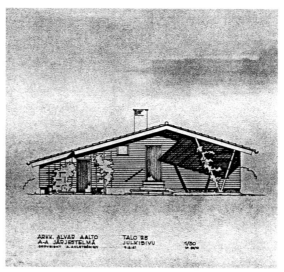

ARKK. ALVAR AALTO   TALO 25
A-A JÄRJESTELMÄ   JULKISIVU   1/50
COPYRIGHT A.AHLSTRÖM OY

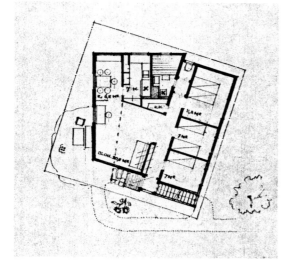

26. Three of the many
AA system variations on the
plan of the small wooden
house. Floor areas 68.4, 75,
and 80 m².

27. The AA house exteriors
also offered considerable
potential for variation.

tic support of the company's managing director Harry Gullichsen, and should have appealed to everyone. What actually happened has been told in the second part of this biography (*The Decisive Years,* p. 141). The company's general meeting indignantly voted the whole flighty project down, and the house factory concentrated on the production of a handful of easily sold types of 'AA houses', as they were dubbed in advertisements after the initials of both designer and manufacturer. During the Continuation War, the house factory made virtually nothing but 'Jurtta' plywood tents for the German army, and soon the Aalto types were so modified that they became indistinguishable from the very ordinary products of other Finnish house factories. Unsatisfactory sales later prompted the company to sell the whole factory to its main competitor, Puutalo Oy, after which the AA house definitively disappeared from the market.

How inevitable this sequence of events was is hard to judge. Aalto's vision of the infinitely variable house permitting enlargement, assembled from prefabricated units, was undoubtedly interesting, and it seems preposterous that it should have been rejected only because the Ahlström shareholders could not bear the thought of providing working-class families with running water and modern plumbing. Whether the house factory really would have been successful if it had been backed up by the experimental village, the nationwide campaign for better living, and the more harmonious environment called for in Aalto's programme, is another matter.

The definition of the purpose of architecture given by Aalto in his 'Sermon on the Mount' was based on the idea that a building should relate to the surroundings in a way that provides for the greatest possible physical and mental well-being, while the environment as a whole must remain in equilibrium. The thought is beautiful, and the general quality of life would certainly be raised if it could be carried out. What Aalto failed to consider was that people also make a whole series of irrational demands on the buildings they live in, such as that their homes should enhance their prestige, mark their affinity with certain traditions and groups of people, satisfy their needs for individual expression, and so on. In real life, a construction business that indulges these wishes and lures customers with cheap rich man's villas, the vagaries of fashion, the appearance of luxury, and pretentiousness, false traditionalism, or a mendacious idyll may have better sales than a builder who provides the correct angle to the sun, well-protected views, a quiet site, heat economy, and enlargement potential.

No doubt this was another Aalto project with a certain measure of fantasy about it – perhaps not 'artistic' but idealistic in this case: an unrealistic hope that people can be protected from the misfortunes that result from short-sightedness, vanity, and the indiscriminate application of the gifts of technology.

Another set of problems that came to Aalto's attention in his work for the Ahlström company was linked to regional planning. The company had its administrative centre in Noormarkku, with factories in both Pori and Pihlava.

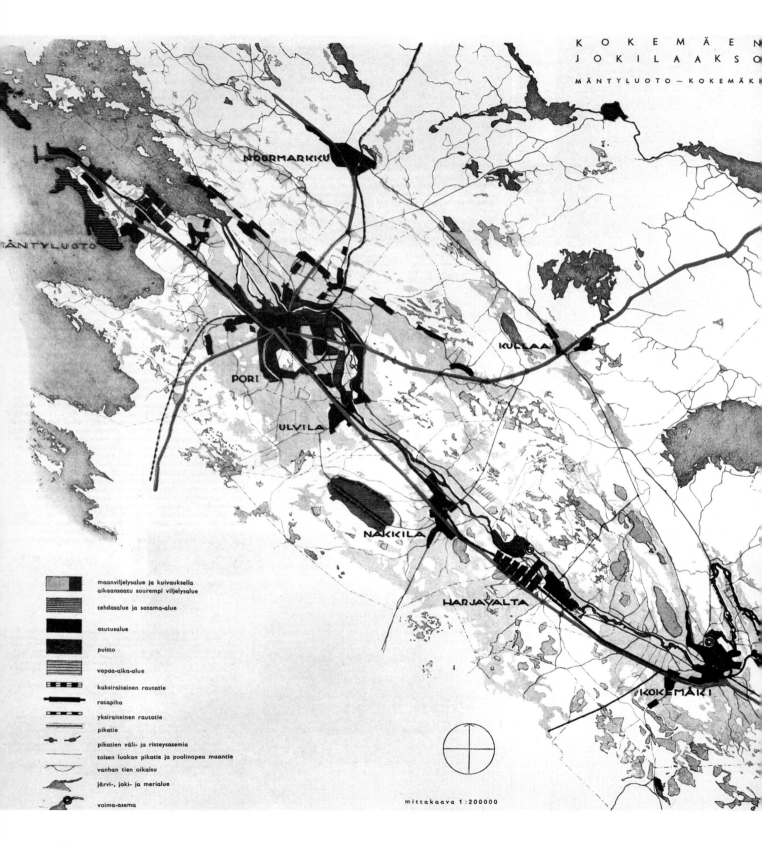

K O K E M Ä E N
J O K I L A A K S O

MÄNTYLUOTO—KOKEMÄKI

NOORMARKKU

MÄNTYLUOTO

KULLAA

PORI

ULVILA

NAKKILA

HARJAVALTA

KOKEMÄKI

maanviljelysalue ja kuivauksella
aikaansaatu suurempi viljelysalue

tehdasalue ja satama-alue

asutusalue

puisto

vapaa-aika-alue

kaksiraiteinen rautatie

ratapiha

yksiraiteinen rautatie

pikatie

pikatien väli- ja risteysasemia

toisen luokan pikatie ja puolinopea maantie

vanhan tien oikaisu

järvi-, joki- ja merialue

voima-asema

mittakaava 1:200000

58

28. Aalto's Kokemäenjoki
regional plan treated the
whole river basin from
Mäntyluoto harbour to the
village of Kokemäki as an
organic whole.

Harry Gullichsen, the broad-minded managing director, was concerned at the virtually random exploitation of the entire region, the Kokemäenjoki river valley. New settlements, production facilities, and communication routes were being built by uncoordinated local initiatives. In spring 1941, Harry Gullichsen persuaded the municipalities affected to commission Alvar Aalto to produce a general development plan for the Kokemäenjoki river valley.

Regional planning was virtually unknown in Finland at the time. Attempts in that direction had been made only by Otto-I. Meurman in the province of Viipuri and Bertel Jung in the Kymi river valley; the detailed plan worked out by Aalto for the project was truly a pioneering effort.

As usual, Aalto could not take the assignment as an isolated project: he immediately raised it into an all-encompassing cultural question of principle. This is made quite clear by a long article he published at the end of 1941 in *Arkkitehti* journal under the title: *Rural building, a key issue for the reconstruction effort, for the architecture of our whole country, and for our inner social equilibrium.*

The following main points can be extracted from this lengthy and rather chaotic text. Aalto starts by recalling the pre-industrial era, when a certain balance prevailed between man and nature. Town and country were two completely different environments. Towns were dominated by an ancient urban civilization, while nature was predominant in the rural areas; in both, problems had to be solved case by case, taking local conditions and individual alternatives into account. As a result, all things formed a coherent, functional system tending towards balance and harmony.

Then came "a break in the developmental curve", "a cultural crisis, when the old production methods were superseded by industry" and "the inner balance of the system built upon tradition and handicraft was shaken". This happened when technology gave man the power to perform simplified, repetitive tasks independently of local conditions. The consequences were fatal to the environment. The old, balanced contrast between town and country was also disturbed. Cities began to spread into the countryside, rural areas became urbanized. Previously unknown evils appeared when industries and new housing areas were located in agricultural settings and former backwoods. Communications problems, wasteland, pollution of water and air ensued. Short-sighted, feverish exploitation gave rise to often insoluble long-term problems; in brief, growing chaos and deteriorating living conditions were the increasingly conspicuous result of an uncontrolled transformation.

Aalto points out in his article how illogical it was that all regulation and competent planning focused on the cities, while the development of rural areas, on which the country's future really depended, was completely uncontrolled. Landowners decided what to build and how to do it outside the planned urban areas. Market forces were given free rein in the scramble to obtain short-term advantages.

Aalto's criticism was more than justified at the time, since the ruthless exploitation of rural land and natural resources was not curbed until 1952, when new building legislation covering rural areas gave local governments jurisdiction over planning.

His American experience evidently enabled him to lay the foundation for Finland's later regional planning at this early date. Jussi Rautsi, who trained as an architect at Aalto's office in his youth, published a praiseworthy if somewhat fragmentary master's thesis in 1984 on "Alvar Aalto's unrealized regional plans and experimental towns". In it Rautsi points out the impact that the work of the Tennessee Valley Authority had on the Kokemäenjoki river valley plan, and notes Lewis Mumford's observation that the 'neighbourhood' unit strikes an ideal balance between the human needs for belonging to a group and for individual freedom. Aalto opposed the scattering of the Finnish rural population to isolated farms that gave rise to untenable social and economic conditions after the war and contributed to a rural exodus. His regional plans advocated small villages which would foster a working community of interests and an economy based on a realistic mix of agriculture and small-scale industry.

The principal innovation in Aalto's regional plans was that he ignored administrative municipal boundaries and concentrated on the links arising from topography, economy, and communication. He saw these as living organisms covering whole regions of mixed urban and rural character. To master the problems of these areas, it was not enough to impose a handful of prohibitions and statutory obligations; creative imagination and the ability to stake out general plans were needed in order to define and combine the various components, such as jobs, housing, services, farmland, forests, recreational areas, and traffic arteries, into a functioning unity.

Ultimately, of course, comprehensive planning would be needed for the whole country, but pending this Aalto suggested that regional plans should be drawn up immediately for twelve areas in which the pressure was strongest and the danger of irreparable mistakes greatest.

We should not entertain any exaggerated notions about the value of Aalto's regional plan for the Kokemäenjoki river valley as a model. It was no utopian, ideal plan that he produced for his clients, simply a preliminary overview of the problem and an analysis of possible solutions. In his practice, Aalto tended to keep within the bounds of the possible and the compromises that had to be made, but somewhere in the background was always a vision that stimulated the imagination and lent a special aura to everything he designed.

Aalto believed, quite rightly, that the task of regional planning was exceptionally demanding, both because of the complex relationships that must be taken into account and because the planner must be free from the influence of individual economic interests and local ambitions. Thus the task could not be entrusted to anyone employed by the industries, interest groups, or municipalities affected. The only power that adequately represented the public good in this instance was the national government. However, he distrusted the government and the bureaucracy too much to suggest that a government office be made responsible for the needed plans. Instead he suggested that the government should set up "a group of experts" comprising "one or more persons who are fully conversant with all phases of architecture and construction, from regional and town planning down to the smallest detail of construction engineering". Reading between the lines, we understand that really only one person in Finland was qualified for the job (perhaps in collaboration with a few colleagues he would be allowed to select), and that person was Alvar Aalto.

His report on rural building was not confined to regional planning. He also discussed housing in the rural areas, a significant aspect of the environmental problem. In his Swiss 'Sermon on the Mount', Aalto had already touched upon the "cultural crisis" caused by industrialization, when houses built by carpenters began to be replaced by factory-made type houses. He had also recommended a cure: a shift to growing, variable houses made of prefabricated units. He noted: "Recently there has been a rather sharp reaction against prefabricated buildings and groups of housing made up of them. This reaction, which expresses criticism of fragmentary, unharmonious construction methods in rural areas and casts doubts on the results of a superficial, inexpertly directed machine culture, is correct in itself, but arises from a not very penetrating analysis. The appearance of a building and its so-called style are not independent of its function in society." Aalto wished to emphasize "the housing biology aspect".

By this time, late 1941, Aalto seems to have drawn his own conclusions concerning the Ahlström company's lack of interest in genuinely progressive housing production. Here again, he saw the government as the only possible salvation. Neither the Rockefeller Foundation, MIT, nor the Ahlström company had been prepared to give him an architectural testing ground for trying out flexible, growing houses in practice and for experimenting with designs that satisfied human needs. He now came up with a new plan and, as was his wont, presented it in extremely specific form. "On the land of a wholly or partly state-owned industrial facility with an urgent need for dwellings, a test project should be set up for rural housing." Moreover, "a similar test site should be established on the grounds of some large farm belonging to the state, with the purpose of developing housing on agricultural land."

It scarcely needs saying that the dream of a "governmental group of experts" on regional planning and governmental testing stations for housing production found no response in the refractory reality Aalto was still trying to reform at the time. We may also note that his ideas about a cultural crisis brought about by technology, environmental problems, and the need for the "step by step transition of industrialism into what it is in any case destined to be some day – a harmonious factor of civilization", defined problems that are only beginning to be taken seriously in our day, but which even we do not have the power to solve.

We still allow technology to serve our short-term interests; we still think that a few simple bans of the worst abuses are enough to avoid disasters. Aalto believed that creative planning and an active vision were needed to achieve a

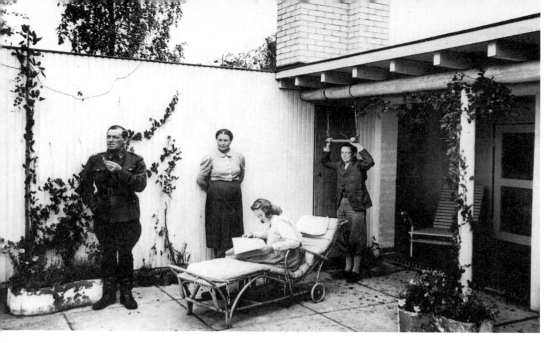

29. Alvar and Aino Aalto with their children Hanna Maija (later called Hanni) and Heikki (later called Hamilkar) on the roof terrace of their home in Munkkiniemi during the Continuation War.

30. The Aalto family at home at Riihitie 20. Note the paintings by their friends Léger and Moholy-Nagy on the wall, Calder's mobile hanging from the ceiling, and Marcel Breuer's Wassily chair, all significant sources of inspiration for Aalto. On the grand piano, the music for Sibelius's *Finlandia*.

balanced whole. Here, however, we come up against the difficulty of designating those competent to draw up plans that affect our environment, and ultimately our whole planet, whether on a small scale or on a large one. The truth seems to be that such creative experts are hard to find, and that people are just as unwilling to listen to self-appointed saviours today as the Finnish authorities were to listen to Aalto in 1941.

Finland's Continuation War

Finland was drawn into a new war with the Soviet Union on June 25, 1941 for a variety of reasons. One was concern over the Russians' real intentions regarding the defenceless yet still free country. Finland sought a counterbalance to Russian pressure from the only direction that remained open: the Germans, who were allied with the Russians at the time. The growing German presence in Finland following the invasion of Norway and Denmark meant that Finland was no longer wholly at the Russians' mercy. The general reaction among Finns to Hitler's attack on Stalin was relief. Karelian refugees, in particular, greeted this chance to regain their homes with undisguised joy.

It was also inevitable that the apparently irresistible German advance in the East should give rise to *Schadenfreude*, satisfaction at Russian misfortune, among people with the memory of the 1939 attack still fresh in their minds. Relatively few Finns saw the situation with such clarity and accuracy as did Nils-Gustav Hahl in the previously quoted letter.

Once again, Finland's able-bodied men had to risk their lives at the front. We already know about Hahl's fate. Three architects from Aalto's office, Jarl Jaatinen, Eero Urpola, and Erkki Taimi, had already been killed in the Winter War. Another three died in the Continuation War: Trygve Ahlström, Halfdan Cederhvarf, and the Danish volunteer Poul Anton Hansen. Aalto does not seem to have even dreamed about active service. Fortunately, nor did his military superiors, and he was allowed to keep his safe job at the Government Information Centre. He was actually promoted to lieutenant. In practice, he continued to correspond with his foreign friends about reconstruction aid, and travelled to Sweden and Denmark to give lectures. Otherwise he continued to handle his own architectural assignments for Finnish industry.

The prevalent attitude among Aalto's circle to the political situation can be seen from the following letter written by Maire Gullichsen shortly after the war broke out:

Mairea, July 13, 1941.

Dear Alvar,

I cannot miss this chance to dash off a letter to you, since it can be done so that the censors and their "half-German professors" can't get hold of it. I'm giving it to a friend of ours who is going to Helsinki today. Wondering what you're up to. Are you at the Information Office or do you have a private office? I just can't picture you, a genuine Westerner, in the new mentality that's sweeping across the country and making people change opinions like others change shirts. All this German propaganda and crusade ideology our newspapers are adopting has such a depressing effect. So we are now definitely on the wrong side, and all we can do is make the best of a bad job. I just think everything, the whole future we must build, seems pretty hopeless, whichever way the war ends. Stuck here in the country like in a sack, with nothing but the scarce and biased news on the radio, and no menfolk to talk to except Jonas Gylphe (one of Ahlström's directors), *but he is living in higher spheres with a portrait of Hitler on his desk, perpetually celebrating the imminent fall of* (the Soviet naval base in) *Hanko so loudly that the Horst Wessel Lied can be heard right up to here. Otherwise just people who take their daydreams for reality . . . So I would be very glad to know how you two see things. Obviously I realize that you are active in the right way.*

Headquarters has ordered Mairea and Havulinna to be commandeered for use as hospitals, but so far there doesn't seem to be any rush. Quiet and peaceful here, Mairea more beautiful than ever. It's just hard to sit here so completely out of touch with the whole world, with no active work to do. That's why I've started planning to arrange summer camps for children from the bombed cities. Did you hear that our friend Nils-Gustav (Hahl) *has enlisted as a volunteer in a 'death battalion', and is packing hand grenades in his knapsack rather than medical supplies this time? An idealist to the very last. Getting field messages from Harry* (Gullichsen) *from time to time. He is stationed at a lake near the border, Simpele to be exact, swimming and bathing in a smoke sauna, and waiting for the order to break camp. They know just as little about what's going on as we do. But when it finally does get going* (that is, the offensive against the Red Army), *it will surely be pretty rough . . .*

Affectionate regards to you both,
Maire

31. From the village of Miitkala in Uhtua, eastern Karelia. Photo: I.K. Inha, 1894.

32. East Karelian archi-
tecture: House of
D. Bombin at Suojärvi.
Photo: G. Grotenfelt.

33. Courtyard side of
D. Bombin's house.
Photo G. Grotenfelt.

Aalto's loathing of Hitler and abhorrence of all Nazi propaganda were at least equal to Maire Gullichsen's, but in one instance his reaction may seem surprising from the modern perspective. The incorporation of Soviet 'Far Karelia' and its Finnish-speaking population into Finland seems to have been a natural and pleasing thought to him. An undated letter, probably written in late autumn 1941, from 2nd Lieutenant Alvar Aalto to the head of the Government Information Centre proposes the establishment of a special Karelian department at the Centre to disseminate "accurate information" about "the not only racial and linguistic but above all cultural affinity" between Finland and Karelia. Here Aalto drew on his old enthusiasm for turn-of-the-century Finnish expeditions to "the lands of song", citing the journeys made by Akseli Gallen-Kallela, Louis Sparre, and J.K. Inha to the eastern backwoods villages, and the inspiration Finnish architects such as Sonck, Saarinen, and Armas Lindgren had found in Karelia.

This letter is related to a newspaper article by Aalto published in the newspaper *Uusi Suomi* on November 2, 1941 under the title *Architecture in Karelia* (quoted on pp. 229–230 of *The Decisive Years*). The main idea of the article was that Karelian architecture had not been affected in any way by eastern influences, having sprung up directly out of the Finnish soul and the primitive local conditions. However mistaken and absurd the idea may seem in the light of cultural history, the dream expressed in the article of a spontaneous, self-generating architecture interestingly reflects Aalto's idea of the primal force of architecture.

In spring 1943, Aalto was sent by the Information Centre on an architectural

34. Sauna built in 1945 for the Ahlström company in Varkaus, clearly reflecting Aalto's Karelian ideas.

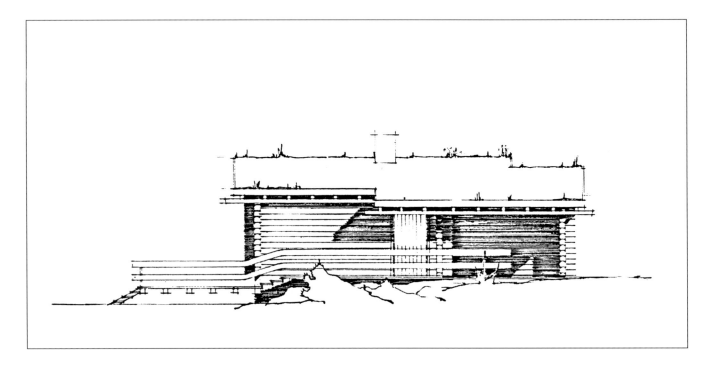

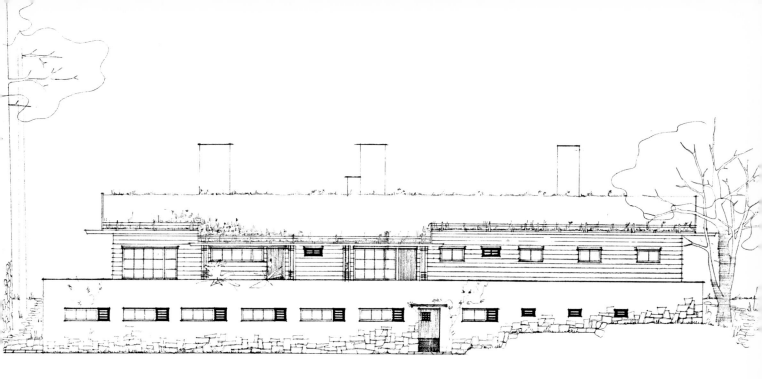

35. Sauna and laundry, Kauttua 1944, also from Aalto's Karelian period.

field trip to the Karelian region of Aunus. His own architecture during this period shows the distinct influence of Karelian folklore, as shown by illustrations 34, 35 and 40 in this book.

For all his antipathy to Nazism, Aalto could not avoid some collaboration with the German comrades in arms. The Information Centre passed on his articles to German publications, such as *Nordlicht*. The Association of Finnish Architects hosted a lecture by the German professor of architecture Ernst Neufert in Helsinki in December 1942, just ten days after Aalto had been elected chairman. Aalto had in fact probably initiated this visit, as Neufert was in charge of the standardization programme in Germany, and Aalto, as we shall see in a later chapter, wished to start up a similar project in Finland.

Aalto's reluctant contacts with German authorities culminated in the summer of 1943, when the Association of Finnish Architects was invited to send a delegation to Germany to inspect, under Neufert's guidance, the progress of standardization throughout the country. The hosts requested that Aalto, as the association's chairman, head the delegation, but he found various pretexts not to go, and four other architects left for Germany without him. When the hosts sent a military plane to pick him up a week later, Aalto could no longer wriggle out of going.

Kirmo Mikkola interviewed (February 18, 1976) one of Aalto's fellow travellers, professor Esko Suhonen, about their experiences during that memorable visit to Germany long ago. I quote a passage from Suhonen's account in an unfortunately unpublished interview series edited by Tapani Virkkala for the Finnish Society of Architecture:

I shall not go into what we learned about standardization in Germany, however significant and unique those lessons may have been. Especially in industrial architecture and in certain building projects for the Army, the Germans had achieved technological standards that were completely new to us. We were also shown installations that were considered top secret: in Hamburg, for instance, we visited the Uboots Werke, a shipyard built into an artificial hill. We were shown how this hill was made by injecting concrete from two-foot thick pipes into gigantic formworks full of steel. None of us had ever even dreamed of technology like this. Another of the significant building projects we were shown was the new Reichskanzlei, the Chancellor's office in Berlin, which had just been completed and which no Finn, and precious few Germans, had seen.

As for Alvar Aalto's attitude: he took the trip more or less as a joke. When he joined us on the night train from Hamburg to Munich, he invited us to his luxury compartment, where he had somehow or other managed to conjure up a real smorgasbord, though Germany was suffering from serious food shortages during the war. Alvar acted as host, dressed in a silk dressing gown with a red fez on his head. He said to us: Look, boys, don't you think we should treat this trip as a game? He then presented us with a scenario for how the game should be played, and assigned each of us a grand role of our own. He made me a college professor, though no-one could have dreamed that is what I'd be one day.

36. The newly erected Reichskanzlei in Berlin was designed by the Finnish architects' host, then-Reichsminister for armaments Albert Speer.

37. The congress hall for 5,000 people in Nuremberg was never completed because of Allied bombings.

And of course he paid special attention, as always, to the female sex during this trip. A little later, we took a day train to Nuremberg. The female conductor was dressed in long trousers and a uniform jacket, with a dashing uniform cap on her head. When she read the sign on our compartment door saying that we were Finnish guests of Reichsminister Speer, this young lady, who was really good-looking, started dutifully reciting every station that the train stopped at. In those days there was only one train a day, and it stopped at every little village, so the trip took an eternity. When Alvar noticed how pretty the girl was, he talked her with a little effort into sitting down among us. When the conductor said that it wasn't really proper since she was in uniform, Alvar said that was easily fixed, and soon more than just the jacket had come off. I should point out here that we had been told before our trip that it was very difficult to get hold of any alcoholic beverages in Germany. Revell, who acted as our quartermaster on this trip, carried in his suitcase 50 kilos of spirits, mainly Finnish brandy. So that's how Alvar was able to offer a few swigs to the conductress. We hadn't passed many stations before she cheerfully joined in with our singing with her arm around Alvar's neck, and no-one announced where the train would stop and where *we were going any more. They also agreed to meet in Nuremberg that night, though I didn't have the chance to find out if they really did. I was a little worried about the young lady's future prospects in her profession. Note that we were accompanied everywhere by Professor Neufert and a younger architect, Dr. Burckhardt, who accepted this behaviour without a murmur, obviously out of politeness to their Finnish comrades in arms.*

Well, that was a glimpse of the romantic side of the war years – the unpleasant side is not worth talking about.

In any case, I want to tell you of the last function we attended at which Alvar behaved in a very . . . how shall I put it? . . . manly way, at the same time showing his unique sense of humour. We had been invited to a farewell dinner at an engineers' club by Berlin's Wannsee. All five of us Finns were placed at separate tables – some of the tables were small, some large, all of them round. Until then Alvar had stubbornly kept to his declared decision not to make any speeches during the trip, but after two weeks he had softened up enough to agree to make the obligatory farewell speech. Both our German hosts and we Finns awaited this with great excitement. I remember that we had visited the most famous German sculptor, Arno Breker, in his castle, and had been treated so well there that we were still in a jolly mood, to put it mildly. Our German hosts, however, came to the dinner stone-cold sober. The evening began with a bowl of punch, which tasted like some kind of lemonade to me, but must have contained some proof, as our hosts became visibly elated, though its effect on us was sobering more than anything else. Then we started getting worried, as time passed and Alvar still didn't get up to speak, while our hosts were already getting rather tipsy. A couple of us went over to Alvar to remind him: wasn't it time for that thank-you speech?

At last Alvar got up and there was instant silence in the room. This is what they had all waited for. There must have been a hundred people there. Alvar spoke fluent German, and he started by saying that we Finns are neither Nazis nor Bolsheviks. We were a little worried and wondered whether he was so drunk that he would start talking politics. How would it all end? But Alvar went on quite calmly: "We are actually forest apes from the land of Eskimos, Waldaffen aus Eskimoland." Then he went on – and I'll try to give it in direct speech. Alvar:

"I do not know very much about what has been built here in the Third Reich, as because of my work in Boston I have been here so rarely. But once when I was waiting for Lawrence Rockefeller at the Harvard Club, my eyes happened to fall on a book with red covers on the shelf. I took it down, and discovered that it was written by an author completely unknown to me by the name of Adolf Hitler. I opened up the book at random, and my eyes fell on a sentence that immediately pleased me. It said that architecture is the king of the arts and music the queen. That was enough for me; I felt that I did not need to read further . . . "

This brought down the house. Everyone appreciated Alvar's speech. This is how he acted throughout the trip. In our discussions with our hosts, he kept just barely within the limits of the acceptable by always coming up with a mitigating joke at the end.

The Finnish architects were also received with great cordiality by their official host Albert Speer, who had just been appointed Reichsminister for armament. At this meeting, Aalto expressed his concern about the fate of a former associate of his, the young Danish architect Nils Koppel, who had just been arrested by

38. Finnish architects' delegation visits Arno Breker's studio near Berlin. Left to right: Aarne Ervi, a German architect, Alvar Aalto, Esko Suhonen, Jussi Paatela, their host Breker.

the Gestapo in Copenhagen. Koppel, who was Jewish, was about to be sent to a concentration camp in Germany, when he was released without explanation, evidently on Speer's direct orders. He immediately fled to Sweden, where he soon found work as an assistant to Aalto in a Swedish architectural project that we shall examine in the next chapter.*

*The author found out about Aalto's contribution to Koppel's release in an interview with Koppel in Copenhagen on March 13, 1986.

Swedish Divertimento

During the difficult war years, Aalto, like the rest of us, lived under the psychological stress that was part of this time of confrontation and violence. War compels people to live in the here and now; whether good or bad, that is all there is. War follows the ruthless law of either-or: victory or defeat, life or death.

Obviously these conditions were completely out of tune with Aalto's mentality and personality. For him there was no either-or, only both-and. He always strove to reconcile opposites, to find a harmonious balance between alternatives. He did this by distancing himself from the present, by shaping a vision through which conflicts could be resolved. He saw reality clearly and harboured no illusions, but it provided only the raw material for his optimistic creative imagination.

We cannot understand Aalto's actions during the war years unless we keep this aspect of his character in mind. His life during the war was completely different from just about everybody else's, which is reason enough to marvel at his own obstinacy as well as at the forbearance of the people around him. We know already that Aalto did not categorically commit his future to Finland, but considered several alternatives. If things went badly at home, he could move his practice to the United States or Sweden. He had no wish to kill enemies; he believed that he could influence them by appealing to reason and the common good, *the human side*. While the rest of the world concentrated on bombing and destroying, Aalto was already living in the period of peacetime reconstruction that must come sooner or later. He could only create, and since there was nothing for him to build in Finland but emergency housing for the homeless and factories for the war industry, it was natural for him to seek work in neutral Sweden. People led normal lives there, the economy was booming, and a normal architectural practice was possible.

In December 1942, Aalto was granted an exit visa for a one-month stay in Sweden. His application was accompanied by a certificate from the Nordstjernan shipping company, which promised to cover the expenses of "Professor Alvar Aalto's visit to Sweden for expert consultations in architecture". This and several later visits to Sweden during the war had momentous consequences.

Aalto had made the acquaintance of his colleague Albin Stark on lecture and propaganda tours to Sweden. Stark was a highly successful architect who had a greater flair for business than for artistry. His work included commissions from Axel Axelson Johnson, director and principal owner of Johnson, a leading Swedish company. Stark greatly admired Aalto's architectural ability, and the two gentlemen got along very well socially. The General, as Axel Axelson Johnson was known because of his title of consul general, ordered Stark to solve a whole series of architectural problems at the end of 1942. Stark suggested that Aalto should work with him. Aalto responded enthusiastically: at last he would be able to create instead of just talking. The collaboration did not present any difficulties of form. Stark had a large, efficient office in Stockholm, where the plans could be drafted; Aalto had the ideas; the General had the money. As Stark had anticipated, the General and Aalto also established a close rapport: both were bold visionaries and shared a worldly, gentlemanly attitude to life. A friend of Lawrence Rockefeller and Frank Lloyd Wright could not fail to strike the right note in his dealings with Axel Axelson Johnson. The tone of their relationship is reflected in the ceremonious New Year's greetings they cabled to each other every year up to 1947.

At Christmas 1943, the General thanked Aalto FOR YOUR BROAD-MINDED PLANNING OF COMMUNITIES AND INDUSTRIAL ESTATES FOR MY COMPANIES THIS LAST YEAR, and received the following reply: YOUR MAGNIFICENT PLANS AND

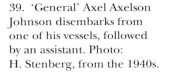

39. 'General' Axel Axelson Johnson disembarks from one of his vessels, followed by an assistant. Photo: H. Stenberg, from the 1940s.

INSTRUCTIVE PRESENTATION OF PROJECTS ARE A SOURCE OF JOY TO ME AND AN
INSPIRATION TO TACKLE THE PROBLEMS STOP PRELIMINARY DRAWINGS IMMEDI-
ATELY ON JANUARY 1. The following year, the tone was more direct. Aalto cabled:
THANK YOU FOR THE PAST YEAR DURING WHICH YOUR DELIGHTFUL ASSIGNMENTS
GAVE ME MORE PLEASURE AND ENJOYMENT IN MY WORK THAN ANY OTHER, to which
Axel Johnson replied: I HEARTILY RECIPROCATE YOUR KIND NEW YEAR'S WISHES
AND THANK YOU FOR HAVING COMMITTED YOUR EMINENT SKILLS TO THE
QUESTIONS I HAVE PUT TO YOU DESPITE YOUR IMPORTANT AND RESPONSIBLE
PROJECTS IN FINLAND DURING A DIFFICULT TIME.

Since Albin Stark's drawing archives in Sweden are not fully accessible, his
joint projects with Aalto are only partly known. According to the Swedish Aalto
scholar Gösta Salén, Aalto probably drafted various plans for the Johnson
company's Södra Verken plant in Avesta, and designed a coin museum fitted
into an old building in the same city. He also designed bus terminals for a
transport company belonging to Johnson in central Sweden. Fortunately some
of the drawings for Aalto's two most important assignments for the General
have been preserved in the Aalto archives in Helsinki. Both projects probably
stemmed from the substantial profits made by the Johnson shipping company's
international freight transport operations as a result of Sweden's neutrality
during the war. Unfortunately, neither plan was carried out, probably because
of the changed economic situation after the war.

The first design was for a magnificent private residence, the Villa Tvistbo,
which the General wished to build on a large, forested estate across Lake
Schissen from Schisshyttans Manor, some distance from the town of Ludvika.
The design is fascinating in that it is the only work that fully reflects Aalto's
enthusiasm for Karelianism, which flared up in 1941 but subsided quickly.
More precisely, it reflects his idealized image of a wilderness architecture that
grew spontaneously in the deep forests of East Karelia (cf. p. 66 above and pp.

40. Sketch for the Villa
Tvistbo, the Karelian-
inspired residence
designed by Aalto for
Axel Axelson Johnson
in 1944.

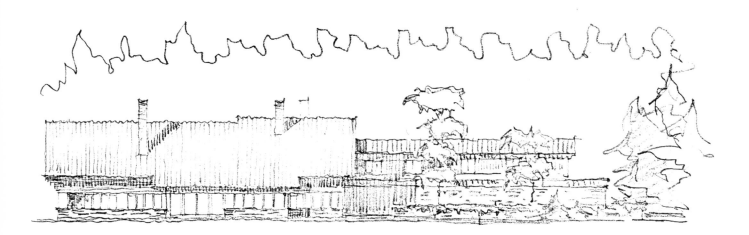

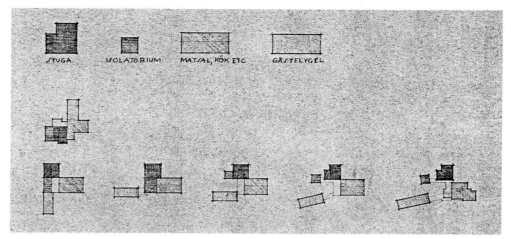

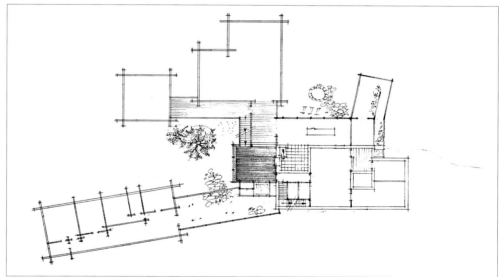

42. Villa Tvistbo. Alternative with diagonal guest wing.

43. Villa Tvistbo. Plan of the compact version with ground-floor living room and kitchen area. The bedrooms and guestrooms are upstairs.

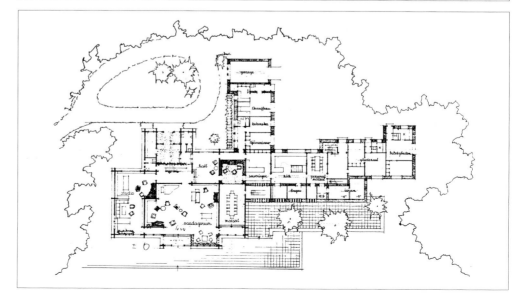

229–230 in *The Decisive Years*). The aspect of Karelian architecture that interested Aalto most, and which he tried to incorporate in even his simplest prefabricated housing, was the principle of growth. The old Karelians built their houses by superimposing new building volumes when needed to the original kernel, which was built of horizontal timbers: the contact surfaces – that is, the partition walls – were thereby doubled. Roof pitch was completely free. In designing the Villa Tvistbo, Aalto first determined the requisite elements. These included a kitchen area and dining room, a living room, a bedroom, a guest wing, and a 'meditation room' for the master of the house, all treated as separate units and combinable in various ways in the manner of building blocks.

Sketches for two such combinations have been preserved. Both feature projecting wings, placed diagonally in one design. The materials – logs of dry standing pine, sod roof, and stone walls – underline the primitive hut character of the house. The interior, however, is anything but primitive. It provides all the modern comfort that a magnate of the time could desire, including numerous bathrooms, a clothes closet for the lady of the house, a playroom for the children, a library, a servants' wing, a garage, and an underground vault for securities and valuables. It also has the floating room sequence Aalto had used in the house for Maire and Harry Gullichsen (cf. *The Decisive Years,* p. 160). The Villa Mairea is in fact the only Aalto building with which this unbuilt Swedish residence could have been compared.

Aalto's most extensive project for the General was the 'Johnson Institute', which was to have been built on Nyby hill, overlooking Avesta's industrial district. The design comprises a dozen largish buildings spread out over the hilly, forested terrain in a manner reminiscent of an American university campus. The main buildings include a mining museum with five successive exhibitions halls terraced diagonally from a large entrance area, as in Aalto's Tallinn museum design. A seafaring museum with a similar room arrangement and a virtually freestanding glass pavilion displaying the Johnson shipping company's collection of figureheads from old ships – Sweden's largest collection of the kind – form an elegant group. Further on is a four-storey building containing scientific laboratories for research into heat, magnetism, radiation, pyrometry, calorimetry, and other physical and chemical disciplines. Next, on the other side of a small plaza, come five testing departments: separate, workshop-like pavilions. The 'Avesta Hall' has display space for the Avesta ironworks' products and a wedge-shaped auditorium seating 285, with staggered tiers and an extremely elegant, shell-shaped ceiling. An enormous bowl-shaped depression outside contains a Classical open-air theatre, with up to 30 rows of seats forming a semicircle around the round orchestra, providing seating for more than 1,000 spectators. The nature of the events to be held there is not specified in the drawings. An outdoor regional museum, a hostel and restaurant, housing for the curator and guard, and sites for a school and faculty housing to be added later, round off the ambitious plan.

44. Master plan for the
Johnson Institute in Avestä.
The laboratories surround
the courtyard at the top.
In the central area, left to
right: hostel and restaurant,
Avesta Hall with auditorium,
seafaring museum with
figurehead display room,
central court, and mining
museum with open-air area
for local culture exhibits.

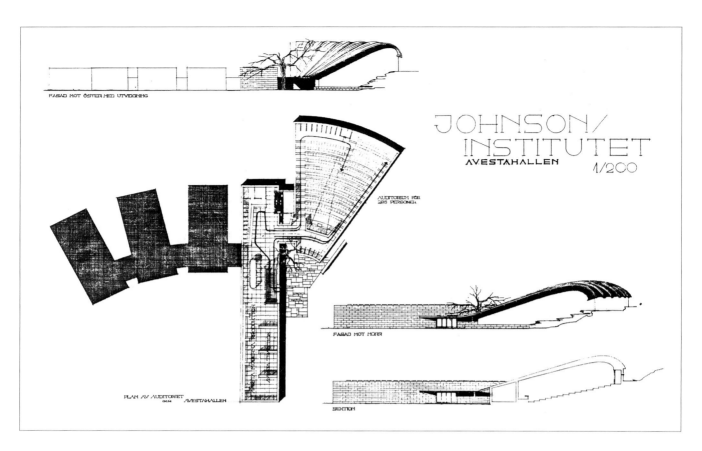

JOHNSON/
INSTITUTET
AVESTAHALLEN 1/200

FASAD MOT ÖSTER MED UTVIDGNING

AUDITORIUM FÖR
285 PERSONER

FASAD MOT NORR

PLAN AV AUDITORIET OCH AVESTAHALLEN

SEKTION

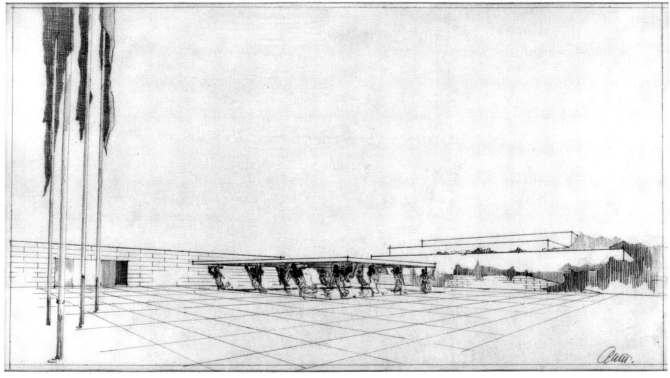

The Johnson group probably could have financed construction of this institution, but the operating costs, comparable to those of a technical university, must have seemed an excessive burden to the family business. The General and Aalto appear to have been drawn into a contest in visionary extravagance, leaving the prosaic realities far behind them. As for Aalto's share, the architectural inventiveness of the design and the brio with which he made use of the potential of the terrain and landscape reveal the starvation diet his creative genius had been on during the war years. Here, as in the Villa Tvistbo, he gave free rein to aspirations repressed for a long time.

Let us now turn our attention to two equally significant projects in which Axel Johnson was not officially involved, but which were obviously linked with the interests he represented.

The first was a proposed new town centre for Avesta. This small town in Bergslagen, the Swedish mining region, was chartered in 1919. Its economy, dominated by the Avesta Jernverk (ironworks), owned by the Johnsons, benefited from the company's success during the war years. Amid this new-found wealth, the town fathers realized that Avesta lacked many of the central buildings and institutions that a self-respecting community must have. In spring 1944, the town council innocently turned to the Johnson company's trusted architects, Albin Stark and Alvar Aalto, with the question: "Is it possible to combine under one roof several key needs of government, assembly, representation, various aspects of public life, associations and educational facilities, and so on?" (excerpt from Aalto's official description of his proposal). Among the facilities required were a new town hall, library, theatre, 'People's house', town hotel, and courthouse. Knowing Aalto's positive mania for multipurpose buildings, we can imagine his excitement. That autumn he went to Avesta to present his brilliant, detailed, carefully studied, and even economical response to the town council's question.

Aalto's Avesta centre, the first and in many ways most interesting of the proposals for new town centres he was to present in his later years, was based on the idea that the kind of town hall a small town like Avesta needs and is capable of building can be little more than a modest office building with no pretensions to dominating the townscape. Public buildings in general tend to be dwarfed in our times by commercial and residential development. However, by bringing several such institutions together, a building complex can be made that both meets the need for a monumental town centre and provides a gathering place for the townspeople. From dawn to dusk, citizens of all ages have reasons to visit a centre that houses local government offices, a library, a restaurant, a workers' club, a hotel, a dance floor, a theatre, and numerous shops and outdoor facilities. This kind of centre provides for socializing rather in the manner of a collective home.

The people of Avesta received the proposal with astonishment. It decidedly did not correspond to their idea of serious architecture. Aalto's renowned charm and persuasiveness had an effect on only a handful of people, chief

79

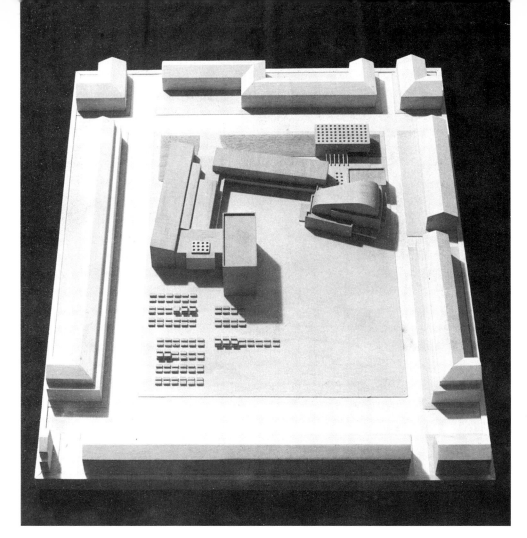

47. Aalto's proposed Avesta city centre. In the middle is the Citizens' Court, with the office wing of the City Hall jutting into it. Left, the council chamber (with 12 round skylights), then the assembly hall and restaurant. Hotel at far left. On the far side of the Citizens' Court, the workers' club, next the theatre and lastly the skylit library.

among whom was Ernst Sundh, engineer, master builder, and local business genius. He became a sworn Aalto supporter, and fought gallantly for the centre plan. He later became Aalto's business partner when the Swedish Artek factory was set up in Hedemora. He even built his own Aalto house, known as the Sundh Center, in Avesta (1955–60).

Most of the people of Avesta, however, did not want Aalto's town centre. They had all sorts of objections: some asked why it was placed at an angle to the rectangular grid of the town plan. According to Aalto, this made for "a charming contrast", but his critics thought it completely unnecessary. They particularly objected to the idea that offices, cafés, shops, the library, and the workers' club had not been kept separate; for example, the town hall wing had boutiques on the ground floor. This might be acceptable in the carefree South, but "did not suit the Swedish temperament". The proposal was altogether "foreign to the town's character", had no specific local flavour, and could have been placed in "any mid-sized town in Sweden or abroad" (quote from the local building committee's minutes, January 29, 1945).

A surer way to torpedo the plan was with financial arguments. The town council suddenly discovered that Avesta could not possibly afford the project. It made no difference that master builder Sundh offered to build the entire complex for 3,050,000 kronor (less than half a million dollars) and that the annual maintenance costs for the centre would be 30,000 kronor after subtracting rental income.

The plan was shelved and forgotten. But thirty years later, when a travelling Aalto exhibition came to Avesta and the model for the centre was put up, the townspeople rubbed their eyes in disbelief. How could this unique opportunity have been passed up? All the institutions brought together by Aalto had been built later on scattered sites at many times the cost. Instead, Avesta had carried out a completely different plan for Markustorget, the central square. It is the site of the 'Plus complex', a gaudy, ugly shopping centre, containing various department stores and chain stores peddling their wares. This development says a good deal about the Swedish double standard, which in theory lauds the social goals of cultural offerings and human contact that the Aalto centre would have served so well, but in practice favours commercialism and consumerism.

The second major project undertaken by the team of Aalto and Stark during the war was the master plan for Nynäshamn, completed in 1945. The official client was the newly-designated town, but since it was built on land detached from the Johnson family estate, Nynäs, and was home to a number of large industrial enterprises, primarily Nynäs Petroleum, a member of the Johnson group at the time, the real client was obviously the General.

Aalto naturally took part in a competition held by Nynäshamn for the design of a town hall. With his usual sensitivity to the natural environment, and out of respect for the rocky archipelago setting, he submitted an entry with several organically linked building volumes unfettered by geometry. The jury's criti-

48. Avesta city centre seen from Markustorget. Left to right: hotel, city hall, and theatre.

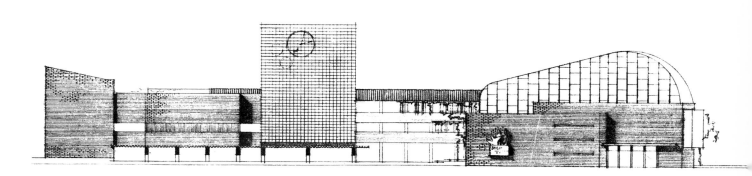

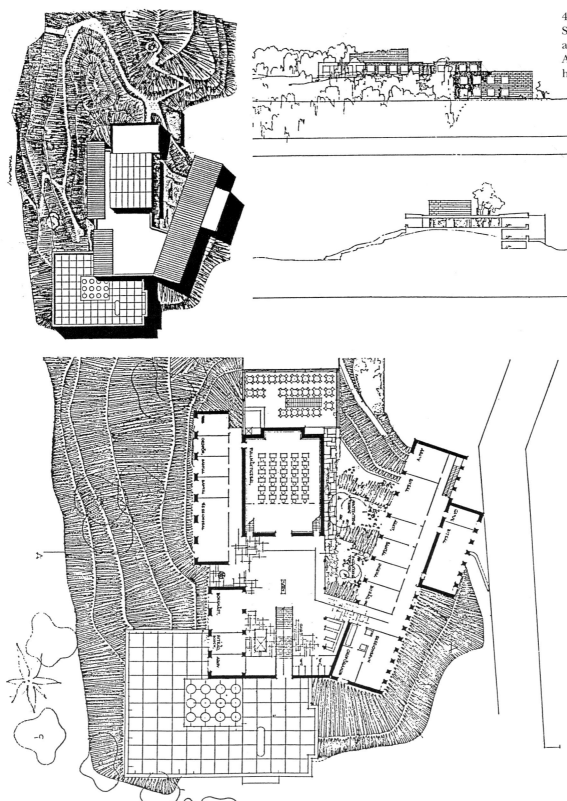

49. These drawings in the Swedish journal *Arkitekten* are all that remains of Aalto's entry for the Nynäshamn town hall.

cism of a few practical weaknesses in the design seems petty, as these could have been easily corrected. Aalto's entry did not win a prize, but it was purchased for 750 kronor.

The Nynäshamn town plan gave some direction to the town's expansion, and a point block designed by Aalto but distorted beyond recognition by Stark was eventually built in the Heimdal area. Sadly, these are the only visible marks of all of Aalto's ambitious efforts in Sweden in the 1940s. A row house, a heating plant, and an apartment hotel in the Skatan quarter of Avesta, mentioned in a letter from Aalto to Stark, never got off the drawing board. The same goes for the town plan of the Hufvudsta district of Solna, a Stockholm suburb. Aalto worked on this plan, which also started as a joint project with Stark, from 1945 to 1960.

The reasons for these failures are not easy to find, but Aalto's many later setbacks in Sweden suggest a fundamental incompatibility between Aalto's boldness and Swedish caution. His work with Stark was also hampered by external circumstances. The Swedish architect, who was to have been the dynamo and practical executor of their joint projects, suffered a stroke in 1945 that led to his death a few years later. For his part, Aalto was drawn into so many commitments after the war, in the United States and elsewhere, that he no longer kept up his contact with the Johnson group.

50. One of Aalto's point blocks for the Heimdal area in Nynäshamn, showing entrance bridge and wedge-shaped plan. Albin Stark 'normalized' the house so completely during construction that Aalto disclaimed all responsibility for its design.

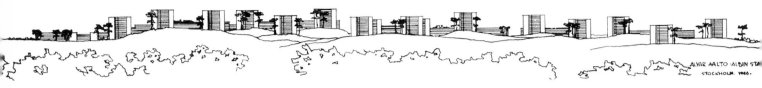

This did not mean that he lost sight of Sweden altogether. In fact, he toyed with the idea of moving to Hedemora in 1946, as we shall see in a later chapter, and took part in some of the most important architectural competitions arranged in Sweden in the 1950s and '60s. Because Sweden and Swedish culture had been important to him from his childhood, and because some of his best friends were Swedes, he nursed a lifelong ambition to build something significant in his second spiritual homeland. It was a bitter disappointment to him that this never happened.

51. Aalto's bold skyline for the Heimdal housing area in Nynäshamn provided wide sea views for inhabitants and emphasized the wave movement of the terrain. As built, the design was greatly watered down.

Chairman of the Association of Finnish Architects

When Alvar Aalto was admitted as a member of the Association of Finnish Architects (or SAFA, as it is usually called after its complete name *Suomen Arkkitehtiliitto Finlands Arkitektförbund*) in the early 1920s, the association was a small coterie composed overwhelmingly of Swedish-speaking Helsinki architects, who met at the venerable Kämp Hotel. It was more like an English gentlemen's club than anything else. By 1941, SAFA had 260 members recruited from around the country, and the majority were Finnish speakers. The old spirit lingered on surprisingly long, however, as the established, well-connected older members set the tone. All architects considered themselves standard-bearers of culture and worldly wisdom, an attitude represented with great authority by Alvar Aalto himself. The architects were politically liberal, which is why SAFA avoided all major schisms among its collegial membership during the 1930s, a time of extreme divisiveness in language and party politics.

A typical example of the lofty but genuinely liberal spirit that still survived untarnished in 1945 is provided by Aulis Blomstedt's memorandum to the SAFA leadership on the question of whether the association's journal, *Arkkitehti-Arkitekten*, should continue to be published in Swedish as well as in Finnish:

We architects, whose only purpose in life is to learn to speak the lapidary, universal language of architecture as fluently as possible, should not in this, or in any professional matter, be concerned with the petty interests of any micro-community grouped around this or that minor Germanic or Finno-Ugric dialect. Our true mother tongue is the petrous language of architecture, the living, clear tones of which still ring out in the architecture of Egypt, Greece, and Rome, while the corresponding spoken languages have long been hidden away in the dark corners of libraries.

As long as the membership remained reasonably small and all knew each other and were on good terms, SAFA remained a gentlemen's club and a school for civilized manners. Aalto, too, learned there to restrain the intolerance that is one of the worst flaws in human behaviour. The confrontation between traditionalists and modernists in the 1930s had put Sirén, the designer of the Finnish Parliament House, and Aalto at sixes and sevens. Whenever they happened to meet in the street, Aalto would cross over to the other side to avoid having to greet his rival. It is edifying to see how well they behaved at SAFA board meetings once they had both been elected. In later years, they could actually deliver encomiums to each other, though the old antagonism still smouldered under the surface. When in 1955 SAFA was discussing which works to include in an exhibition entitled "The Modern Breakthrough in Finnish Architecture" to be sent to the United States, Aalto thought that the Parliament House should not be included, while Sirén wanted to reject Aalto's Paimio Sanatorium on the grounds that "it was an extreme example of the breakthrough of a Neo-Functionalist nuance in our architecture".

In the democratic annual elections among the members, Aalto was first elected to the SAFA board back in 1935, and in 1939 he became vice-chairman. However, he seems to have been burdened by a perception of his wartime behaviour as disloyal. He remained on the board, but there was considerable opposition to him from autumn 1939 on. The story of how he overcame this opposition step by step and gained the chairmanship in 1943 is an extraordinary chapter of his chequered career. His desire for this post was due in part to understandable personal ambition, but also to his firm belief in the reconstruction ideas he had formulated in the United States, which he had no chance of carrying out without SAFA's support.

He began his offensive soon after his return from the United States. At the time, SAFA had already set up a reconstruction committee headed by its chairman, Otto Meurman. At a meeting in February 1941, Aalto spoke of his "American Town in Finland" and his institute at MIT, and hinted discreetly that Finnish architects might receive scholarships to work there. He published his extensive article, "The Reconstruction of Europe", in Arkkitehti journal that summer, and the one on "Rural Housing" in the autumn along with another article suggesting that the 1939 housing exhibition should be turned into a travelling, constantly updated exhibition on reconstruction.

In December, he launched the decisive attack. In an inspired speech to the SAFA annual meeting, he depicted the dangers of the uncoordinated, inferior reconstruction work that had begun, partly under Army supervision, partly directed by incompetent agricultural societies and ministries which had no clear idea of the larger issues involved. He explained that only the "creative force", design skills, and humanist attitude represented by trained architects could steer the programme into the right path. Directives, bureaucracy, and technology cannot in themselves achieve anything positive; at best they are a necessary evil. However, it is obvious that architects alone cannot design and manage everything. The Association should therefore seek a coordinating and supervising role in reconstruction.

The architects responded enthusiastically to these arguments. There and then they decided to set up a Reconstruction Office, and turned to the national government, which seems to have favoured at least parts of the initiative. This was confirmed when the SAFA Reconstruction Office was placed under the supervision of the Ministry of Public Works. In May 1942, the Reconstruction

Office opened its own offices, and architects Viljo Revell and Aarne Ervi (Aalto's former assistants) were ordered from the front to take up service there. It went without saying that Aalto was in charge, and that he was now a member of all SAFA committees which had anything to do with reconstruction.

As Aalto had thus proved his mettle as SAFA's most innovative force, it seemed reasonable that his colleagues would vote him into SAFA's highest office at the next election on March 15, 1942. The election did not go as he had hoped, however, showing that there was still aversion to him. Meurman, the incumbent chairman, was re-elected with 44 votes to Aalto's 7. Aalto took his defeat in stride, however, and proceeded to dominate subsequent SAFA meetings with his verve, humour, and charm. The following election (for the 1943 term) took place on October 27, 1943, and Aalto mobilized all his supporters. Of 40 members present, 24 voted for Aalto and 12 for Meurman; Hilding Ekelund was elected vice-chairman, a position he held for many years.

Aalto was chairman of SAFA until 1959, when he decided not to run again. In the early years, he attended meetings assiduously, but later, especially when he was teaching at MIT, he was conspicuously absent. He was re-elected unanimously without opposition on several occasions, but now and then another candidate would get a few stray votes. The chairmanship gave him excellent opportunities to cultivate his foreign contacts. Many of the visiting lecturers at the Association's meetings were old friends of his, including Sten Branzell, Gregor Paulsson, Gotthard Johansson, Hakon Ahlberg, Sven Ivar Lind, Albin Stark, and Nils Ahrbom from Sweden, Kay Fisker from Denmark, Sigfried Giedion from Switzerland, and F.R.S. Yorke from Britain. Aalto represented

52. Aalto in his role as SAFA chairman, here shown conferring the Association's silver plaque on his colleague Sigurd Frosterus. Photo: Sandström.

the Association brilliantly at international architectural conferences; on select occasions in the home country, such as SAFA's 60th anniversary in 1952, he was the natural focus of attention.

That particular occasion, celebrated with an "Acanthus Ball", filled the entire Helsinki Art Hall. Characteristically, Aalto sent Prime Minister Urho Kekkonen an invitation in which he wrote that the celebration was very informal with no official guests of honour, but that "if it should amuse you to see what the architectural corps with ladies look like when they are merriest, I would be happy to have you and your spouse come as my personal guests." K.A. Fagerholm, Speaker of Parliament, received a similar invitation, but with no mention of the corps' merry ladies. A letter from Aalto to Kaarlo Hillilä, director of the National Pensions Institute, gives us an inkling of how the party went for him. The letter deals with practical issues involving current plans for the Institute's head office. Aalto wrote: "I would have liked to talk about this at the party in the Art Hall, but I was so blind drunk that I couldn't get hold of you there. Grogs internally and women's breasts externally don't seem to do me good."

As for SAFA's official meetings, Aalto often managed to give them, too, a festive touch. No literary genre can be more sterile than the rigidly schematic,

53. Some of the participants in SAFA's 'Acanthus Ball' at the Helsinki Art Hall in 1952. Aalto sitting on the floor, Speaker of Parliament K.A. Fagerholm and wife standing to his right. Photo: Hilli.

paragraph-ridden minutes of meetings, but the minutes of board and general meetings in the SAFA archives show time and again how the various people who kept the minutes were captivated and stimulated by the chairman. A typical example is provided by Einari Teräsvirta's minutes of the Association meeting in Otaniemi on May 24, 1952, when the architects first saw the 'Tech Village' designed originally by Aalto, and then gathered at its restaurant. After reporting the formal business, Teräsvirta concludes:

5: Established that "no-one has been wronged".

6: The chairman gave an account of his recent trip to Italy in his amusing manner.

7: The meeting continued and concluded in the form of a "dancing congress". Inspected: A. Aalto. In witness whereof: E.T.

Dinners with the ladies were part of standard protocol throughout Aalto's reign.

Examining Aalto's actions as chairman and his real contribution to the Association's work, two key initiatives stand out. The first was the *Finnish Standardization Office,* which started as a branch of the Reconstruction Office and was headed by Kaj Englund. Right from the start, there seems to have been some confusion regarding objectives. The Office started diligently preparing 'building cards' that would assign standard measurements and fixed designs to all the various elements of house construction, from doors, windows, and staircases to joists, wall insulation, and sanitary facilities. By March 1943, close to 100 cards with comprehensive technical specifications had been prepared. They were sent regularly to subscribers – architects and master builders – who only had to specify card no. x in their drawings and building programmes to show what they wanted done. Ten years later, 188,090 cards had been sold, and standardization continues today with purely practical goals.

For Aalto, the plan embodied the idea of flexible standardization he had formulated at MIT in 1940. Instead of unifying housing construction to make it cheaper and more efficient, the goal was to permit individual and local variation despite industrial production. At a SAFA meeting on March 15, 1942, just before the Standardization Office began its work, Aalto discussed the standardization issue at the after-dinner coffee:

The body responsible for standardization should be like the French Academy or Gustavus III's Academy, following the development of the language and determining which forms should be considered correct.

He defined his conception of the parallelism between architecture and literature in a short paper entitled *Architecture and Standards,* based on his dictation and published by SAFA in 1942.

The work of the architect can be compared in many ways with that of the writer. As the author uses a certain vocabulary to create a work, so the designer of buildings creates a work from a variety of elements which can be compared with the words of a language. In some ways, however, the author is more fortunate than the architect. The elements he uses, the words of a language, have a precisely defined meaning and orthography – they are

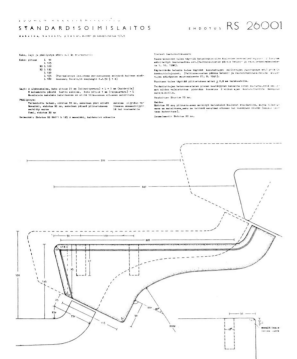

54. A Standardization Office building card, printed September 30, 1942, showing Aalto's invention of *the standardized concrete stair* with flexible use for staircases with varying stair depth and grade.

'standardized' and can be retrieved in systematic order in dictionaries. A dictionary naturally contains a large number of rare words which are not commonly used, but even with the limited vocabulary of everyday speech the author can describe a great variety of things, present his ideas, and give expression to shifting emotions, depending on his skill in using the language. The architect's plight is different. He has no access to an authoritatively approved 'dictionary of building'; he works with elements that are in a state of complete anarchy. For the most part, the words of the language of architecture, the articles of building, have not been standardized: there are any number of articles which differ unnecessarily in forms and dimensions. The superabundant vocabulary of the 'language of architecture' resembles written Chinese, which has thousands of characters that can take ten years to learn. In fact the architect tends to spend a disproportionate amount of time familiarizing himself with articles with varying 'signs' . . .

The purpose of standardization in architecture must be to provide the elements, the 'cells', of which the building, the 'organism', is composed. Just as in nature every cell is related to the whole, so in architecture the parts must be 'conscious of the whole'. When designing the parts, one must know the desired result; at least, one must have a notion, a conception of it.

Not until 1958 did the discrepancy between these humanist goals and the Standardization Office's real impact come to light. That year SAFA set up a committee to find out what had gone wrong with the Standardization Office. It was admitted that conditions in the early years of reconstruction had made it necessary to concentrate on economic considerations "which are misleading, however. Now we must raise standardization to a higher level in harmony with cultural values. We must distinguish between technical standardization, which leads to uniformity, and qualitative standardization and norm-giving, yielding a completely different result. SAFA has a special responsibility to work for this deeper goal. Mass production belongs to the sphere of business, only indirectly to architecture."

The committee did not get any further than this declaration of principles. How to put 'cultural standardization' into practice remained moot, perhaps because Aalto's theory of flexible standardization had contained 'a certain measure of fantasy' from the very beginning. There is probably an inherent contradiction in seeking unlimited organic freedom and at the same time building up a strictly mechanical system such as that of the building cards. In contrast, the individualized architecture produced today goes quite far in spontaneous 'flexible standardization', since the technical production methods of building components have automatically resulted in varied combination potential.

Another item at the top of Aalto's agenda, which he pursued even more energetically during his chairmanship, was the *architect's professional role.* As I showed in Part I of this biography, Aalto inherited from his father and maternal grandfather an old-fashioned belief that the civil servant has a responsibility to society and should be above all private interests. Thus, government officials had to be politically and financially independent servants of society. Aalto extended the same responsibility to two specific independent professions: physicians and architects. Their duty was to think only of their patients' or clients' best, naturally for reasonable financial compensation so that they could lead a life consistent with their station.

This meant that Aalto thought of the architect as *the client's trustee,* a specialist who looks after his client's true interests to the best of his ability, in the same way as a doctor does. This is possible only if the architect enjoys his client's full confidence and manages to convince him of what is best for him. The client must be sure that the architect is not trying to take advantage of his ignorance or cheat him for the benefit of a third party, such as a building contractor or a manufacturer of building supplies. The special, direct relationship between architect and client is sealed by the architect's signature on each drawing, the equivalent of a doctor's name under a prescription.

Aalto was not alone in these beliefs, even if he embraced them with unusual fervour. The whole corps of architects had adopted these principles, whether consciously or unconsciously, because they enhanced the prestige of the profession. However, new times and new economic and political realities meant new pressures. The government, various corporations, and large building contractors engaged architects to work anonymously in their offices together with master builders and engineers, who were showing an increasing propensity to design buildings without the assistance of trained architects. At the same time, various companies started manufacturing and marketing architect-designed interior decoration details. These problems became particularly pressing in the conditions created by postwar reconstruction.

The struggle to ensure a leading role for SAFA in reconstruction was part of Aalto's effort to defend the architect's role in society. Minor skirmishes were fought, as when SAFA decided in 1941 on Aalto's suggestion that architects should not be allowed to accept subordinate positions other than as assistants to other architects, which led in 1943 to the Association's forbidding architects to work for the central association of agricultural societies. In 1944, SAFA drafted the following recommendations for its members:

1) *Architects should not act as middlemen for others, but should sign and answer for their drawings personally.*

2) *Architects should not work for anonymous clients, except in the case of type drawings available to all.*

3) *It violates professional ethics for an architect to work for building contractors (with the possible exception of national and local government).*

4) *An architect may not approve his own works as a building inspector.*

To these guidelines, Viljo Revell added the comment that the purpose was *not to gain advantages for the profession but to create conditions conducive to the best possible work.*

This policy obviously set the Association on a collision course with reality. At a meeting of the Federation of Nordic Architects in Gothenburg in 1945, it turned out that the Norwegian architects' stance was as rigid as that of the Finns, whereas in Sweden and Denmark it was acceptable for architects to be employed by incorporated organizations such as the Kooperativa förbundet (Swedish Cooperative Union and Wholesale Society), which had a very progressive and reputable office in Stockholm.

The inevitable showdown came fairly quickly, and with no less a body than the Finnish National Board of Building. The Board had decided in 1951 to appoint two engineers to positions previously held by architects, and two years later appointed a new general director who was unacceptable to SAFA. Finland was in severe economic straits, and the Cabinet wished to place the main emphasis in governmental building projects on realism and economy. SAFA had recommended Viljo Revell, whose magnificent but expensive business complex, Palace, had just been completed in Helsinki. This showy building was probably seen as a negative recommendation. The government instead chose Jussi Lappi-Seppälä, who was an architect but no longer a member of SAFA, as he had acted in direct defiance of the Association's requirement of unselfishness and impartiality in financial matters.

The appointment was a slap in the face for SAFA, and was taken as a special challenge by the Association's chairman. He staked all his prestige on persuading the President of the Republic to fire Lappi-Seppälä, but President J.K. Paasikivi was just as stubborn and unyielding in this affair as Aalto. To give weight to its demand, SAFA decided to declare a blockade on the National

55. Jussi Lappi-Seppälä, appointed general director of the National Board of Building in 1953, a former employee of Aalto's who became a bitter adversary but ended up as his ally.

Board of Building for as long as its objectionable chief remained in his post. This meant that architects who were already employed there would be permitted to continue, but no new vacancies would be filled.

Lappi-Seppälä countered by unofficially bringing to SAFA's notice a forged internal government document according to which no governmental commissions would be awarded to SAFA members as long as the blockade lasted. The forgery was exposed, the Chancellor of Justice was brought into the affair, and in 1955 SAFA published a pamphlet with the title *A Battle for Justice*. There was infighting at SAFA meetings. One member went so far as to say that "young architects had unthinkingly followed the stars in the decision to blockade the Board of Building". Aalto was so upset at the insinuation that he unceremoniously turned his opponent out of the meeting room. This resulted in some other architects accusing the chairman of "acting like Franco", and some twenty members withdrew from the Association. Aalto here showed a passion that may seem surprising in the man of compromise and synthesis that he really was, but on this occasion he could not come up with a conciliatory vision. His belief in the complete irreconcilability of the architect's role with financial profit was so strong that he did not see the contradiction in his own financial interest in Artek, which in his eyes was a purely altruistic cultural institution.

The struggle lasted two years, and drained much of Aalto's mental energy. Fortunately his friend, Prime Minister Fagerholm, suggested a compromise in 1957 that satisfied both parties. Lappi-Seppälä was allowed to stay, but the architects were given greater influence in the government building committee, which wielded authority over the Board of Building. They could thus at least theoretically control the architectural quality of government building projects, which they felt was threatened.

Aalto also had to compromise in his personal grudge against Lappi- Seppälä. The Jyväskylä Pedagogical Institute, which Aalto designed following his victory in the 1951 architectural competition, was built under the supervision of the National Board of Building. Moreover, the building of the University of Technology in Otaniemi, which was originally directed by a commission headed by the university's vice-chancellor, was made the responsibility of the Board of Building in 1959, bringing Aalto into close contact with the enemy he had fought so bitterly. One of the subjects they had to discuss was architect's fees. So Aalto bit the bullet and invited Lappi-Seppälä to make peace over lunch at the Savoy. Lappi-Seppälä eventually became an ardent supporter of Aalto's, and took his side in the prolonged controversy over the Helsinki centre plan.

During Aalto's chairmanship, SAFA exhibited more frequently than ever before. The transfer from Stockholm of a major architectural exhibition called *America Builds*, which opened in Helsinki in autumn 1944 shortly after the armistice between Finland and the Soviet Union was signed, was all Aalto's doing. He was also an initiator of *Finland Builds,* the first overview of contemporary Finnish architecture, which took place in autumn 1953. Two years later, SAFA sent a similar but smaller exhibition to the Smithsonian Institution in Washington.

The most important long-term initiative by the Association during the Aalto years was the founding in 1955 of the Museum of Finnish Architecture, an independent, government-subsidized institution. Aalto was not particularly active in the committees that made the practical arrangements, but he was obviously the museum's godfather. The idea of an institution that differed entirely from all other European museums at the time, a modern museum based not on a permanent collection but on an outward orientation and a variety of activities, could not have arisen in Finland without Aalto's special experiences and contacts in the United States. The link is clear in the manifesto for the planned museum published by Aalto in *Arkkitehti* in spring 1954:

The old museum concept is being replaced by a new form of activity, the prime example of which is the Museum of Modern Art in New York. The museum is a synthesis of a large conservation centre and an institution for exhibitions and scientific research. Some 80% of MOMA activities take place outside the central institution proper.

The museum of architecture Aalto had in mind was not, however, the kind of institution based on foreign PR, retrospective exhibitions, and historical research that it eventually turned into, but a rendez-vous for creative architecture and a forum for Finnish architects to present constructive proposals for the solution of tomorrow's problems. To this end, he designed a 'House of Architecture' in 1966 with 4,000 m^2 of exhibition space, incorporated into his grand plan for the centre of Helsinki. He imagined that the cities and provinces of Finland could display their achievements there and vie for the best architectural ideas. Characteristically, he connected this vision with the ancient Greeks. According to Aalto, Delphi and Delos had been 'cultural clearinghouses' for the rival Greek city-states of the Achaean League, which kept their own 'treasuries' there. Why should not Finland's cities follow this example with equally impressive results? Aalto knew his fellow countrymen, but on this occasion their – and his – patriotic illusions were defeated by adverse reality. The proud House of Architecture in Helsinki, along with the dream of Finland as a cultural trend-setter, remained one of Aalto's many unfulfilled 'artistic fantasies'.

Since this chapter deals with Aalto's relationship with SAFA, and not with the Association's history, I shall conclude my account with the note that by the time he resigned as chairman, membership had risen to 522, having doubled during his fifteen years at the helm. As this implies, SAFA was turning from a collegial social club into what it is today: a trade union with 1900 members, focusing on promoting its members' financial interests and establishing their terms of employment. Thus Aalto's increasing dissociation from the Association was understandable. His interests and goals were different.

Return to America

Throughout the war, America remained a dream for Aalto from which he had been too precipitately torn away, a dream of the epoch-making architectural laboratory that was to solve the problems of building in the industrial age, and of the modern furniture he hoped to develop further through Artek. The beachhead gained at MIT was important to him, and he kept up his contact with the university as long as possible to show that his absence was due only to force majeure. In a letter to MIT President Compton, which he managed to send via diplomatic courier in March 1942, he said that his work at MIT "has to me become like a life's calling".

All the same, he might very well never have had the chance to return. But fortune smiled on him once again. In the second volume of this biography, I told the story of how three young Americans, William W. Wurster and Betty and Tommy Church, arrived unannounced in 1937 at Alvar and Aino Aalto's door in Munkkiniemi and rang the bell. In autumn 1986 (having made arrangements beforehand) I rang the doorbell of the Churches' small house close to San Francisco's fashionable Fisherman's Wharf, and was received by the eighty-year-old Betty Church. She is the last survivor of this set of friends, but the house is the same in which Aalto stayed on several occasions, and the sprightly lady gave a detailed account of the meeting fifty years before which led to a lifelong friendship. It seems that Aalto knew only a hundred words or so of English at the time, but he used this vocabulary so expressively that afterwards his guests regretted that they hadn't written down everything he said – it would have made the most exquisite modern poetry. I was surprised at the account of the overwhelming architectural experience that the Aalto home had given these specialists: they had already visited England, Denmark, and Sweden, without finding anything so modern and close to nature at the same time (Tommy Church was a landscape architect).

One of the main reasons for Alvar and Aino's visit to California in 1939 was to see Wurster, who had designed several private homes around San Francisco

56. William W. Wurster in
the early years of his long
friendship with Aalto.
Courtesy of Richard
P. Peters.

in an idiosyncratic style that earned the epithet "Bay region style" from Lewis Mumford. Wurster's architecture had very little in common with that of Aalto, and Wurster's genuine enthusiasm for Aalto was based on personal esteem rather than any stylistic affinity.

We now come to Lady Luck's intervention in Aalto's life in 1945. That spring, Wurster was unexpectedly summoned from the sunny West Coast to Cambridge to become Dean of MIT's architecture department. One of his first acts was to write to Aalto via the U.S. War Department (normal postal service to Finland was not yet working), asking whether Aalto wished to return to MIT for, say, six months a year in order to be able to go on working in Finland. The letter arrived a whole month later, and Aalto's reply (dated July 14, 1945) took the same time to reach the United States. Aalto declared that the world's enormous reconstruction problems could be solved only in the United States, and he would be glad to take part in this work. For this purpose, MIT should arrange through the War Department in Washington for Aalto to make a study trip to several devastated European countries. He also proposed a method for the project: research in how to counteract the anti-individualistic mechanization of life and the environmental uniformity to which industrial construction threatened to give rise: "What I am at is a special architectural liberation from the grip of technical standardization."

Wurster was obliged to curb Aalto's plans to some extent. MIT could not even afford to pay the transatlantic air fare, let alone a costly tour of Europe, so Aalto would have to settle for a sea voyage. As for the programme, Wurster prosaically suggested that Aalto should come for a preliminary three-month visit to "enable you to sense the temper of America". The courses to be taught did not have to be defined in advance: it was enough if Aalto was willing to "give the students the lift which your brilliant personality can give".

With all the formalities and negotiations at last completed, Aalto finally set off on November 6, 1945 (he flew from Stockholm; citing lack of time, he had at least won this concession from MIT), and word was sent to the relatively few students who were studying at MIT's architecture department immediately after the war. According to this announcement, Aalto would "give lectures, have conferences with students who are doing special problems and be critic of design of one of the two groups".

Aalto was far from being the open, spontaneous person his friends imagined. Behind his sociability and charm, he concealed a certain restraint and reticence; on a deeper level, we should perhaps consider his personality closed and hypersensitive. He was critical of virtually all those around him, which they rarely realized as he gave them the illusion of perfect fellowship. The letters he

57. Aino 1940-luvulla. Alvar Aallon kynäpiirros.

sent Aino from America therefore have a special interest. He spoke more freely and confidentially with her than with anyone else. These letters are also a direct and very lively source of information on the contacts he made in America and on the very eventful life he led there.

Let us begin with the warm and flattering reception he had on the other side of the Atlantic.

On November 7, 1945, he sent the following chivalrous telegram in English to Aino: LANDED IN NEW YORK VIA BERMUDA MIRRORLIKE OCEAN REFLECTING YOUR SMILE ALVAR. A few days later (undated), he reported his first impressions of Cambridge, which is situated on the left bank of the Charles River across from Boston:

Dear little Aino. I am sitting on Gropius's top floor, it's a peaceful holiday just after my arrival in Boston. I still think of the flight over the water, of the feeling that the distance wasn't so far from where you are, and that during the quiet night flight high above the clouds I sat under the starry sky reading your letter in the light of the small night lamp, as we flew from the Azores to the coral islands of Bermuda. My thoughts are with you all constantly, I follow what you are doing from hour to hour, and when I walk down Commonwealth Avenue with Wurster around 5–6 p.m., I think that you may be in bed by now and I hope you have peace of mind and sleep well . . .

A few days later, still undated:

Dear Aino. The work here has begun. A little chaotic to start with, as Wurster is a little overly eager. For example, he has brought an aristocrat from India who is an architect and has been commissioned to build a hospital somewhere out in the jungle. * The poor boy says he came here to get a little continuing education à la Paimio Sanatorium, and now I am becoming responsible in some way for what he is building for his government. Wurster is very cordial, and so are Catherine (Wurster's wife) and baby. I have been to their home nearly every day.

America has been marked by the war much more than one would expect. Almost impossible to get a hotel room; the same goes for air and train tickets. The people are somehow psychologically tired, much more impolite than before. I have finally found an apartment, at Marlborough Street 430, Boston. A big room, bed with curtains, masses of colonial bric à brac and a large bathroom, all on the upper floor of a little old private home, where I am the only lodger. Getting this required all the contacts and family relationships that MIT could muster. MIT is conveniently just across the river.

Sandy Calder opened an exhibition the other day. I flew to New York, where all our old friends gathered at a suburban Italian restaurant. Léger with a new blonde, the Sweeneys, Sert, Miss Willard and dozens of others we know but I don't have the slightest idea of their names. All sent their love to you. I left early, at midnight, and slept 9 hours. There's no point wasting my strength, even though they were all good friends.

I haven't really suffered from travel fatigue, though New York is a hard city, as you know, and the time difference gives me some trouble. It's peaceful here in Cambridge, and

---

*This was the young architect Durga Baipai, whose father was later India's ambassador to Washington. Durga Baipai trained with Aalto in Finland in 1946.

now that I have a place to stay, I'm living very quietly. The weekend starts tomorrow. May take the train to Maine to some forest inn, if I can get a room. The surroundings would be closer to you and the children. A little walk in the mossy forest Saturday and Sunday, or perhaps I'll stay here and paint a watercolour for you – if I do, on such thin paper that I can send it airmail.

Here is the following letter, written at Marlborough St 430, Boston:

Dear little Aino. Writing this on a peaceful Sunday morning. Just visited New York, went to a Sibelius concert with the Saarinens. Supper with them afterwards, of course: Eliel and Loja send their love, they are just like before. The following morning Frank Lloyd Wright woke me up, had breakfast at the Plaza, three hours of really pleasant conversation. Both he and Olivanna (FLW's wife) send their love.

Friday I attended something of a summit. NY architects, among them Howard Myers, George Howe, Stone and a dozen others, arranged a big lunch at the Manhattan Club. Two guests of honour: FLW and myself. Two speeches were made, one to each of us. Howe harangued me as "the world's finest enemy" (Finland's participation in the war on the German side was still fresh in American memory) *and then proposed "three cheers for the most creative architects in the world – from double A to double U". Everyone here asks about you and the children. I have had many offers for private commissions, but have said no to all. Perhaps I shall make a building for MIT, however. They need a new library, a new gymnasium, a new professors' club, and a new dormitory, all at once. Very few cocktails here, but lots of kisses for you. Your A.*

A letter postmarked Cambridge, December 5, 1945 describes a memorable visit to Taliesin:

58. After the lunch both Wright and Aalto received a small photo album documenting the event, but designating only one of them as the guest of honour. This is Aalto's album.

TO HONOR

ALVAR AALTO

LUNCHEON

MANHATTAN CLUB   NEW YORK

NOVEMBER 23, 1945

GUESTS

HUGH FERRIS	HENRY WRIGHT	FRANK LLOYD WRIGHT
EDWARD D. STONE	PHILIP JOHNSON	WALLACE HARRISON
GEORGE HOWE		Host: HOWARD MYERS

59. Aalto at the head of the table, talking with George Howe, a pioneer of Modernism in the United States.

My dear Aino. Taliesin, just for two days, but that's enough. Met FLW in Milwaukee, where he was waiting for me. The small hotel was pleasant, too: the porter immediately asked for my autograph for his Finnish wife. We then went to the Art Institute, which had a large FLW exhibition. He lectured at 4, and took me with him up on the stage, where I sat next to him all through the lecture. I was naturally introduced as "Europe's most distinguished architect" and in the newspapers we were shown "arm in arm". In the evening we drove the 160 miles out to Taliesin. Supper just as in the photographs: Frank, Olivanna and me in the special seats of honour, the boys and girls passing the food around small Japanese tables. Then music and performances by the students, each in turn. Slept like a log for 10 hours. Today I have strolled around. The place is agreeable and the atmosphere is right. The school is much bigger than you'd think, though some of the rooms are so low that FLW's son-in-law, an architect of course, can't stand up straight in them. The main drawing office is about 40 x 30 metres, and there are many different studios, all built by the students and local farm boys with their own hands. I am enclosing a

*landscape sketch of the view from the window at which I am writing this letter. Tonight
I take the flight or train back to Boston. I have been in a very optimistic mood all through
these last few days. Your work, Artek's resources, the fantastic opportunities here in
America, and the crystallizing direction for our joint work, all this builds up to a harmony
that I shall write about another time. Many kisses little Aino from your Alvar.*

Immediately on returning to Boston, Alvar wrote a brief thank-you letter to
FLW that began: *Dear Frank. Words cannot express how much the visit to Taliesin
meant to me both in head and heart reactions.* A letter to his colleague Aulis
Blomstedt back in Finland provides a less formal comment on his visit. It gives
us an unvarnished glimpse of Aalto's puckish side, but also of his awareness of
the fundamentally positive attitude to life that gives flavour to Wright's
architecture, as it does to Aalto's own:

*Taliesin 3.11.45. My dear Blomstedt, You see where I am . . . It is so damned beautiful
here. You could call this place the heart of America. The building is simple and sweet –
built by farmers and students of the school with their own hands, using stones straight out
of foundations and the soil. But it isn't built on rock. My research indicates that Taliesin
is built on cunt, and you can really feel that foundation here. It's a good foundation. Tuus
Alvar.*

Before going into the plans for the future that the visit to Frank Lloyd Wright
seems to have crystallized in Aalto's mind, I should like to dwell a moment on

the positive human contacts and flattering offers he received during his visits to the United States. On December 13, 1945, he wrote:

Dear Aino. This was supposed to be that "Christmas letter"; we'll see if it gets to you in time. I was sitting in the bar with Gropius, who just left, so I started to write to you instead. You know, I have great difficulties because of people's excessive friendliness. Today Harvard offered me a full professorship (on a par with Gropius and directly under the university board). And Saarinen suggested that we should divide up his commissions and I should start up an office of my own near Cranbrook. Wurster and especially Burchard are offering me the MIT annex. I think, little Aino, that we shall not accept any of these "world-class offers".

In a letter a few days later, he provided an interesting piece of information:

In January I shall present the MIT board with a programme and drawings for an Institute for architectural research. I have made this my main project here. But the people who are helping me in this are so bad and so used to a mechanistic way of thinking that I don't dare hope that the plan will come to anything at least in the near future. The work would be fun if the atmosphere here wasn't so wrong. FLW told me: "My America no longer exists, nor do the England, Germany, and Japan that I loved. Democracy has yielded; various fascisms and such have given us a worldwide mobocracy. America has become much more imperialistic than in our days, and so self-sufficient that the civilized people who matter so much to us are no longer as important as they used to be."

Of course this was a spontaneous emotional outburst on my part and not all that significant in itself. But right now I am a little pessimistic because Wurster is directing the faculty a little like a schoolmarm (as you know, he's a bit of an old woman for all his heartiness). Burchard is so often in Washington that I haven't had the chance to talk to him properly (he's the grandiose type and recently discharged from Germany as a general). Burchard, then, is looking for great things to accomplish, and Wurster is dreaming of hopeless improvements at the school. My job is really a matter between Burchard (=the Bemis Foundation) and myself, but Wurster keeps bothering me with his narrow mind. I'm also bothered by Harvard's unexpected move. As I told you before, they suddenly and quite solemnly turned to me and offered me a full professorship. Now that the Harvard school is becoming an academy, they think it will be flooded by so many students that they'll have to set up two parallel schools of architecture, one led by Gropius and the other by myself. I have a feeling that the matter isn't quite that simple, and they're going to set up a murderous rivalry between Gropius and me, just to avoid criticism by having two of the principal modern trends in architecture represented at Harvard. Then the Trustees will find a suitable opportunity to throw one of us out.

I'm continuing this letter in New York. Just flew in and am sitting at the bar in good old Plaza. Two beers (for my thirst) and a jam omelette (composed by myself) with a little port (no cocktails), and then to bed (no girls). I'm living like a millionaire nowadays (that is, extremely frugally), but I have reservations with American Aviations for the New York – Boston – New York flight every week. Just got back from 'dinner' at Horn & Hardart: main course 30 cents, buttermilk 5 c, and bread-and-butter 5 c. Tomorrow I take the train (Pullman) to Cranbrook.

Aalto went to Cranbrook to spend Christmas with the Saarinens. He had received three invitations for the holidays. Calder wanted him to come to a party in Roxbury, and wrote that it would be "a little crowded", but that he could sleep on a sofa in the studio. Edgar Kaufmann Jr. invited him to Fallingwater with Museum of Modern Arts director Alfred Barr, but Aalto preferred (as he wrote to Aino) to "sit snickering quietly with Saarinen, telling Finnish jokes".

On December 26, 1945 he wrote from Birmingham, Michigan:

Dear Aino. Am sitting with Eero Saarinen at their office in Birmingham on the second day of Christmas. They looked after me very tactfully at Christmas. I got Christmas presents from everybody, even the Swansons (Eliel's daughter and her husband), *in the form of food packages ready packed to be sent to Finland; that is, to you. Will mail them tomorrow, a weekday, so they should get there eventually. Going back to Boston the day after tomorrow. My private life is rather dull, as I avoid company (the parties I can't say no to are more than enough), but it's also dull because of my sense of alienation in this world. I'm trying to find the right path, but have all the American indifference to Europe against me and all these efforts to tempt me personally with "the moon and the stars". Besides Harvard, this office is now trying to offer me Saarinen's inheritance and many commissions here. You know my answer to that offer, too, but write me what you think about it all anyway.*

If it was ever clear that Aalto was not intent on his own career or financial profit, but was ruled by the ideas or chimaeras he believed in, it was at this crossroads in his life. On one side, "the moon and the stars" in the United States; on the other, the uncertain future offered by his vision of society.

Before concluding this chapter on Aalto's social success in the United States, I should like to quote his account of the honorary Ph.D. he received from Princeton University on the occasion of its bicentennial celebration on February 22, 1947. The ceremony took place only a few days after Aalto had flown across the Atlantic from Finland for the fourth time after the war. Here is the story in his letter of February 28, 1947 to Aino:

The takeoff was elegant, the plane rose smoothly and then I spent hour after hour in my seat without getting any sleep. When we approached Newfoundland, the most magnificent aurora borealis I have ever seen appeared against the northern sky. Something like this. (Aalto depicted the phenomenon on a page of the letter.) *In Newfoundland we had the usual landing problems, nor could we touch down in Stevensville, but had to go on to a small place called Moncton in Canada. Arrived in New York at 3 a.m., and then in Boston around nine and MIT at 10. Two days of work on the dormitory – it's beginning to shape up into a building – and then to Princeton. I stayed with the Dean, Sherley Morgan. One hour to change clothes, then dinner with the President; only the Ph.D.'s and faculty heads present. The company reminded me of the people we used to meet at Walter Ahrensberger's* (famous collector and patron of the arts) *dinners: scientists in creased formal clothes, a little pathetic in the manner of Toivo Hirn* (Aalto's former schoolmaster and friend). *There were more dashing types, too, "domestic careerists" as my neighbour at the table called them. The following morning, ceremony at the university chapel. First we were dressed in our black silk gown with the requisite square cap. Then we marched, first the so-called master's degrees and then us doctors, to the chancel, where*

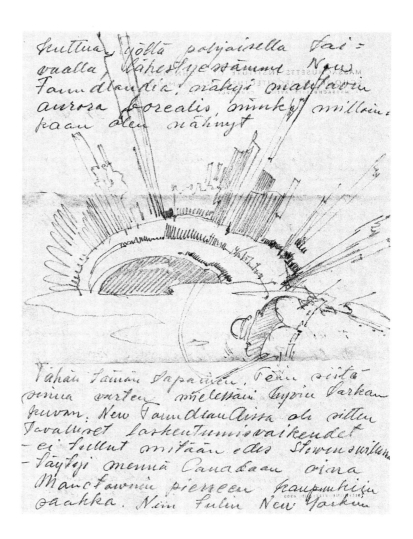

61. Page from Aalto's letter to Aino dated February 28, 1947, with a drawing of the northern lights beyond the plane's propellers.

we sat with the president and the MC in the middle. After the speeches, we were escorted one by one to the chancel steps, where we were dressed in a new gown of yellow silk, mine with brown trimming as a sign that I represented the fine arts. Here we were told about all the good things we had done, and the president stuck a roll of parchment in our hands. And that was that. At the lunch that followed, (U.S. Secretary of State) *Marshall was the guest of honour. I was told that FLW and Tony Garnier will receive their Ph.D.'s later, as Wright was ill and Garnier had not got going in time because of his age. Everyone was extremely friendly to me and I returned to work in a very good mood.*

Ten days later he wrote another letter:

Just got back from my second trip to Princeton (for a seminar at which Aalto gave a short talk). *All of the colleagues are here, even Giedion has come from Switzerland, the whole set of friends from San Francisco, and new faces from Brazil, Mexico, etc. FLW was well this time. The assembly hall was decorated for the bicentennial with photomontage all along the walls. On the wall behind the chairman, your works and mine were shown, on the wall to the left FLW's, and on the short wall at the back Tony Garnier's. Our names*

62. Aalto received honorary
degrees from many Ameri-
can universities. This photograph is of a ceremony at
Columbia University, New
York on December 1, 1964.

*were on a frieze above the photographs, and beneath them some words about the triumph
of truth over falsehood. The conference opened with a speech about our nobility and other
rubbish. Together with FLW, we then strutted like two roosters on a rubbish heap and
amused ourselves at the expense of these innocent souls. I skipped some of the sessions, and
took long walks instead. As you remember, there are woods around Princeton, and this time
there was even snow. Tried to take care of myself as best I could and thought that I would
soon be coming back to you. America continues to slide in the same direction. The taste
is getting worse every day, but they have the best intentions and the speeches at the seminar
were long.*

Ten months later, Aalto was invited by the Royal Society of Arts to receive the
insignia of honorary membership from the hand of Princess Elizabeth. He felt,
however, that he did not need to be present in person, and the Finnish
ambassador to London represented him at the ceremony. Aalto certainly had
his share of personal vanity, but he may have learned from Wright that ignoring
an honour enhances it.

The striking part of the letter just quoted is its dawning criticism of life in the
United States. As we have seen, Aalto was very attracted to the vitality, spirit of
freedom, and spontaneity he thought he found in America during his first visit.
Closer acquaintance with American technocratic excesses and dollar worship,

and perhaps even more the contact with critical spirits such as Lewis Mumford and the Museum of Modern Arts circle, led him to pay increasing attention to the dark side of American society. His principal goal as an architect, which was to humanize industrial culture and create a counterbalance to the obsessive quest for efficiency, was obviously in utter contrast to the prevalent mentality in the United States.

His assistant in the Cambridge dormitory project, Veli Paatela, told me a charming anecdote which highlights Aalto's attitude in this key issue. Paatela and Aalto had been invited to a seminar at MIT, where Professor Burchard spoke of the rising standard of living in the world. Out of politeness to Aalto, he made a comparison between United States, the pioneer country, and little Finland. Applying the criteria customary at the time, Burchard cited the number of cars, telephones, refrigerators, washing machines, etc., per thousand inhabitants, concluding that Finland was woefully backward in this comparison, and still had a lot of hard work to do to cut down the American lead. After the lecture, the audience was invited to ask questions, and after answering the students, Burchard turned to Aalto and asked him if he had any comments. Aalto replied that he had nothing at all to add, but purely out of curiosity would like to ask a few supplementary questions: Could Burchard tell him how many rowboats there were in the United States per 1,000 inhabitants. "I don't quite see the point", Burchard replied. "The point is that in Finland it often happens that a boy lives on one side of a lake and a girl on the other. Rowboats are really very useful things, and we have at least 250 of them for every 1,000 inhabitants." Aalto went on to ask a few more questions: "How many American hairdressers can put on their skis at their front door and set off? How many city-dwellers in the United States can reach unpolluted fishing waters 15 minutes away from their home?"

The seminar concluded with deafening applause for Aalto from the students.

Artek Center and Aino Institute

Even before the war, Aalto's furniture had become popular among progressive architects and designers on both sides of the Atlantic. Peace brought huge reconstruction projects and a general need to reform the world; by this time, the Aalto furniture was fully developed and could be mass-produced. Many thought of it as tomorrow's furniture. That, at any rate, was the opinion of Mr Boumphrey, owner of Finmar Ltd, Aalto's London representative. In the 1930s, Boumphrey had imported large quantities of Aalto furniture, but had been compelled to close shop when deliveries from Finland stopped. After the peace treaty had been signed, he immediately wrote to Aalto about his intention to reactivate the business, but that Aalto must transfer both the production and the copyright to him, since Finland was officially an enemy country and could not do business with the U.K. "Later, when times have changed, Finmar will try to compensate you financially."

It must have given Aalto great pleasure to be able to reply to the devious Boumphrey that he was quite unnecessarily worried about the hostility between the countries. By then, Aalto had almost completed implementation of the plan he first conceived in 1941 to start up an independent Artek company and factory in Sweden, which did not suffer from the serious shortage of raw materials like glue and textiles that hampered the production of Aalto furniture in Finland. By 1945 *AB Svenska Artek* (Artek Sweden) in Hedemora (with Ernst Sundh, Aalto's faithful standard-bearer from Avesta, as its principal shareholder) was busy building a furniture factory expected to open March 1, 1946 with three times the capacity of the Turku works. Summer 1946 saw the opening of Svenska Artek's exhibition pavilion in Hedemora, one of Aalto's most charmingly original designs despite its temporary character and relatively modest size. There would therefore be no difficulty for Mr Boumphrey to import new-made Aalto furniture . . . It need scarcely be added that Finmar Ltd was never reactivated.

An even more unscrupulous attempt to cheat Aalto had already been made in the United States. As mentioned in an earlier chapter, during his visit to

63. The Svenska Artek pavilion in Hedemora, a display building that was used for only one season.

New York in 1940 Aalto had signed an agreement with a businessman by the name of Clifford Pascoe, setting up a jointly owned American company called Artek Pascoe, with a sales outlet on Madison Avenue and its own furniture production at the Eggers works in Wisconsin. When the good Mr Pascoe saw in the next few years how wildly the little ship Finland was tossed about on the storm waves of the war, he concluded that he would never have to render a detailed account to the Finnish shareholders or to the designer himself. He engaged in ever bolder manipulations to promote his own interests, and finally to take over the entire company. He started by failing to redeem the last major consignments of Aalto furniture from Finland, which were in a Manhattan customs warehouse. They were auctioned off by customs for a song, and naturally purchased by Mr Pascoe. A little later, the company was discreetly relieved of its assets, and closed shop. Pascoe instead started a new company, wholly owned by himself and a partner named Brennhaus. To crown their efforts, they decided to 'improve' the Aalto designs to suit the more streamlined and extravagant American taste. Sales were brisk throughout. The only problem was that Aalto turned up in New York quite unexpectedly on November 8, 1945. At this point, he did not have a clear idea of what was going on, but he immediately sensed that something was wrong. He wrote in his first report to Aino:

Looked up Pascoe to talk with them. Some 15–20 typists at the central office, and the rest to match. Business must be good. They have a big new exhibition and sales space at 16 East 49th St, just off Fifth Avenue. They were having a trashy "post-war season opening". Their entire team of representatives were gathered at the cocktail buffet, and I was naturally the sensation of the day. Everything else was all right except the furniture. What damned 'streamlined nonsense' they had, some of it a corrupted rehash of our models, some their own rubbish. Well, we haven't been here, so maybe that part can still be corrected. But they were much too ingratiating with me . . .

In a later letter:

Pascoe and Brennhaus are very eager about cooperation, but I cannot fraternize with them or suggest compromises before my lawyer has given me some necessary figures. The problem is artistic rather than financial. Tell Maire that her money (invested in the old company) *is not lost; on the contrary, the business is thriving. We could probably immediately get a few thousand in royalties out of them, but the heart of the matter is "the right to artistic decisions", and to get that back we may have to give up some of the money.*

Aalto had a good lawyer, Harmon Goldstone's brother John, who eventually defeated Pascoe in a drawn-out lawsuit, which swallowed up most of the damages awarded. At any rate, Aalto got rid of an unscrupulous partner, and could plan his American furniture sales on a completely new basis.

One possibility, and probably the best, would have been to accept an offer made by his old friend James Sweeney in the summer of 1947 to set up a New York Artek together. Aalto was interested, but by then he was involved in more extensive plans which eventually became so fanciful that Sweeney backed out. Aalto's dream was to set up a new sales network covering all of North and South America as well as a non-profit organization called *Artek Center,* which would handle distribution and work together with the *Aino Institute,* a foundation-type body for experimental furniture research. His letters to Aino outline the development of this plan.

He first took up the subject immediately after his visit to Frank Lloyd Wright in Taliesin.

I think, little Aino, that now is the time for us to look for some peace. I have been thinking that we should concentrate on Artek for a year or two. We could work on furniture, lamps, and so on. We would travel around, inspecting sales (South America next summer), and design just a few buildings. No routine factories for directors. That way we would be able to work more closely together. We would have time and a fixed goal. This "peace treaty" should be appropriate in a Christmas letter. Drop me a line to say what you think.

A few days later, he continued:

My plan is for us to concentrate on a forest life in Hedemora (or somewhere else). We'll build a little institute where we can do what we please. The big Rockefeller Foundations and suchlike, MIT and Harvard, too, are just too 'tricky'. The Americans will draw up any kind of programme you please to Save the World, and professors of all kinds come up to me to discuss various plans, but I know that the result will be exactly nil. People have no sense of proportion, neither professors nor students.

Here we come to a theme Aalto would often revert to: his increasing

64. The Aaltos in 1947,
ready to direct the Aino
Institute and to launch
furniture sales through a
worldwide organization.

discomfort in the United States. A typical comment from a letter dated May 11, 1948:

I have tried to paint (oil paintings) for some days, but strangely enough nothing comes of it. I remember Léger said the same last time we met, and Miró's big fresco in Cincinnati (that Sweeney showed to me) was a flop. It's a repetition and a summing-up of his previous work, but there's something wrong with the scale.

After spending Christmas 1945 with the Saarinens, Aalto visited the Kaufmann family at Fallingwater, where old Mr. Kaufmann gave him detailed advice on how to set up his Artek Center and Aino Institute. Aalto laid out his conclusions in a letter dated January 1, 1946:

Dear little Aino. I'm feeling particularly lucky right now because snowstorms on the way from Pittsburgh (the Kaufmanns) to Boston messed up all air traffic, so that I couldn't make it to either Hudnut's or Gropius's New Year's vigil. I'm sitting all alone at the empty Switch Grill of the Gotham Hotel, and it's 11.30 in New York. I had accepted both Hudnut's and Gropius's invitations for 8 o'clock by mistake, so now I've cabled my excuses to both. My plane to Boston won't be leaving until 1.30 tonight, so I've ordered ham and scrambled eggs – just one gin and bitters. I'm feeling pretty good, for around my neck – as always in the air – I have your stocking. Here is my philosophy concerning our future:

1) As a centre for the Artek organization, we will found a laboratory, the Aino Institute. It will be located and built in Hedemora to start with, then in Finland. 2) All new contracts with wholesalers will require a basic fee to be paid to this foundation, at least $10,000 for American companies. Retailers must be members of the foundation, and pay an annual sum of e.g. $500 (1,000 according to Mr. Kaufmann). 3) The Aino Institute will be a non-profit institution broadly performing laboratory research into furniture design problems and building details. This will make it unlike anything else in the world. About 10 architects will work there full time. 4) According to calculations done here, we'll need $40,000 a year to run it. That would come from membership fees and royalties, from Britain and other countries, too, and from our own royalties. I tried to make Finland the centre for the Institute, but in that case we won't get a nickel here, and everyone agrees that a sufficiently strong central organization is a sine qua non. We can later move the whole shop or part of it to Finland. 5) Instead of setting up a large trustee or committee organization, it's simplest to start with a laboratory of our own and an affiliated school. The school could also be a continuing education centre for MIT students. 6) The Institute will have a branch in New York. 7) The commercial companies – the new Arteks in the U.S., South America, Britain, etc. – will come under the scientific institution. 8) All architectural work there must be independent of the commercial line. 9) The Institute should start with furniture, lighting, textiles, and a little ceramics. Building details later – or maybe at once. Shall write about this immediately to Sundh.

Now my flight is leaving, must rush. The Kaufmanns asked me to give you their warmest regards. I spent two nights there and am well rested. Two Australian girl architects had been ordered there on my account. They had been told that I never lie down unless a lady at the side of the bed presents a diploma of completed studies in "architecture and planning". But the invitation tempted me no more than the offers from Harvard and Cranbrook. I wanted to sleep, so I slept alone. How incredibly one's morals develop. But seriously, dear little Aino, I wish you a happy new year from the heart. You are the world's most beautiful person and I send you many kisses.

This plan may not seem crystal clear, but it does give an idea of how the Aino Institute was envisaged. As for the American Artek Center, it grew in Aalto's imagination on the basis of real possibilities that seemed to be opening up. In a 1945 letter to Aino, he wrote: *The situation here is that our design has now reached the general public, and that our 'sales value' is now as high as high can be.* This optimistic assessment was not contradicted by appearances. Pascoe's sales success has already been touched upon. In San Francisco, Aalto's old friend Tommy Church was eagerly awaiting new consignments, and an architect in Washington, F.A. Gutheim, who published the first book on Aalto in 1960, wanted to start up another retail outlet for the furniture. After Pascoe's swindles were revealed, Aalto energetically sought to start up a new company in New York. Very opportunely, a promising candidate for the position of director turned up in the Danish-American architect Marshall Christensen, who already had suitable facilities on Park Avenue. A new potential manufacturer of Aalto furniture also expressed interest. The Hagerthy family of Cohasset, Massachusetts owned a boatyard which could easily be converted for the purpose.

Retailing candidates virtually stood in line throughout the country. Besides Church in San Francisco and Gutheim in Washington, Christina Nute in Boston and Harry Weese in Chicago became Aalto furniture dealers. A lively correspondence ensued concerning the sales areas of each company. Christensen, who had special ties in Latin America, wanted Mexico and South America. William Cabaniss opened a retail outlet in Denver in 1948. One of Aalto's students at MIT, Enslie O. Oglesby, started a Louisiana branch of Artek in New Orleans, and Norman Yeon was the representative for Oregon. As the supplier for all these, Aalto planned to set up a new company, *American Artek Inc*, with the Finnish and Swedish parent companies as majority shareholders. In preparation, Aalto started adding to his contracts for deliveries from the Hedemora factory a 10% premium for American Artek Inc and 1% for the future Aino Institute. These fees were paid to Aalto's New York lawyer, John Goldstone.

The deliveries from Sweden got under way in summer 1946, and Aalto was very eager to have the American retailers place as large orders as possible. The Hedemora factory, however, was not prepared to give its clients prolonged sales credit, and required cash payment at customs clearance in the United States. This was the beginning of a sad tale in which Aalto persuaded the factory to grant credits which the companies had increasing difficulty in paying back. The friendly letters from Aalto to "Dear Chris" (=Christensen) passed through a stage of wonder at non-payment to the chilly announcement to "Mr Christensen" in summer 1947 terminating the relationship. When in 1948 the New York company managed to "raise new capital" and started paying off its debts, it was "Dear Chris" again. Things went worse with Christina Nute, who never paid her debts and whom Aalto did not hesitate to call a crook and a bandit in their correspondence.

On the basis of the scanty material in the Aalto archives, it is hard to tell exactly what went wrong with sales of Aalto furniture in the United States and why. Possibly Mr Pascoe's Americanized 'improvements' found buyers among the public more easily than the ascetic original models. Probably the retailers Aalto chose were intellectuals without business contacts or sales ability. What is sure is that Aalto himself had no feeling for financial affairs, however convincing his calculations on the financing of the Aino Institute and his reports to Aino about his frugal life in the United States may seem. Genuinely thrifty friends of Aalto's were always shocked by his habits. Aalto told me once about a tête-à-tête dinner at Gropius's, after which he offered to help his host by doing the dishes. Gropius came rushing into the kitchen and said: "If you go on running the hot water, you'll ruin me." Gropius also had his secretary write to Aalto in Finland to request payment of two long-distance calls to New York that Aalto had made from his home. If Aalto had had just a fraction of this attitude, the fiasco of his furniture sales in the United States probably could have been avoided. The only consolation was that in spite of everything, the Hedemora factory was able to deliver and collect payment for large consignments of furniture for the Aalto

65. The intimate "Poetry Room" at Harvard, furnished by Aalto in 1948, was long a forgotten gem. Photo: Göran Schildt 1982.

66. Charles Eames's DAR chair from 1950.

dormitory in Cambridge and for the Poetry Room and Lamont Library at Harvard.

Along with these incidental obstacles, which perhaps could have been overcome, there was a deeper reason for the difficulty in introducing Aalto chairs as 'tomorrow's furniture' in the United States. Plastic was beginning to compete with wood as a material for industrial furniture production. It all began with a series of competitions arranged by the Museum of Modern Art in the 1940s for new furniture designs. Eero Saarinen and Charles Eames won prizes with chairs that were basically developments of Aalto's bentwood furniture. The modern furniture developed at Bauhaus had been based on a geometry inspired by the De Stijl architects. In creating the Paimio chair on the basis of Breuer's design for the Wassily chair, Aalto not only replaced steel tubes with wood, but above all substituted organic lines adapted to the body for abstract geometric composition (cf. *The Decisive Years,* pp. 79–80). Aalto's chairs, however, were organically bent in only one plane; they did not form soft hollows, only seats adjusted to the human shape. Saarinen and Eames took their designs one step further. New production techniques allowed their first prize-winning chairs, though made of plywood, to be moulded in every dimension. This meant giving up all the form-giving properties of wood. Total pliability, however, was a characteristic of the new materials celluloid, bakelite, and fibreglass, which became available around this time. It was natural for Saarinen and Eames to turn to plastics, which were better suited to their needs, and came into their own in designs like Eames's streamlined 'DAR' chair of 1950 (F 66). This and other plastic furniture developed into the mass-produced and mass-marketed modern furniture that Aalto's designs, which still required some craftsmanship and were thus relatively expensive, could never be.

The link between the furniture of Aalto and Eames is spelled out in a telegram preserved in the Aalto archives, dated February 25, 1946, from Eero Saarinen to Aalto in Boston. He says that Eames absolutely wishes to meet Aalto to show him "a most interesting moulded plywood furniture developed by him". His two younger colleagues repeatedly tried to arouse Aalto's interest in the method of making three-dimensional moulded furniture, but he remained cold to the idea. He would not give up what he called "the language of wood fibres". As I have pointed out (*The Decisive Years,* pp. 84–85), the repertoire of forms Aalto had developed through his experimental wood reliefs and bentwood furniture pointed the way for his architectural designs as well. Wood was quite simply an element of what could be called Aalto's individual style.

Interestingly, Saarinen and Eames also carried over the forms inspired by their plastic furniture into their architecture, as Saarinen's famous TWA terminal at New York's Kennedy Airport shows. Two styles were thus contrasted here: Aalto's monumentality inspired by the natural material, wood, against

67. Eero Saarinen's TWA pavilion at Kennedy Airport in New York, 1962. From the book *Eero Saarinen: On His Work.*

Saarinen's monumentality, inspired by the technology of plastic. The American people, infatuated with technology, naturally preferred the work of Eames and other plastic artists to Aalto's. Our time, which has begun to distrust the promises of technology and to try to readapt man to the natural order, may find another message in Aalto's furniture.

68. Aalto's architectural style was rooted in the 'language of wood fibres', as this detail of the ventilation system in Vuoksenniska Church shows.

Aalto at MIT

69. Ink drawing of the Ice-landic volcano Hekla, seen through the window of an aeroplane on a flight from Finland to the United States, 1947.

There has been great confusion about the time Aalto spent in the United States in the 1940s, what he did as professor at MIT, and how his students felt about him. After trips to Boston, New York, and Berkeley, where I went through archives and interviewed surviving witnesses; after correspondence with younger American researchers, who generously communicated their findings to me; and especially after perusing Aalto's own rich but chaotic archives, I have managed to clarify the matter somewhat. Before going into detail, let me give a list of the seven periods during which Aalto really taught at MIT.

In 1945–46, he made three visits to the United States: from November 7, 1945 to February 2, 1946, again from June 17 to August 9 (this is the only occasion

Island Hekla   47

on which Aino accompanied him), and from October 30 to December 6. He returned home from the last of these journeys on the *Gripsholm* liner to Gothenburg; he made all his other trips by air. He was in the U.S. twice in 1947, from February 18 to April 20 and from October 21 to December 3. He also made two trips in 1948: from April 7 to May 14, and from October 7 to November 14, when he returned home because of Aino's serious illness.

Apart from the first four and a half month visit, as we see, he spent no longer than two months at a time in the U.S., and considerably less in the last year. This being so, there could obviously be no question of any systematic, long-term instruction at MIT. As Wurster expressed it in a letter in 1950, one might better say that Aalto, along with some other celebrities, were "like meteors flying through the school", where they gave sporadic guest lectures. It was originally intended that the San Francisco architect Vernon de Mars should alternate with Aalto as professor, and the Institute gave them a room to share. De Mars, whom Aalto later chose as his partner in designing the library for the Benedictine abbey of Mt. Angel in Oregon, told me in 1986 that because Aalto always arrived late, they were regularly at MIT at the same time. As a result, they became good friends, and de Mars managed to pick up some useful philosophical pointers

70. Ink drawing from 1946: "Cape Cod, hurricane".

from Aalto. Among other things, de Mars was astonished by Aalto's habit of placing all letters that were not from Aino on an unread pile on his desk, where they soon formed a small mountain. "They might be very urgent and important letters, from the school's President, for instance?" de Mars took the liberty of asking. "Believe me", said Aalto, "even the most important letters soon become less important if you let them lie."

This bohemian style does not seem to have given rise to any protests from the MIT directors. Three weeks after Aalto first came to MIT, Wurster wrote to a personal friend in San Francisco: "It is exciting to have Aalto here. He is well filled with energy and our term's work will be wonderful because of him."

As we have seen, Aalto considered his main tasks at the time to consist of designing an architectural research building for MIT and gaining acceptance for his programme for its laboratory. On January 3, 1946 he wrote to Aino: *Today I'm in a fairly good mood. The sun has been shining all day over the snow drifts and the frozen Charles River, a pretty rare combination for Boston. The work is going well, 'The Project'* (the architectural laboratory) *that I am designing together with the boys from the master's course will soon be ready to be submitted to* (President) *Compton.*

Clearly a good deal of Aalto's teaching took the form of real planning work and drawing. Another indication of this is a paper in the Aalto archives from the 1945 autumn term detailing an assignment for the grade II students. They were to place a three-car garage on a wooded, sloping plot already containing a house and garden (a map of the plot and house was attached).

His lectures seem to have dealt largely with the reconstruction of Finland. As a concrete example, he presented his plan for the city of Rovaniemi, to be built on the ruins of a town which had been totally destroyed by the Germans. He also took up the subject in a series of lectures elsewhere: Princeton, the Museum of Modern Art, and other locations. The MOMA lecture on February 5, 1946, attracted such a large crowd that many could not fit in. Among the audience was a young Italian called Bruno Zevi, who was so impressed by the lecturer that during his subsequent influential career as a teacher and leader of the "organic school of architecture" in Italy he never missed a chance to praise Aalto. This kind of instruction, based more on personal magnetism than logical arguments, may seem pedagogically suspect, but it is basically the artist's way of influencing and teaching others.

It is difficult to establish a list of the MIT students who really studied with Aalto, as many who may have heard no more than one lecture have later wished to appear as his disciples, while others have disappeared to fates unknown. However, I was able to track down a handful of indisputable cases and to interview them about Aalto's teaching methods. Herbert Beckwitch of Boston told me that he had taken part for five or six weeks in a graduate students' group project initiated by Aalto. The assignment consisted of furnishing a shop using wood, stone, and textiles as materials. However, Aalto's most important contribution came in informal discussions with small groups of students. Another Boston architect, Robert B. Newman, told me that he had been involved in building full-scale models of some rooms in Aalto's student dormitory design, after which various furnishing arrangements were tested in practice. "His sessions with us in the design studio were always interesting – when they happened. It was group discussion rather than dialogue. He liked the girls." Another student, Enslie O. Oglesby, later practised at Aalto's office in Finland and established himself in the 1950s as an independent architect in New Orleans.

The most detailed and best description of Aalto as a teacher, however, was provided by Lee Hodgden in a highly articulate letter. After studying at MIT, he, too, worked for a while at Aalto's office in Finland, and is now a professor at Cornell University in Ithaca, N.Y. His letter starts with the observation that Aalto "was a great practitioner and more an inspiring and charismatic personality than a professional teacher". His instruction often consisted of talking to students about his own work or taking them for walks.

I remember that he took us on a tour of Beacon Hill (in Boston) *in order to point out the quality of design and detail of that era. (Among American architects, he particularly admired Bulfinch.) He also told us a lot of anecdotes about Frank Lloyd Wright (but influence is minimal, as Aalto didn't see FLW's work before his first U.S. visit in 1938.)*

Aalto was very much an intuitive architect, and at that time he did not like to discuss architecture on any abstract or theoretical basis. He encouraged the students to sketch freely and to invent rather than to rely on standardized technology. He would say such things as (faced with meaningless hard-line drawings by unimaginative students): "You should throw away the tee-square – Throw the Sweet's Catalogue out the window – think and

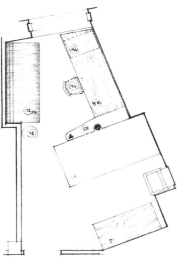

71. Plan of a student room in the MIT dormitory. 1) bed, 3 E) desk, 12) sofa, 8 E) bookshelf, 5) clothes cupboard.

72. Room for two students in the MIT dormitory. Furniture part standard Aalto, part specially designed.

draw." "We don't talk about architecture – we just draw beautiful lines." The whole idea was to cultivate the 'eye' for form, there is no method for this.

It is hard to say how an intuitive architect teaches, as there is no dogma, just responses to the student's attempts to solve the problem. His approach was also anecdotal – he was a marvelous raconteur, and would tell us long, funny stories, most of which had a serious philosophic point to illustrate. One of Aalto's stories was in the end more educational than hours of criticism over the board, if, and the 'if' was the problem, if one was able to see the point of the story. And if one could transfer the wisdom of the story to one's own design work. These stories often had only a grain of factual basis (he always improved a good story), but there was a higher truth in the fable most of the time. I suppose he was sort of the architect's Aesop; he loved to make the point with a good story, complete with drawings.

Of course much of the inspiration was in Aalto's own design work: every Aalto building was didactic in the sense that he intended those who could read the lesson to see how the problem ought to be solved.

Aalto's office was run very much the same as a design studio in school. After the initial parti sketch, the architect on the job would try to bring it all to scale and see that it was workable. Then began the long process of over-the-board criticism by the maestro – a process which continued until the minutest detail was solved to his satisfaction. Every job received intimate personal attention. He was amenable to any intelligent suggestion, which is the way one uses good collaborators, and always exercised remarkable patience with those who were slow to see what he was trying to create. Many study models were built in order to refine the design. He had a remarkable grasp of details.

This testimony from one who knew Aalto both as a university teacher and as the head of an architect's office has great value in that it so strongly emphasizes Aalto's constant pedagogical activity. His students at MIT were few, and perhaps not all equally receptive, but the list of Finnish and foreign architects who started their careers at his office comprises several hundred names, and includes a surprising number of prominent architects. Aalto's office was a much more important school to many than any university.

In retrospect, it is clear that Aalto did well in not becoming a professor at Harvard. Wurster, who knew him, had no trouble keeping him in a very loose arrangement with MIT. In a letter dated January 3, 1946, Aalto tells Aino that MIT had reduced its requirement for his presence in the United States to just one term annually, had considerably raised his salary and travel allowance, and above all had commissioned him to design a new student dormitory on a demanding site on the banks of the Charles River. Aalto did not cut down on his teaching because of this commission; in fact, it provided him with the practical example that he considered essential to his instruction.

The basic idea of the dormitory, with its twisting, serpentine form following the river, illustrated some of Aalto's most important principles. First, by lengthening the facade, the form made it possible to have all students' bedrooms face southward towards the river. This also improved the view from most of the rooms by putting the river and, even more important, the intense traffic along the shore in longitudinal rather than transverse perspective, which

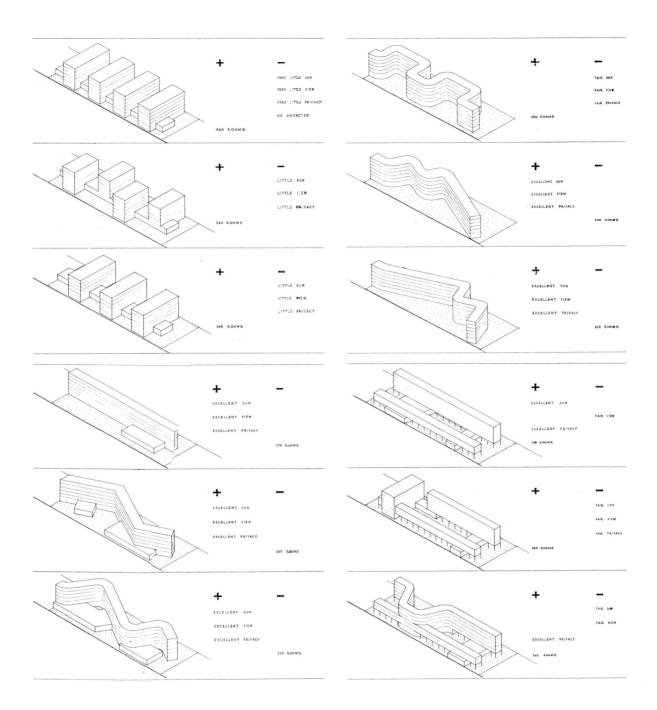

73. Aalto prepared a report for the building committee on the advantages and drawbacks of various basic dormitory plans. On the plus side, he cited the possibility of fitting in more than 250 rooms; on the minus side poor, inadequate, or only moderate sunlight, view, and separation of rooms. None of the solutions is perfect, but the plan he settled for was the best possible compromise.

made for a more pleasant psychological experience. The variation achieved in room form and solar orientation was another important by-product. Variation despite standardization, the humanization of technology, living cells imitating nature instead of the deadly accumulation of mass production were all part of the programme that Aalto had so eagerly urged in his Swiss 'Sermon on the Mount' and which his 'laboratories' were to study. Here at last was the chance to try out his theories in a practical experiment, to show what he meant by 'flexible standardization'.

The building programme, however, gave rise to certain practical difficulties. An architect designing an ordinary hotel need only study the furnishing of one or two room types in detail; these can be repeated a hundred or a thousand times, depending on the size of the hotel. In Aalto's dormitory, every single room had to be designed individually. Since few of the corners were straight angles, furniture types had to be varied; clothes cupboards and other fixtures had to be custom designed. This led to higher costs, and critical voices began to be heard on the MIT board. The economics of the project were based on the principle that rents should cover both capital costs and maintenance; thus, building costs had to be kept under strict control. A letter from the President's office dated July 30, 1946 points out that "the problem here is to provide good housing for our students, not to build an experimental dormitory. If we can accomplish the first objective by following the second, fine, but we must be sure of this." According to the original programme, the dormitory was to contain 150 single and 75 double rooms, with space for 300 students, but in an effort to make ends meet, two ultimatums were issued to Aalto to significantly increase the number of rooms.

This very nearly scuttled the whole plan. Wurster, whose pet project the Aalto dormitory was, threatened to quit as dean if Aalto's design was not built. At the same time, he tried to persuade Aalto to make the compromise that was obviously necessary by placing 54 additional rooms on the north side. This would have brought down costs to an acceptable $5,300 per bed, but it also would have torpedoed Aalto's basic idea besides resulting in some dark corridors, which Aalto had wished to avoid from the start. He therefore categorically rejected Wurster's suggestion in a letter dated August 13, 1947: "If we are poor (that is, if MIT is pinching pennies) we should not make a mixed work and dream of architecture which is logically perfect. I prefer a clean shirt."

Part of Aalto's genius was his ability to be spurred by difficulties and to turn thorny problems into artistic victories. Both MIT demands for more rooms for students led to significant improvements in the plan. The first time this happened, Aalto managed to squeeze in several rooms by lifting the cafeteria out of the building volume and placing it in front of the facade as a separate pavilion. Meeting the second ultimatum called for more ingenuity, but after his return to Boston in October 1947, he was able to send Aino good news:

I managed to fit in the additional boys neatly; in fact I did it by improving the building. I found a superb trick that solved the whole problem; will send you a sketch in my next letter.

I have improved almost every part of the building; now it is really going to be good. It always happens that the real inspiration comes and exact forms appear only after construction has started. As for the additional rooms, it went exactly the way you thought best: keeping the basic form of the building with some improvements, but increasing the number of rooms with a stepped extension on one end, turned out best. As always, your instinct was right.

The MIT dormitory is one of the best documented Aalto buildings, as detailed comments on it can be found in the correspondence that was necessary whenever Aalto was in Finland. Wurster, who was fighting hard for the project on the sidelines, particularly admired the "cascade staircase" of the inner facade, actually a development of the "Venetian staircases" and stairwells outside the main mass which appeared in Aalto's youthful, Neo-Classical designs, and which he was at last able to carry out here (see e.g. W 35 and W 67

74. Aalto managed to increase the number of rooms from 225 to 256 by adding a fan-shaped extension to the west end of the building.

75. The north elevation of the dormitory with the 'cascade staircase' admired by Wurster.

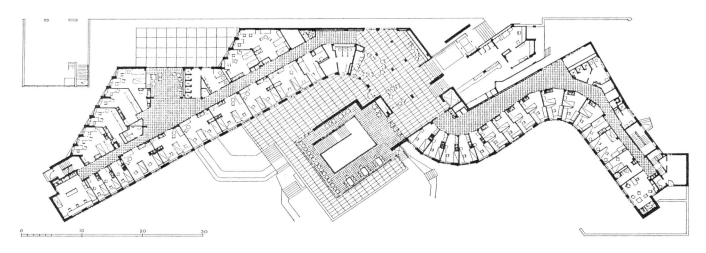

76. Riverfront facade of the dormitory, with the projecting restaurant pavilion. Photo: Museum of Finnish Architecture.

in *The Early Years*). The V form was dictated by the need to have all traffic to all storeys pass by the doorkeeper at ground floor.

As a foreigner, Aalto could not be registered as the building's architect and had to find a local associate, which is why Robert W. Kennedy was cited as "associate architect" for the building. It was more important to Aalto to have a Finnish assistant on the site to develop his sketches and handle the thousands of practical details involved in construction, just as the boys at his office in Finland did. His first assistant in the United States was Veli Paatela, who arrived in September 1946 and returned to Finland in February 1948 after winning an architectural competition that led to an independent commission for him.

A letter written by Aalto to Paatela on January 4, 1947 sheds light on the relative independence and confidence enjoyed by the best of Aalto's assistants:

Of course it's good to ask about things, but I think it still best that you decide on problems there whenever you feel sure. For me the main thing is that the original character of the building remains intact. Don't be too shy about details.

A little later (April 21) Aalto stressed that the dormitory should have "a rather simple rawness about the details; the buildings shouldn't be too too sensitive."

After Aalto and Paatela had completed the official drawings, the contractor made the cost calculations MIT needed to decide whether the design should be built in the first place. The working drawings were then to be done by the local practice of Parrey, Shaw and Hepburn, which had no responsibility for the actual planning. They refused to start work before the decision to build had been made and a contract signed. This seemingly standard approach infuriated Aalto and gave rise to a characteristic comment in a letter (October 9, 1946) to Wurster: "Such a way of working reminds me of something I have heard about a public restaurant. Commercial cooking. It is only a pity that the potatoes, this time, are called architecture."

In April 1948, Olav Hammarström arrived in Boston to replace Paatela. Construction was about to begin, and his first task was to go to Parrey, Shaw and Hepburn to supervise the conversion of the metric system used in the official drawings to inches, feet, and yards. In an interview at Cape Cod on February 8, 1981, Hammarström, who stayed in the United States after the dormitory project, told the author that this apparently trivial operation had as radical effect on the design as translating a book from one language to another. The American 'language of drawing' is harder, and has less nuance and detail than the Finnish system. The result was a shock to Aalto. Hammarström did his best as construction supervisor to save as much as possible of the original spirit.

Aalto's letters to Hammarström are interesting because they mention details that were omitted for financial reasons. A rooftop garden in the manner of Le Corbusier, highly suitable for this big-city environment, was shelved at an early stage and never materialized. More remarkable was "the network of white poles" for ivy to cling to that Aalto hoped to the very end to place over the brickwork of the undulating facade, "forming a gentle transition from solid wall to window" and also providing "softer interior lighting by acting as a curtain when seen from inside". This idea for "making definitive architecture" probably occurred to him on seeing the Classical ruins of Rome, which he visited in summer 1948, but the holders of MIT's purse strings were

77. This perspective sketch shows the "network of white poles" Aalto intended to place over the central part of the south elevation for ivy to climb up all the way to the roof. As the preceding photograph shows, the idea was not carried out.

78. MIT dormitory room
with bunk bed.

not receptive to Aalto's arguments, and the ivy trellises were struck off the programme.

Another tug-of-war, concerning the furnishing for the students' rooms, had
a more favourable outcome for Aalto. Aalto produced figures to prove that
specially designed furniture made in Hedemora would not be significantly
more expensive than the inferior standardized products on the American
furniture market, which, moreover, would be difficult to fit into the free-form
room plans. The cost of the cheapest Artek alternative was $127,786, while
comparable American standard furniture would cost $108,340. Aalto man-
aged to obtain approval for a sample order from Hedemora for ten rooms, after
which a compromise was found, with Artek furniture predominant. Aino
designed the attractive and practical room interiors, using some fixtures and
otherwise furniture that was more robust than the standard pieces to endure
rough handling. The final cost of construction came to about 2.5 million.
Aalto's fee, after having redesigned the building three times to increase the
number of rooms, was $34,000, from which he paid Paatela's salary for 13
months and Hammarström's for 14 months. All that remained for his personal
trouble was $5,460.

A comment on the practical viability of the building is in order. Aalto's idea
of a happy balance between individual privacy and free social mingling
determined the balance between the students' rooms and the windowed

127

corridors that served as community space. It turned out in the 1950s that the students did not appreciate this plan, but spent most of their time locked up in their rooms. Some of the common rooms were therefore converted into lucrative students' units. When I visited the dormitory in 1981, the situation had changed again. The students' demands for community facilities had forced a return to the Aalto plan, and a new, extrovert generation of students generally kept their doors wide open, living in a manner reminiscent of a Neapolitan alley. Only a handful of students preparing for exams kept their doors shut. All doors were decorated with gaudy, humorous collage, indicating who lived in each room and what they thought about sex, politics, or themselves. One of the major problems of architecture is that lifestyles change more rapidly than buildings.

Aalto made his last visit to MIT as professor in October 1948. Only that summer, he and Aino had planned to supervise the furnishing of the dormitory and go on to Brazil in the winter, where they intended to set up an Artek branch and study the feasibility of importing to the Nordic countries "Brazilian woods, which have a leading position in the making of high-quality furniture". That autumn it turned out that the cancer for which Aino had been operated in 1946 had spread and could no longer be stopped. Aalto had been in Boston less than a month, and the dormitory was still far from complete, but he realized that he must go back home to Aino. She had once told him that she would like to have a mink coat some day when they could afford it. In those days, mink coats were much more of a symbol of luxury and success than today. Prices were also prohibitive: "Dark high class wild $3,000" and "light slightly coarse china $1,500", according to one of Aalto's letters; that is, approximately one year's teaching salary for him. He asked his friend Harmon Goldstone's old mother to find the most beautiful mink coat in New York and buy it for him. When Aino died at home in Munkkiniemi on January 13, 1949, he spread the coat over her feet on the deathbed.

The dormitory was dedicated on June 11, 1949. Aalto was not present. He had intended to return to MIT in autumn 1949 to resume his professorship. In September, he wrote to Wurster to announce that he had won the competition for the Helsinki University of Technology in Otaniemi, and construction was to begin immediately.

The plan comprises approximately 70 buildings, the acropolis, different departments, laboratories, dormitories, etc., on a free site of hundreds of acres, the most beautiful spot near Helsinki. You know by yourself this means work, work and work.

Aalto had also won first prize in the competition for the National Pensions Institute, and was working on its design. He therefore wished to limit his stay at MIT to no more than three weeks, during which he promised to lecture every day. The letter concludes:

I could of course for MIT give up one or two of my bigger works but I can of course in no case abstain from building the new Technical University of my own country, which happens once in a millennium. Things like that are labor sacrum.

Wurster replied very understandingly, and suggested that Aalto should return to MIT later, when he had more time. Aalto promised to do so in 1950, but again postponed, and MIT very forbearingly marked him as "absent on leave" on its list of teachers. In fact Aalto did not return to Cambridge until May 1963 for a short visit to meet old friends and to see the dormitory, undoubtedly one of his most important works, for the first and last time almost 15 years after it was completed.

Death of Aino

One of the most difficult judgements I have had to make as Aalto's biographer relates to Aino Aalto's place in his life and her contribution to his work. I made Aalto's acquaintance in 1952, when Aino was no longer alive. Thus I cannot fall back on personal impressions or conversations with her, but must base my opinion solely on existing documents and secondhand reports.

The latter are extraordinarily unanimous. All those who knew Aino Aalto seem to agree that she was a very strong and discerning personality, though reticent and slow to react, and complemented her outward-looking and highly spirited husband remarkably well despite – or perhaps because of – their great differences. In a brief epitaph, Gregor Paulsson found a simile that perhaps best illustrated the difference between the spouses: Alvar was like an ardent flame, Aino was like still water. I trust that the depth of their relationship has been conveyed by the stories of their work and family life, of their common friends in Finland and abroad, discussed on previous pages of this biography.

An outsider can never fathom the deepest layers of a relationship between two people, but recalling the chapter on Aalto's childhood in which I discussed his relationship with the mother who died young, and the apparently incurable wound the traumatic loss seems to have left in his psyche, it is tempting to give a psychoanalytic interpretation of his relationship with his wife. It seems that in Aino he unconsciously sought and found a replacement for his lost mother, and that she became vital to him as a shield against the unresolved pain of Selma Mathilda's death. This hypothesis is clearly supported by a 1932 letter from Aalto to Aino, in which he speaks of his innermost feelings without rationalization or inhibitions: "I lay (on board ship during a trip to Stockholm on his own) and talked with you as never before. Always when I thought of you in my loneliness, it was as if I had begged you to help me in something – I missed you terribly, and at the same time there was something painful about it."

Aino's love had overcome his pain and built a protective wall against the threatening darkness. His work had been given its inmost meaning by her understanding and appreciation. He had to show her everything he did, just as a child shows his latest achievements to his mother. Her approval and understanding were essential for his work to have any value. This is why he named her as an associate in his work, even if her contribution had been only to approve the result.

The correspondence between them during Aalto's visits to the United States in the 1940s gives us a fair idea of both their personal and professional relationship. In November 1945, Alvar wrote from Boston:

Dear, dear Aino, there is nothing in the world so wonderful as our little family, and at the same time I am so glad that there is nothing exaggerated or divisive about it. It is your doing that everything is so natural and self-evident – just like the best architecture in the world. You are the source of security and the steady, quiet warmth that gives our life its stability and fulfils our work.

79. Alvar and Aino in Milan on their last trip together to Italy, 1948.

80. This ink drawing of Aino was made by Alvar on January 2, 1949, eleven days before she died. Does the legend "Mami" subconsciously imply that her death repeated for him the traumatic loss of his mother forty-three years earlier?

Aino replied in a letter dated November 30, 1945:

Read your letter dozens of times, and it moved me and warmed my heart more than I can say . . . Naturally I realize that there is still much room for improvement between us, particularly on my side. I have often been filled with wonder at your instinctive composure and optimism. In our little conflicts, you are the one who has usually been right. I have a tendency to 'exaggerate' that I want to get rid of. Life seems good when there is someone like you to share it with.

In autumn 1948, when Aino was virtually incapacitated by illness, Alvar wrote:

The dormitory has progressed to the stage that construction can no longer be suddenly stopped. I shall probably have to come back for a couple of weeks next spring for the finishing touches. The prospect of coming home soon makes me happy – America is somehow a country that does not agree with me. Another thing that contributes to my balanced state of mind is the thought that this period of travel in my life is coming to an end and a new period of work is beginning. I have now drawn as much as I can on my own, and this has reminded me of the days of intense competition design and other work we have shared – the highlights of life. We shall steer our lives towards them again now. Away with routine jobs and in with work that is "not too big" but done at home and with you.

As we see, Alvar could not face up to the thought of losing Aino even in the cruel last weeks of her illness. He still spoke of "our life", and assumed that they would continue to share it. Throughout his life, he refused to confront death, shutting his eyes to it in panic.

The next years were very hard for Aalto, who went through his life's worst crisis and often appeared unbalanced and confused. His work seems to have been the only thing that kept him going, and he clung to it desperately. During and after Aino's last illness he worked on a competition entry for the University of Technology campus in Otaniemi near Helsinki, a work in which Aino partici-

81. The winning entry "Ave Alma Mater, morituri te salutant" in the 1949 competition for the new campus of the Helsinki University of Technology in Otaniemi. Aalto's final design for the campus, built between 1951 and 1978, was largely based on the competition entry.

pated, at least in discussions. He sent it in on April 11, 1949 with the motto "Ave alma mater, morituri te salutant" (Hail university, those who go to die salute you). The reference was to the Roman gladiators' well-known salute to the emperor upon entering the arena (Ave imperator, morituri te salutant).

Feminist-inspired attempts have been made to overestimate Aino's architectural contribution at Alvar's expense. It has been claimed that all fresh ideas were hers, and that after her death Aalto only repeated himself in his work in the 1950s. To some extent, Aalto himself caused this misunderstanding. He had grown up in contact with three strong women, his two mothers and his aunt Helmi; this had instilled in him a respect for woman as an intellectual being that was quite unusual for his time. Add to this his previously mentioned need to exaggerate Aino's contribution and involvement. He always spotlighted Aino at his own expense, and did not object even when it was said that the bentwood furniture was entirely her work. It seems almost as if she was a kind of tutelary goddess to him, as is shown by his idea that the research laboratory he dreamed of should bear her name. When we get down to facts, and study what original clients and contemporaries had to say about Aino's work, we arrive at a different conclusion. Aino's contribution was not in creative ideas, but on a different plane which may in itself have been just as important.

82. Photograph in the Pöytyä parish newsletter of the parish centre designed by Aino in 1930.

Pöytyän Seurakuntaterwehdys

1932

Toimitti: Pöytyän seurakunnan papisto.

Sisältö: Jumala auttaa. — Seurakuntaelämän merkitys. — Käykäämme ahkerasti kirkossa. — Seurakuntatalomme toiminnassa. — Pyhät sakramentit seurakunnan käytännössä. — Pöytyän seurakunnan raamattutunnit 1932. — Koti ja rakkaus vanhempiin. — Seurakuntamme lapset. — Pöytyän Toveruusliitto. — Nuoret, varjelkaa elämänne. — Seurakuntamme vanhukset ja sairaat. — Seurakuntatyötä Pöytyällä 1931. — Kirkkoherranvirasto. — Kirkonisäntä. — Rippikoulu. — Kinkerit. — Hautaukset. — Olkaamme ehdottomasti raittiita. — Pöytyän seurakunnan kirkonisännät 1645—1932.

Jumala auttaa.

Herrassa rakastettu Pöytyän seurakuntalainen.

Meillä on Jumala, joka auttaa. Oletko sitä kokenut?

Moni ajattelemattomuudessaan luulee, että ihminen tulee toimeen ilman Jumalaa. Ja moni elääkin siten kuin ei taivaan Herra ihmistä näkisi. Jokainen ajatuksemmekin on hänen tiedossaan. Ja kerran on meidän kohdattava hänet. Meidän elämämme on perin epävakaista. Joka aamulla terveenä työhönsä menee, voi jo illalla maata paareilla. Moni onnettomuus vaanii ihmistä elämän matkalla. Avuton on lopultakin itseensä luottavakin ihmisraukka elämän suurten kokemusten edessä. Miten autamme itseämme ja omiamme kuoleman edessä. Mistä saamme rauhallisen mielen ja todellisen tyyneyden?

Jumala auttaa.

Jumalan käsivarret ovat pitkät ja voimakkaat. Ne tapaavat ihmislapsen läheltä ja kaukaa. Missä olemmekin, aina olemme Jumalan kasvojen edessä. Emme häntä voi minnekään paeta.

Jumala auttaa. Oletko hänen

Pöytyän seurakuntatalo.

Seurakuntaelämän merkitys.

Olemme jäseniä Pöytyän seurakunnassa. Sillä on suuri merkityksensä. Kasteen hetkenä Herra liitti meidät jäseniksi hänen ruumiiseensa, hänen seurakuntaansa. Kristuksen seurakunta on uskovien yhteys, jossa Jumalan sanaa viljellään ja sakramentteja Herran käskyn mukaisesti hoidetaan. Vaikka ulkonaisessa seurakunnassa onkin

Käykäämme ahkerasti kirkossa.

Jumala puhuu meille kyllä joka paikassa, mutta kirkkomme on se Herralle pyhitetty paikka, jossa kokoonnumme hänen sanaansa kuulemaan ja siitä saamaan sielullemme virvoitusta. Sen vuoksi onkin meidän ahkerasti kirkossa käytävä. Älköön mikään este meitä pidättä-

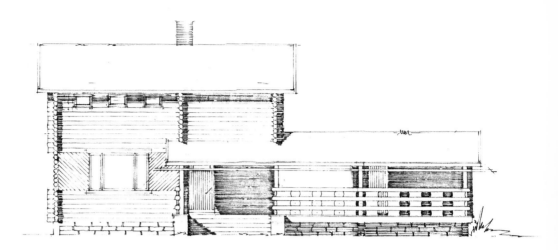

83. Aino Aalto's elevation drawing for Professor Kauppi's villa in Heinola rural municipality, 1947.

It is not easy for an outsider to judge exactly what Aino brought to the work designated by Aalto as joint projects, but a number of designs exist for which she alone was responsible. An early example is the Villa Flora (W 77), the family's summer home in Alajärvi. This was definitely a small masterpiece, although the strong Asplund influence indicates that Aalto was involved in the basic design or at least suggested ideas for it. A better opportunity to judge Aino's ability is afforded by her competition entry for the Finnish pavilion at the 1939 New York World's Fair, which she submitted in competition with Alvar's designs (W 220). As I pointed out in the second volume of this biography, however, it went back to Alvar's sketches for the planned hall of the Villa Mairea (cf. *The Decisive Years*, F 181, 182). Other buildings designed by Aino include the competition entry for Jyväskylä vicarage (W 84), Pöytyä parish centre (W 152), and Professor Kalle Kauppi's summer villa near Heinola (F 181, 182). With the best will in the world, one cannot call these three designs architectural masterpieces; they are closer to the low-water mark in the Aalto canon.

Aino had indisputable success, however, with her glass design, such as the prize-winning Bölgeblick service (W 165), with her textiles, and especially with her interior design. Even before her marriage, in 1922, she had designed dining room furniture which won a prize and was built (cf. W 76), and as a newlywed bride she had furnished the ladies' room of the Hämäläis-Osakunta in Helsinki (W 52) and a hatter's shop (W 65). During their years in Turku, she designed nursery interiors, with which she experimented in her own home, furnished a model flat in the Tapani Building (W 108), and built her own experimental kitchen for the 1930 Minimum Apartment Exhibition in Helsinki (1930, W 150). With the founding of Artek, she became a full-time interior designer. Commissions completed with great success under her direction included such prestigious jobs as the furnishing of the Savoy restaurant in Helsinki (W 211) and the seniors' dormitory in Cambridge. She gave definitive form to much of Artek's standard furniture, and made new variants of Aalto's

135

84. The Savoy restaurant in Helsinki was furnished in 1937 by Aino with standard Aalto furniture.

basic types. She was also something of an exhibition specialist, and arranged many of the significant displays of their output which established Aalto as the leading name in Finnish architecture and design. She handled the Aalto exhibition at the 1936 Milan triennale together with Hahl, and did most of the work for the first Aalto retrospective, which opened in Helsinki in 1947. This was a magnificent summing-up of the husband-and-wife team's twenty-five-year collaboration, a farewell of sorts to the Aino period of Alvar's life.

This brief overview gives an idea of how Aino's and Alvar's collaboration worked. Since both were very strong, independent personalities, they increasingly refrained from working under the same roof. Aino found various niches within their joint projects: exhibitions, interior design, and the management of Artek, where she was in sole control. The Aalto archives contain a draft for a lecture given by Aino in January 1943 to female colleagues at the Architecta club, which she had taken part in founding. In her lecture, she stressed how important it is for the female architect to concentrate on the things most important to her: housing, the needs of children and families in planning, day care, schools, libraries, and gathering places for young people. We may assume that she devoted special attention to these sectors in many of Aalto's major assignments.

Her most important contribution to their collaboration, however, seems to have been to act as her husband's best and most reliable critic. He could discuss all of his most difficult problems with her, and he always trusted her judgement. A small example of how their collaboration functioned is the letter from Boston in which Alvar told Aino how he had finally solved the problem of increasing the number of students in the dormitory by following her suggestion of adding a cluster of wedge-shaped rooms to the enlarged west end of the building.

Holding her own so well in her personal life by the side of a person like Alvar Aalto, both inward with the family and outward with friends and the public, was no mean achievement. Aino was admired and warmly appreciated by everyone who came into contact with her, from the many assistants who worked at the office over the years to Alvar's foreign colleagues and friends. Typical of this was the letter about Aino that Ellen Harrison, née Rockefeller, sent me in 1985, in which she especially stressed the contrast between the effusive Alvar and the warm, silent, maternally protective Aino.

The most eloquent obituary for Aino was written by Carola Giedion Welcker, a close friend of Aino as well as of James Joyce and Constantin Brancusi. Note that she emphasized Aino's role as tutelary goddess, which I indicated was so important. Here is the obituary from the first 1949 issue of Arkkitehti:

Far beyond her eminent ability in directing her office and in her profession, Aino Aalto, with her retiring humility, embodied a universal world of feminine grace, maternal care, and human confidence: great, elemental qualities, which are essential for real life to germinate and prosper.

Her relaxed outward charm matched her inner being, matched the light colours she loved, even better matched the colour white, which was inextinguishably hers. Memory projects her stubbornly in this light: I see her dressed in festive white in New York, in sporty white in Zurich, and in summer white in Italy, with white sandals on her feet. The gentle tilt of her head when she greeted someone, her feminine smile and her blue eyes, in which thoughts seemed to swim like silverfish; everything about her was a remarkable blend of humility and dignity. Yes, everything about Aino was unobtrusive and quietly concentrated, self-contained. Aino was uncompromising. She was a pure spring from which one could seek strength, imbibe faith, and find encouragement. In Antiquity, she would have been depicted as Demeter, carved in stone. The Middle Ages would have made her a Madonna carved in wood, with the protective mantle. And our era? For us she, who so heroically and harmoniously resigned herself to her cruel illness, helping her husband in his work and directing the Artek company to the very end, is a symbol of the purest and most perfect human endeavour.

The most deeply considerate and consoling letter of condolence (in French) came from eighty-six-year-old Henry van de Velde, whom Aalto greatly admired. Van de Velde had fled during the war to Switzerland, where he lived alone with his daughter in a small hut. Alvar and Aino had visited them several times, and a warm friendship had sprung up between them:

85. Alvar Aalto on a visit
to Henry van de Velde
in Switzerland, 1948.
Photo: Aino Aalto.

Oberägri, "Le Bungalow", February 6, 1949

My dear Alvar Aalto,

As a passionate, enthusiastic worker, you will surely throw yourself into your work – in which you are now alone, compelled to endure all its weight and worry in solitude. This dedication will help you, dear Alvar Aalto, it will ease your pain. But it can only bring temporary relief. It is not enough. To be able to go on, you must bravely and perseveringly face the new situation you find yourself in, the life and the future that lie ahead. You surely suspect what your friends expect of you. And also the importance that I personally attach to you, with your special talent and skill, maintaining your worldwide prominence within the movement that has appeared and conquered as the special style of 'our' era.

Refrain from excessive work. It can only anaesthetize you, without bringing the calm you will need to take up a new life and to become aware of the moral responsibility which rests upon you. It is to you more than to others that the young generation of architects and designers look. Dear Alvar Aalto, come here to Switzerland before you start any major projects – a few weeks of deep meditation will give you a clear view of the position you should take at a moment when both the practical and the aesthetic conceptions of the right direction for architecture are in great danger. Come back to us. Our devotion, our deep admiration, and the confidence we have in your creative power will strengthen your faith and redouble the talents you possess.

I squeeze your hands hard.
Your very devoted van de Velde

Rekindling the Light

Van de Velde's unreserved recognition of Aalto's creative talent and his responsibility to continue to develop it were surely of help in Aalto's time of need. But van de Velde was himself too Apollonian in spirit to be able to judge how a Dionysian like Aalto would react at a time like this. Aalto had no strong sense of duty; he could not find solace in the discipline of work or in philosophical contemplation. His work had been motivated by joy and delight, and sustained by Aino's motherly encouragement. Now that the joy was gone, the balance between work and relaxation in his life was shattered. No quiet days in the Swiss Alps or the Finnish forests could help him. He sank into chaos and discouragement; he kept company with Dionysus, who is the god of earthly wisdom, but also of unbridled chaos. Aalto generally had a healthy attitude to drinking: alcohol allowed his personality to blossom forth in an acceptable way. Sometimes he got into trouble, however. During the year after Aino's death, he often went astray, to the great concern of his children, friends, and colleagues.

He had appealed to two major assignments, the Helsinki University of Technology and the National Pensions Institute, in postponing his return to MIT and in not taking part in the final stages of construction of his dormitory there. Nor was he present at the dedication in summer 1949. In fact there was no immediate rush at all for him to start working on the two major commissions at home. The problem was his reluctance to return to the United States, and his chaotic, aimless way of life. The current work at the office was more than enough for him, and was largely handled by his assistants. Only occasionally did he have the energy to commit himself more deeply, as in the case of Säynätsalo Town Hall. He had started working on it back in 1948, and the official drawings were completed in March 1950. This design, complete in every detail, was perhaps his warmest and most beautiful, and shows that his skill did not fail him at this difficult time.

He also took part in two new competitions in 1949. The first involved two funeral chapels for Malmi graveyard, obviously a theme that suited his state of mind. He won comfortably. He sent in another competition entry, for a customs and passenger terminal for Helsinki's South Harbour, with the ironic motto "Entrez en paradis" (Come in to paradise), but the design did not find favour among the jury. Otherwise, the office continued to work on the master plan for the Helsinki University of Technology in Otaniemi. He also designed an enormous wooden indoor sports building for Otaniemi, on which construction

86. Säynätsalo Town Hall, with the staircase to the "Citizens' Square".

87. The Otaniemi sports hall, with "the world's longest wooden roof trusses". Photo: Göran Schildt.

began immediately. At a press preview of this building, he showed that he was still the same old Aalto. He had used roof supports known as 'HB trusses' made up of intersecting boards. According to him, these trusses, with a span of 45 metres, were "the world's longest – Amsterdam has similar ones just 43 metres long".

Aalto's many inessential trips abroad in 1949 show that he was uncomfortable in his empty home. He went several times to Stockholm, and visited Copenhagen, Zurich, Paris, and Holland. The ostensible reason for the last visit was to design the interiors of the *Enso,* a ship built in Rotterdam for the Finnish industrial giant, Enso-Gutzeit.

In Paris he met his old friends Le Corbusier, Léger, and Brancusi, and new friends such as Braque, Arp, and Kandinsky. Le Corbusier introduced him to Eugène Claudius Petit, Minister of Reconstruction, and to André Bloc, founder and editor-in-chief of the influential professional journal, *L'Architecture d'aujourd'hui.* Aalto's association with these two gentlemen led to a very stimulating event which helped him shake off his despondency. They arranged a major exhibition of Alvar and Aino Aalto's architectural output.

The exhibition was at the Ecole des Beaux Arts from April 24 to May 17, 1950, in conjunction with a comprehensive exhibition of Finnish painting and sculpture. The Aalto show was funded by the Ministry of Reconstruction, and *L'Architecture d'aujourd'hui* contributed by publishing a special issue which functioned as the exhibition catalogue. The Aalto show was in the school's Galérie Foch, with a direct view of the riverfront. Aalto could hardly have had a more flattering return to Paris after his triumph with the Finnish pavilion at the World's Fair of 1937. Maire Gullichsen told me of a cocktail party given at the Hôtel des Saints Pères, where she and Aalto were staying. There they met all of Aalto's French artist friends and the entire cultural establishment headed by Minister of Education Delbos.

Aalto's letter archives also recount a somewhat less edifying episode which shows that Aalto still had some way to go to regain his self-control. L'Union des Artistes Modernes had invited him to a reception to praise him and award him a token of their esteem. Aalto accepted politely, and ministers, high city officials, and union members gathered to wait for him. The guest of honour, however, never appeared: he had strayed into a bar. The gift was sent to him, accompanied by a letter which was a masterpiece of polite irony.

Around this time, a meeting took place to which Aalto referred fifteen years later in a letter to Claudius Petit concerning the death of Le Corbusier: "I shall never forget our *dîner à trois* at your place, nor the friendship that united us . . . I loved and admired Le Corbusier." Whatever the differences in their personalities and architecture, there was a mutual sympathy between Aalto and Le Corbusier that went back to the CIAM congress in 1933 (cf. *The Decisive Years,* p. 98), and was also expressed in their correspondence. Le Corbusier's reply to an invitation by Aalto to visit Finland is illuminating:

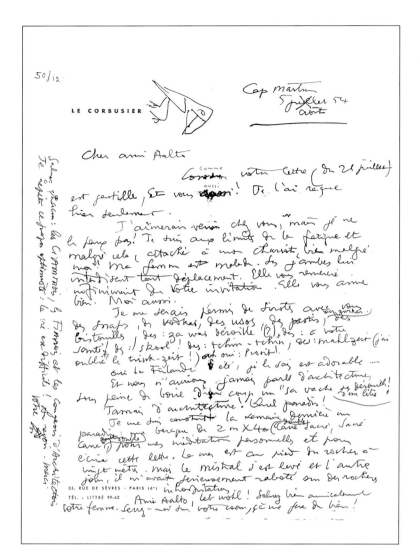

88. In a letter to Aalto dated August 5, 1954, Le Corbusier regretted that he was unable to come to Finland. Note the two raven signatures (*corbeau* = raven, crow).

Cap Martin, August 5, 1954

My dear friend Aalto,

How amiable your letter of July 21 was, just like yourself. I should love to visit you, but cannot. I have no strength left, and yet I must bear my burden . . . I know that Finland is lovely in the summer. If I could come we should not say a word about architecture. What a paradise!

A week ago I built myself another kind of paradise, a shack, two by four metres (double sacred square) for my personal meditations and to write this letter. The sea is 20 metres away at the foot of the cliff. But the mistral has been blowing, and the other day it pushed me alarmingly towards the sharp rocks.

Aalto, my friend, leb wohl, my best regards to your wife, and press me hard to your heart – it will do me good. I repeat my optimistic slogan: Life is hard! Thank you, au revoir, Yours (drawing of a raven)

A few months after the 1950 exhibition in Paris, the Association of Finnish Architects, acting on Aalto's suggestion, made Le Corbusier its honorary member. Le Corbusier, in turn, expressed his collegial feelings by proposing a joint business deal. He wrote that he had designed seven Aubusson tapestries with a total size of 52.3 square metres. The tapestry maker was asking 1,600,000 francs for them, while Le Corbusier's own fee was 530,000 francs. He now suggested that Aalto should sell the weaves to friends and galleries in Scandinavia for twice the sum, yielding a profit of 2,130,000 francs. The factory could also make three variants of each of the seven tapestries, bringing Aalto's share to 6,390,000 francs. The offer shows that Le Corbusier did not know Aalto very well, and that he automatically expected everyone to share his business mentality. Aalto replied through his secretary that the economic situation in the Nordic countries was so poor that the deal was unfortunately out of the question.

Aalto's trip to Paris did, however, give rise to another advantageous deal for Aalto, although it was completely involuntary. He had told Léger of his assignment to design a 'town hall' for the tiny industrial village of Säynätsalo, where Communist workers held a majority in the municipal council. This pleased Léger, himself a Communist, so much that he offered to make a painting for Aalto's town hall. Since he was formally bound by a contract with his dealer, he could not donate the painting, but the price would be nominal. Aalto gratefully accepted on behalf of the people of Säynätsalo, and designed a special niche for the painting in the rear wall of the council chamber. He sent

89. Alvar and Elissa Aalto in their studio in the early 1960s. Behind Elissa is the painting Léger did for Säynätsalo Town Hall. Photo Havas

the measurements to Léger, who in turn delivered the painting. But when the town fathers heard what the painting cost, they refused to take it. "Do you expect us to pay 200,000 marks for such rubbish?" (200,000 marks in those days was equivalent to 865 dollars.) Aalto could not tell Léger for fear of hurting his feelings, so he paid the money and kept the painting.

In the early summer of 1950, there was another stimulating event in Aalto's life: a prolonged visit to Britain. This was in fact the first European country with which he had been able to reestablish contact after the isolation of the war years. His colleague and friend from the days of the 1933 London exhibition, F.R.S. Yorke, came to Finland on the invitation of the Association of Finnish Architects in September 1945, and the next year Aalto was invited by the British Council to represent SAFA at the International Conference of Architects in London. Besides meeting Yorke and Morton Shand again, with his usual aplomb he made so many new friends that he was made a Fellow of the Royal College of Art in 1948. In 1950 the Architectural Association invited him to teach at its school for two months, but he declined: "I am a practising architect, and cannot successfully combine my practice with architectural criticism and theoretical instruction." It was agreed instead that he would give some informal lectures based on his own buildings.

Having done so, he spoke at an extra general meeting of the Architectural Association in London on June 28, an event which attracted a large number of British architects despite the holiday timing. As usual, he spoke freely and improvised, but an able stenographer was present, and the lecture was published in the association's annals. It shows Aalto at the height of his ingenuity and skill in adapting to his audience – in this case, a crowd of English gentlemen. The key question for Aalto at the time was how to reconcile industrial production with adequate quality and individual variation. He asked his audience:

Is it possible today for everyone to enjoy the qualities and quantities that were previously the privileges of the happy few? It is very, very difficult to socialize quality so that the general public can enjoy it. I hardly think there is a better way or a better means than that accomplished by Christ at the wedding at Cana, when he mixed water with the red wine.

Imagine that you are inviting twelve guests to dinner and intend to serve a good burgundy. No problem. But if we are inviting three thousand men and women to dinner, the question arises: how can we serve them all a good burgundy? Some of them will be sitting half a mile from the distribution site, and burgundy cannot endure transport for such a long distance. When it arrives, it is no longer burgundy but a mediocre wine. That is the tragedy of our age: we do not have the technical capacity to provide quality across the social spectrum – which is what our goal should be today.

Aalto spent the remainder of the summer of 1950 in Finland, but in September he was travelling again. This was partly in the form of study trips to metropolises on the Continent in connection with the design of the National Pensions Institute, but he also had business in Holland, where Sandberg, director of Amsterdam's Stedelijk Museum, mounted the extensive exhibition of Aalto's work that had been in Paris that spring. The show was in Amsterdam from October to November.

By this time, there were signs that Aalto was spending more time at the drawing board. He entered and won a competition for a new parish church in Lahti. In Säynätsalo, a topping-off celebration was held in December for the important town hall project. Moreover, two very extensive projects appeared on the horizon: an enormous nitrogen products factory in Oulu for the chemicals company Typpi Oy, and the Jyväskylä Pedagogical Institute, which soon grew into one of Finland's liveliest universities. One might venture to guess that Aalto's victory in the competition for a college in his old home town gave him a special lift and speeded up the recovery of his mental balance.

The last outbreak of travel fever came in 1951, when Aalto flew to Barcelona to deliver two lectures (in French), on April 7 and 10, at the *Colegio Oficial de Arquitectos de Cataluna y Baleares*. The subjects were *L'humanité et l'architecture* and *L'élasticité des constructions d'architecture,* clearly variations on his earlier lectures on *The Humanizing of Architecture* and *Flexible Standardization.* In Barcelona, he made a useful contact in Antonio de Moragas, secretary of the architects'

90. The door to the main building of the Jyväskylä University campus. For Aalto, his work on the new university opened the door to a new life. Photo: Alvar Aalto Museum.

association, to whom Aalto referred in a letter as "the prominent leader of young architects". From Barcelona, he made excursions to Madrid and Palma de Mallorca. He returned via Rome, where he made a secret rendezvous with Elsa Mäkiniemi, a barely thirty-year-old architect employed at his office, who travelled there by train, in third class.

In late November, he returned to Spain to repeat his lectures to the architects' association in Madrid. In the capital, he befriended Spain's national conservator Francisco Preto Moreno, with the result that Preto Moreno and his

91. From Aalto's sketch-book from his 1951 trip to Morocco:
Sidi Bou Oth.
The walls of Marrakesh.
Meeting on the road.
Aalto obviously did not know an olive tree from a fig tree.

(according to Aalto) very pretty wife offered to accompany Aalto on a tour of southern Spain. Among other sites, they visited Granada, where the Alhambra was a veritable "stimulation architectonique", as Aalto expressed it in his quaint schoolboy French in a thank-you letter to Preto Moreno. Lured on by the beautiful winter weather and their excellent spirits, the travellers crossed the straits to Tangier, and wandered through various Moroccan towns and villages until they reached Marrakesh, where they turned back. Aalto's return journey passed via Tunis, Rome, Zurich, Copenhagen, and Stockholm; he returned home just before Christmas.

The Aalto archives contain a manuscript in French in which five Spanish architects give their impressions of Aalto during his visit to Madrid. It is probably a translation from some Spanish architectural journal. The immediacy and detail of these comments provide us with a unique opportunity to catch the vital, fifty-three-year-old Aalto 'in flight', mirrored through the eyes of a group of young, intelligent Spaniards. Fernando Chueca writes:

There were a few of us Spanish architects waiting for our Finnish visitor in the lobby of the Hotel Nacional. He came, affable, dressed in black, corpulent but very agile. He looked like a peasant. He sat with us a while, talking lightly about his travels and plans. Then he wanted to go shopping, and I offered to act as his cicerone. I discovered pretty soon that

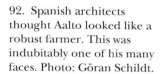

92. Spanish architects thought Aalto looked like a robust farmer. This was indubitably one of his many faces. Photo: Göran Schildt.

he would have preferred to go on his own: here was an architect who liked his independence. Perhaps this is typical of the people from the still forests and the hidden lakes. But I was determined to accompany him, for even if he was not delighted by my presence, I wanted to get to know him personally.

He wanted to buy various knickknacks, or 'espagnolades', for his family and his lady friends in Finland. At Linares, he bought some bead necklaces in Gypsy style, and while I was talking with a friend I had met, he bought a pair of castanets. When he was going to pay, I was startled: the bill was 600 pesetas. The shop assistant explained that Mr Aalto had unknowingly chosen the most expensive castanets, which were made of a special kind of wood and used only by serious artists. When I pointed this out to Aalto, he was delighted and absolutely refused to exchange them for a cheaper pair.

As we were looking into some other shops, I took the opportunity to ask him whether he thought Madrid resembled any other European capital. He thought for a moment, then said: Madrid reminds me of Vienna, perhaps because an Austrian dynasty ruled your country for so long.

Concentrating more on goldsmith's shops than the architectural setting, we came to the Plaza Mayor and the porticoes of Zaragoza street. Aalto showed no reaction, no interest. He was looking for earrings for his daughter, and finally found them on Prado street. They were large filigree pieces from Valencia or Granada, and he tried them on the salesgirl to find the right size with his architect's eye. Another problem was finding a very dark maroon suiting, which he said was hard to get hold of in Finland even though the climate requires dark clothes.

It is my impression that Aalto is very sensitive to decorative qualities. The curious fact is that these architects who are called Functionalists and whom one expects to think along purely practical, rational lines, are above all artists with an exquisite sensibility. This may be because the naive forms of modern architecture call for great subtlety, and therefore subtle architects use them. Alvar Aalto says that the work of an architect demands intense

93. From Aalto's sketchbook from his 1951 trip to Spain: Aliza de Valladolid. House with columns. Peasant's house. House with tower.

ALIZA DE VALLADOLID '51

148

concentration on the real task at hand, and he therefore insulates himself from distracting influences. In Italy, he closes his eyes to the monuments of the Renaissance and the Baroque, and seeks only the essence of the Mediterranean tradition. He is interested in the spontaneous planning of villages and small towns, especially in the mountains. In the days that followed, he repeatedly asked us to show him "villages rooted in the soil", as he put it.

The outcome of our stroll was that Aalto, who initially had accepted my offer with some reservations, did not want to let me go. We became great friends.

Carlos de Miguel:

Since Alvar Aalto had had the opportunity to see some examples of our recent architecture in Barcelona and Madrid, we asked him how he liked it. "It's very hard to say. I can't oppose a theory to a building; that's artificial. You can only oppose another building to a building." We are very grateful to Aalto for this reply. Instead of reproaching us for 'our architectural backwardness', he thinks that if Spanish architects concentrate on the kind of architecture called traditional, they must have good reasons to do so.

Rafael de Aurto:

Aalto is a man with a square build, with a sturdy neck and arms. He was made to cast iron, bend wood, and carve stone. He gazes at the world through his light eyes, which reflect the silence, the cold, and the clean lines of his native country. Apart from his robustness, like all sensitive people he is characterized by the flexibility of a great mind. His simple, primitive, almost childish architecture shows that he cannot hide his feelings, whereas we Spaniards cheerfully use the transcendent forms inherited from our forebears.

To him the new architecture of Madrid is just as uninteresting as the abbey of the Escorial, clearly a conscious choice rather than incomprehension. Sitting in front of the abbey, he turned his back to it, and when we said: "Don't look at the building", he answered with a fleeting smile which could be interpreted: "No fear!" Later, when we got back into the countryside, he was satisfied and fell asleep.

Francisco de Asis Cabrero:

Alvar Aalto's personality, his naive, upright character combined with his architecture, was very instructive to us. During his visit to Spain, we found that he concentrated on the details, texture, and plastic forms of the buildings in our rural villages, whereas the museum of the Prado and the cornices and ground plan of the Escorial left him indifferent. It is obvious that such ornamentation and strict regularity can never be of any use to him in his architecture. He works without prejudice, dependence, or outside influence in keeping with conditions in the Nordic countries.

Finally, Miguel Fisac:

I knew approximately what we all know: that Aalto was the first exponent of organic architecture in Europe. My curiosity was based on two considerations: first, the disappointment that the realized buildings of the European Functionalists had given me, and second, the photographs I had seen of Frank Lloyd Wright's enigmatic architecture and the knowledge that Aalto had translated this kind of architecture into normality. I was thus very happy to have the opportunity to meet him in Madrid. The personal impression he made is relevant: it revealed to me a natural, naive, cordial man with universal range. He never acts as if he had pretensions to being a mythic personality. He cannot be called either humble or arrogant; he seems unaware of his stature, and avoids judging himself. When asked about the work of his colleagues, he is neither critical nor disdainful. A curious feature is his complete lack of interest in architecture that goes in another direction than his. He does not see it, whether it is good or bad, old or new. Is this due to a fear of losing his aesthetic bearings? What he does see is detail that could enrich his thematic forms: the abstract pattern formed by the rays of the sun on a curtain, or the effect of a whitewashed wall against a landscape of bare cliffs.

Perhaps the most surprising reaction of the Spanish architects was that they all thought Aalto naive. Was this due to the difference in northern and southern mentality, or was it because all those with a clearly defined goal appear naive to doubting relativists?

Despite his frequent travels, 1951 seems to have been the year during which Aalto fully regained his inventiveness and his interest in his work. His most urgent project consisted of preparing working drawings for the buildings of the Jyväskylä Pedagogical Institute. The first stage of the project included the main building and its auditoria, a library, a separate cafeteria, a teacher training school, housing for students and staff, and other buildings. He also won a prestigious competition for the 'Rautatalo' (Iron House) in the centre of Helsinki. This finally gave him the opportunity to make his old dream of a covered, Italianate 'galleria' come true. He also won a competition to design a theatre in Kuopio that year, but his entry in the competition for Glostrup Hospital in Denmark did not win a prize. There was also a long list of minor industrial commissions, including a paper mill in Kotka.

Aalto's recovery obviously had to do with Elsa Mäkiniemi, a young architect who worked at his office. As we have seen, she had discreetly found time that spring during a study trip to central Europe to spend some time with the maestro himself. She was a comely, plain-spoken girl from Kemi in northern

Finland, who had gone in for skiing and skating in the winter and swimming across the swift river from her parents' holiday home in the summer. She was also a gifted student with a great curiosity for the world. Above all, she was an unsentimental woman who accepted life's realities, and liked to laugh at her crazy employer, who was twenty-three years older than she.

Aalto's friends understood from the beginning that he could not live alone for long, and that he must have a new wife. They were sure that she would be a colleague, since his work dominated his life so completely. His friends imagined that some wise woman his own age would be equal to the obviously challenging task.

Great was their surprise when Professor Hugo Alvar Henrik Aalto and Elsa Kaisa Mäkiniemi, graduate architect, were married on October 4, 1952 at the Helsinki City Hall by Mayor W. Henriksson. No one who saw them together, however, could think for long that Aalto would have done better to consider a marriage of convenience. His capacity of raising life to a Homeric level was rarely so much in evidence as on this occasion. If this was not Ulysses wedding Nausikaa, it came close. Elsa Kaisa was now called Elissa, an invention that was soon completely accepted. I became acquainted with Alvar and Elissa shortly after their wedding, and I can testify that the positive attitude, the enjoyment of life's adventures, that was a basic characteristic of Alvar's personality was

94. Aalto designed three balcony levels for the inner court of the Rautatalo, or 'Iron Building', in Helsinki, but only two were built.

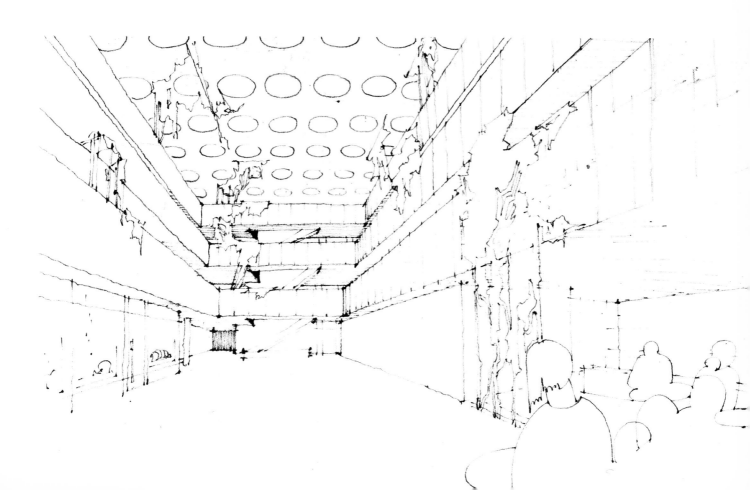

especially striking in these years. Being with them was a constant party, with Alvar's playful whims and Elissa's ready laughter the dominant impressions that remain.

The gaiety that followed this couple was so contagious that even those who met them only briefly were drawn into the magic circle. Typical is an interview published by *The Star* of London in April 1957. Aalto was in town to receive the highest honour of the Royal Institute of British Architects, its gold medal, at a solemn ceremony at the house of architects in West End. Protocol called for Aalto to make a lengthy and serious speech, or 'discourse'. *The Star's* reporter met them at the Savoy, where the Aaltos had just finished a private lunch of wine and shellfish in their suite. As a memory aid, Aalto had written down five words on a scrap of paper for the speech he was to give in a quarter of an hour. We leave the rest to the reporter:

Aalto gives me three minutes and I ask: What are your thoughts about architecture? Answer: It has gone on for many thousand years and I am only fifty years old, so I know practically nothing. Next question: I hear your wife is also an architect? Answer: Yes, in Finland we have a law that says architects must marry within the trade, so when I need

95. The profile of the future Elissa Aalto unexpectedly popped up in one of Aalto's sketches for the Kuopio theatre.

96. Newlyweds Alvar and Elissa, in their new summer-house at Muuratsalo. Photo: Göran Schildt.

a new wife I take a look at my female assistants at the office to see which one has the best lines – on the drawing board, I mean. Here Mrs Elissa, a Wagnerian blonde, interjects: Nonsense, it's just that he's too lazy to look any further.

Aalto's speech, entitled "Fighting Architecture", was written down by a stenographer and it has been a highlight of the editions of Aalto texts published in a variety of languages since 1973. Creative facility, the ability to give his best effortlessly whether as an architect or as a speaker, was a divine gift that made it possible for Aalto to fill his life with new creations and constantly replenished joy.

You Can't Save the World

One of Aalto's most valuable qualities was the ability to turn obstacles into stepping-stones, setbacks into spurs, and difficulties into assets. Even the greatest misfortune of his life, the loss of Aino, turned out to be a blessing for him in the long run. If it had not happened, he would have plunged into the unrealistic and stifling adventure that the Aino Institute could easily have turned into with its concentration on furniture and its worldwide sales organization. His visits to the United States would have continued, and with them his academic activity, which was basically foreign to his nature. Above all, in his activities within SAFA and at MIT, he would have frittered away his strength in a quixotic struggle against the technocratic threat. With all due respect to architectural laboratories, standardization institutes, pedagogical propaganda, and governmental regional planning commissions, these were not the areas in which he could give his best.

Aalto was a child of the Enlightenment, a time of hope that man, through reason, would be able to build a just and happy society. Personal success was not his prime goal; more important was to 'save the world' through an inspiring vision. This goal distinguished his youthful dream of reviving the Italian Renaissance in Finland by transforming Jyväskylä into a new Florence. The theme reappears in his adoption of the Modernist utopia of Le Corbusier and Bauhaus, and also tinges his critique of Rationalism. The realization that pure technocracy is inimical to nature and anti-human forced him to develop a new vision of transforming conflict into harmony.

Aalto's new vision, and his conviction that the future of humanity depends on solving the technological crisis, was such a revelation that at first he looked on it as a universal goal rather than a personal one. He wanted to convince others, to develop an ideology, to embark on a crusade. This is shown by his discussions with Giedion in the 1930s and with Lewis Mumford in the 1940s, in the appeal that he addressed in 1939 to his American colleagues in San Francisco (cf. *The Decisive Years*, p. 177), and in his ambition to turn the entire Association of Finnish Architects into his tool. This was truly a struggle to 'save the world'.

The world, however, will not let itself be saved so easily. People remain imperfect and unreceptive to arguments of both reason and morality. Sooner or later, all visionaries must make this discovery. The way that Aalto handled his disappointment and managed to remain faithful to his vision while accepting the way of the world makes an affecting and instructive story.

It started when he gave up hope that America could subdue the technological threat. His hope that 'the genuine American tradition' could defeat commercialism and 'Hollywood mentality' faded, and he realized that he was ill at ease in the United States. Instead, he convinced himself that small, relatively unspoilt Finland could play a leading role in the drama of world salvation. He thought that flexible standardization of the whole building industry could be achieved there through the influence of all progressive architects. After all, from the very first his own furniture design sprang from his ideas of flexible standardization. The same standard elements, the L, Y, and X legs, reappeared in a variety of combinations, giving rise to a whole range of chairs, tables, shelves, and other furniture. He applied similar principles to his utility architecture and regional planning in Finland, to which he devoted a great deal of energy. These plans repeated a series of basic solutions in ever-changing combinations aimed at achieving the correct balance between the working environment and nature, individual freedom and an enriching sense of community.

Aalto's interest in utility architecture, such as factory buildings and workers' housing, went back to 1930 and his design for the Toppila Pulp Mill in Oulu, and continued through the prewar projects at Sunila, Inkeroinen, Varkaus, Karhula, and Kauttua, to name just the most important sites. During and after the war, he designed new industrial areas for the Strömberg electronics

97. The Varkaus sawmill from 1945 (demolished 1975) shows how Aalto's obsession with nature influenced the external style even of his industrial architecture. Photo: Roos.

company in Vaasa and Helsinki, for the pulp producer Enso-Gutzeit in Summa, and for the chemicals manufacturer Typpi in Oulu. Significantly, his work for the last of these large companies began in 1950. After that, he took no new assignments of the kind, merely completing earlier projects for old clients.

No sharp line can be drawn between Aalto's work of the 1940s and 1950s, but there was an obvious shift in focus. His interest in standardization, furniture design, type housing, utilitarian industrial architecture and housing, and regional planning – in fact, anonymous planning in general – gradually declined. Instead, he concentrated on designing unique, monumental buildings and unique, exemplary total environments. He became increasingly aware that the world cannot be saved, and that even in Finland society cannot be transformed in the desirable direction.

This was hard for Aalto to accept, and even in the 1960s he lapsed into his old optimism in quite seriously suggesting that his country should become an environmental laboratory for the whole industrialized world; that its inhabitants should experiment with and implement model plans for other nations to learn from, all for the greater glory of Finland. This gave rise to a lively public debate between Aalto and myself*, but it did not hurt our friendship. Aalto knew deep inside that his idea was not realistic, and that Finland could not save the world any more than the United States could.

What was there left to do if the world really was irredeemable? With his lively interest in history, Aalto knew that people had always lived in distress, wrestling with overwhelming social problems, but that despite this for short periods certain privileged societies had been able to give somewhat harmonious and civilized forms to community life. The memory of these periods and the knowledge that harmony is possible is what makes life tolerable, Aalto concluded. Thus, anyone who could produce an example of real equilibrium between the conflicting forces in society would make a significant contribution to improving the human condition.

Aalto often said in his old age: *You can't save the world, but you can set it an example.* His first full-blown 'example' of this type was the small administrative complex that he designed for the new industrial village of Säynätsalo near Jyväskylä. He liked to call this building a 'town hall', and undeniably it has the full monumental impact of one.

It would have been natural in many ways for this work, marking as it did Aalto's return from his American detour, to have been characterized by nationalist motifs expressing his patriotism and love of the local setting. Instead, the town hall is as 'Italianate' as the church in nearby Muurame, which he had designed during his youthful Neo-Classical period. Clearly Aalto remained faithful to the belief that a foreign, borrowed motif transplanted with sufficient conviction into Finnish soil becomes genuinely Finnish. The Italian Renaissance was for Aalto an inalienable part of his heritage and his philosophy of life. In his view,

*See Aalto's speech at the Finnish Cultural Foundation's symposium, January 8, 1962.

101. The classic view of Säynätsalo Town Hall, with the now overgrown sod staircase in the foreground. Photo: Mäkinen.

providing the people of Säynätsalo with a setting in which they could live like the 14th-century inhabitants of Siena or San Gimignano was a patriotic act. When the members of the municipal board of building tactfully inquired if a tiny, poor community like theirs really needed to build a council chamber 17 metres high, considering that brick was so expensive, he replied: "Gentlemen! The world's most beautiful and most famous town hall, that of Siena, has a council chamber 16 metres high. I propose that we build one that is 17 metres."*

Aalto envisaged the raised courtyard enclosed by the various buildings as a place for all citizens to assemble in the manner of Siena's Campo. This has not happened so far, perhaps because Aalto idealized community life in Säynätsalo, but the possibility remains.

It is not easy to explain why Säynätsalo Town Hall makes such a strong impression on the visitor, even though it has no eye-catching motifs. A clue is found in a statement written by Aalto in 1956 for a students' journal in Jyväskylä:**

One of the most important tasks of architecture is to find the right scale. Säynätsalo Town Hall, with its small central square and its placing at the end of a larger, wedge-shaped square, is an attempt in this direction. The various parts of the building each have their own distinctive character, but I have tried to merge them into a unified, harmonious whole. The tower is not a tower at all but a culminating mass under which lies the main

* Aalto's assistant, Veli Paatela, recounted the episode to me.
** Original manuscript in the Aalto archives.

symbol of government, the council chamber. Using perfectly simple everyday materials with the right sense of form and rhythm to produce something refined and exquisite is an architectural goal that requires mastery of the art of simplicity . . . Simplicity faces great problems, however. Modern civilization refuses to accept such designs without a struggle. Present-day general education, which is going downhill, has a basic tendency for the vulgarly exotic: people find satisfaction in all sorts of irrelevant rubbish they see advertised. Taste, good taste, which is perhaps the principal distinguishing mark of culture, is so incredibly rare that you would need three or four decimal places to express its frequency.

Aalto's main emphasis was thus on simplicity, proportion, and nuance. The individualism of the various building parts embodied the civic independence he wished to encourage. The same goals were evident in his treatment of materials. Brick, stone, wood, and copper were the main ingredients. Brick had long been one of Aalto's favourite materials, perhaps because it is one of the oldest standardized technological products, and has always been used for flexibility in Aalto's sense of the word.

His first conscious emphasis on the texture of brick came in the design of his own home. Its external walls are not smooth and immaterial in the style of Le Corbusier, as are the walls of the Viipuri Library, but instead allow the individual bricks and joints to show under the whitewash. When he decided to use bare brick for the MIT dormitory, he faced the problem of an excessively homogenized and perfect brick industry. American bricks were all alike in both colour and shape; using them would have given the walls a dead, mechanical look. According to his assistant, Hammarström, Aalto was happy to find a brick factory near Boston that was on the brink of bankruptcy and made "the lousiest bricks in the world". If we are to believe Aalto, however, the matter was not quite so simple. In describing the dormitory, he said:

The bricks were made of clay from the topsoil, exposed to the sun. They were fired in manually stacked pyramids, using nothing but oak for fuel. When the walls were erected, all bricks were approved without sorting, with the result that the colour shifts from black to canary yellow, though the predominant shade is bright red.*

The walls built with these bricks resemble society in that they are made up of a wide range of different individuals.

No bricks quite as individualized as those he found in Boston were available in Finland, but the quality of the bricks used at Säynätsalo is still reassuringly uneven. Aalto attached great importance to giving the wall surfaces of the town hall a living look. His new assistant, Elsa Mäkiniemi, supervised the bricklaying, and when the job was done, Aalto sent the following thank-you note to each of the six masons who had been involved:

Helsinki, April 3, 1951.

The bricks for Säynätsalo Town Hall, which I consider to be an extremely important bricklaying job from the architectural point of view, were laid by Toivo Nykänen, Paavo Asplund, Yrjö Marjamäki, Aimo Renlund, Väinö Puolanen, and Sakari Sundvall. It is

* Text in the Aalto archives.

159

103. Closeup of the sod
staircase at Säynätsalo.

104. The council chamber
as it was built – one metre
higher than that of Siena.
Photo: Kolmio.

very important to me as an architect to promote the art of masonry in our country. This is why the masonry of Säynätsalo Town Hall, both its facade and most of its interiors, consists purely of brick. I must say that I am very satisfied with our collaboration, and that the result is a model example of Finnish brickwork.

*Alvar Aalto**

The most original individual feature of Säynätsalo Town Hall indubitably consists of the butterfly-shaped roof trusses, which have given rise to many different interpretations. According to Aalto, they had a purely practical function:

*The difference between average winter and summer temperatures is 17 degrees: that is, considerable. To prevent condensation in the winter and to keep the heat under control in the summer, ventilation must be provided between the ceiling and the roof. Most of our buildings have two separate structures. My 'butterflies' support both the ceiling and the roof, permitting the free circulation of air between them; there are no intermediate secondary beams.***

This was a typical Aalto 'invention' with a practical function, which naturally did not prevent it from also having an aesthetic purpose. It seems that Aalto intended the associations with mediaeval roof beams evoked by this structure to show that there are traditional techniques that are more appealing to the human eye than the magic tricks of modern technology.

The town hall contains another reference to the ancient harmony between technology and nature, man and his environment. I am thinking of the famous staircase made of sod and split tree trunks at the far end of the courtyard. Such steps, and similar ones made with flat stones, must have been among man's earliest inroads into nature. The use of this ancient technical solution eloquently highlighted the building's message of a humane technology mindful of nature. It is a shame that the municipality, out of misplaced frugality, has allowed this staircase to deteriorate so badly that it has all but disappeared. Replacing the decayed wooden supports every twenty years and mowing the grass of the steps by hand would be a trifle considering the privilege of owning such a unique and invaluable work of art.

As we see, Säynätsalo Town Hall is a backward-looking work, a concrete 'example' of a happy balance between man's technological and ecological aspirations during the preindustrial era. The problems of modern man, however, arise from the new factor of ever-advancing technology. Showing how this dilemma could be solved through concrete 'examples' was the crucial concern of Aalto's mature years.

Vuoksenniska Church in Imatra (1955–58) is a particularly salient example. The basic design idea was to install electrical machinery and a system of ball bearings that could be used to move the inside walls, producing a flexible

* Text in the Aalto archives.
** "The R.I.B.A. Annual Discourse 1957 by Professor Alvar Aalto H.C.M."

church interior. Weddings, funerals, and ordinary services need so little space that only the front part of the church, including the altar, pulpit, and organ, is needed, while the club activities and studies important to the congregation can go on in two rooms at the rear, separated by moveable walls. During major church holidays, all that is needed is a push of a button to open up a large, uniform church interior with vaulted forms that give it an intimate, sacred harmony.

The finesse in this plan is that the machinery, the basic prerequisite for the solution, is invisible and thus entirely subordinate. One could hardly imagine a greater leap from the childish pride at modern technology evinced by Aalto in his youthful design for Paimio Sanatorium, where the main facade was futuristically animated by lifts encased in glass walls. The flying buttresses and vaults of Gothic churches had a strict technical function, but they also had a strongly expressive religious value. The technologically inspired vaults of Vuoksenniska Church similarly express Aalto's faith that it is possible for man to live in harmony with the cosmic order.

In the description of Säynätsalo Town Hall quoted above, Aalto emphasized that the building was designed as part of a larger sequence of open spaces. He had drawn up a master plan for the budding industrial village back in 1945, including a central plaza with statues and fountains setting off the town hall. In 1950, he designed a cultural centre for Säynätsalo to further enhance the significance of this plaza. Unfortunately, only the town hall was built, a fate

105. Frontal view of Vuoksenniska Church. Photo: Ingervo.

106. Plan of Vuoksenniska Church with its 'flexible' interior, which can be expanded or shrunk by using sliding partitions.

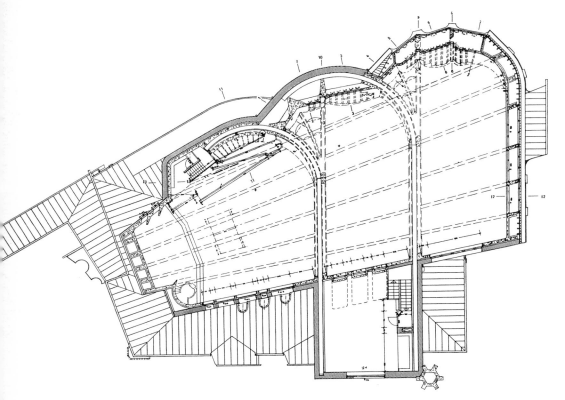

107. Vuoksenniska Church exterior. Photo: Havas.

shared by most of the magnificent proposals for town centres that he dashed off in the 1950s and '60s. Wolfsburg Cultural Centre (designed 1958), Helsinki's Finlandia Hall (1962), and Jyväskylä Theatre (1964) were all fragments of frustrated dreams of central squares. In other instances, such as the Oulu 'river rapids centre' (1943) and the squares with appropriate monumental buildings that he designed for Imatra (1949), Kuopio (1951), Gothenburg (1955 and 1957), Marl (1957), Baghdad (1958), Leverkusen (1960), Montreal (1964), Castrop-Rauxel (1965), Kokkola (1966), and Darmstadt (1969), Aalto's plans remained no more than unrealized visions.

Only in two locations did these plans gradually come to full fruition. One is Rovaniemi, where the library (designed 1961) and theatre (1969) were finally complemented in 1988 by the town hall, designed twenty-five years earlier. The other is Seinäjoki, which could be called "the most Aaltoan city in the world", both because it contains the largest collection and variety of Aalto buildings and especially because it is a brilliant 'example' of how he thought the heart of the modern city should be adapted to nature. To the cathedral-like church and parish centre, designed in 1951, a town hall (1958), a library (1960), an administrative office building (1964), and a theatre (1969) were later added, all grouped around a series of plazas and open spaces.

Aalto's interest in urban centres and monumental buildings did not originate in the 'town hall' of Säynätsalo: it went back to the youthful worship of Italy that marked many of his Neo-Classical designs. The situation was later complicated by his conversion to Rationalism, a movement that denied the value of monumentality and focused solely on technical, functional needs. The famous *Charte d'Athènes*, formulated by CIAM in 1933, did not recognize the need for any monumental centre, or 'urban heart', at all; it articulated the city into separate zones of use with traffic solutions making up the principal motifs. The pronounced monumentality of Aalto's Paimio Sanatorium and Viipuri Library obviously went against the *Zeitgeist,* and he himself passed over this characteristic in describing the buildings in strictly functional terms. Not until his town hall plans for Avesta (1944) and Nynäshamn (1945) did he dare to give his instinct for monumentality freer rein. It blossomed forth fully in Säynätsalo Town Hall.

Aalto's new orientation was clearly connected with his desire to set an example. In contrast to the type house, the monumental building is the ideal 'example': apart from fulfilling a variety of practical needs, it also fulfils an obvious artistic need. The old distinction between art architecture and utility architecture, which Aalto had once decisively rejected, reappeared in his work, though partly for new reasons and without diminishing his awareness of the value of utility architecture. In a 1953 article published in *Arkkitehti,* Aalto wrote:

According to time-honoured European precepts, the centre of a community was divided into two sectors: the housing areas, which were just what the name says – whatever the kind of housing, all the way from slums to aristocratic residences – and areas that were common

108. Seinäjoki city centre, with the library at the far right, the church and campanile in the background, and the town hall on the left. Perspective sketch by Aalto and photo by Rista.

to all, proletarians and senators alike. The public buildings there ran the gamut from the government palace to all the buildings in which some form of public activity took place: offices to which all had access or which all were obliged to visit; community facilities such as baths, libraries, museums; and of course all religious edifices and sacred areas. We must also include the open public spaces, squares, parks, and covered galleries where all citizens without distinction could assemble, and the public monuments and other symbolic and narrative forms which go with them.

This order of things, which has been preserved in Europe through the ages, has now been shattered. The commercialism inadvertently caused by the French Revolution gradually led to a new dominant element in the townscape, the commercial building. This type of building has later reached a scale with which the construction projects of neither state nor associations can compete . . .

During Finland's independence, only a few public buildings have been erected on truly authoritative sites. Our cities are becoming or have already become amorphous masses, in which town halls, libraries, and other community institutions are mere ordinary corner buildings on rented land, without the traditional stamp of government power and social commitment. They have businesses on the ground floor and a random mix of offices and dwellings in the upper storeys. This has become the rule for public buildings, which have thus been relegated to the status of ordinary commercial and residential buildings.

And yet the role of public buildings in society should be just as important as that of the central organs in the human body, if we are to prevent our society from stagnating and

109. Southwestern Finland Agricultural Co-operative Building in Turku (1928–29), with the city theatre embedded in a block of rented flats. Photo: Welin.

becoming mentally repulsive and physically baneful to its citizens. We would probably do best to think of the present – let us hope soon past – period in urban development as a transition, which certainly cannot expect very flattering criticism from the coming generation.

Our society must be restored to health. Perhaps it is wrong to speak of restoration – it would be more appropriate to say that we need to recreate the differentiation necessary to an organized society. The society that is now emerging – which could be called a classless society – is even more sensitive than the bourgeois society to which the French Revolution gave rise, as it comprises more people. Their physical well-being, their civic and general cultural development, depend on the correct planning of public institutions and areas.

For a full understanding of the 'examples' Aalto tried to create in his later years, it is not enough to refer to the monumental – we might also say, artistically meaningful and expressive – function a specific type of building should have. We must also discuss Aalto's special definition of monumentality as the tangible result of complex forces, not as a verbalization or an abstract idea.

Aalto distrusted words, although – or perhaps, because – he himself had an inexhaustible ability to bewitch others, and himself, with words. It is easy enough to 'save the world' with programmes and theories, but even the slightest real improvement in living conditions can be achieved only with the greatest difficulty. One of his favourite anecdotes was the story of how the municipal council of Kauhajärvi decreed unanimously that only beautiful buildings should be erected in their village. Aalto was a sworn empiricist, and believed in plans only when he saw their outcome.

This is the reason for the sharp distinction he made between intellectual activity based solely on words and that which works with matter. As he saw it, painting and sculpture are more difficult and valuable forms of art than literature. Even more important and valuable is architecture, as it provides the material framework for life. Here we find the explanation for Aalto's unwillingness to theorize about architecture, his frequently misunderstood motto: "I do not answer questions about architecture with words, I answer with buildings." Only a building that radiates the special authority which stems from a balanced synthesis of technology and nature, logic and human dignity, can be a source of cultural strength to modern man.

110. Rovaniemi City Theatre (1970–75), a monumental building designed as a unique 'example'. Photo: Mosso.

Aalto delivered a eulogy for Eliel Saarinen in 1950. Inadvertently, it turned into a highly personal confession of faith. He said:

When Victor Hugo pointed out in the 1840s that the printing press had replaced the cathedral as the engine of cultural change at the close of the Middle Ages, hardly anyone could imagine the enormous task that lay ahead, in spite of everything, for architecture reborn. To begin with, architecture appeared to be trodden underfoot by industrialism, which brought about antisocial cities and mere utilitarian, commercial forms. But industrialism brimmed over. Man's most dangerous weapon – the machine – appropriated a power that did not belong to it. It controlled man, instead of man controlling it.

A return to the past was impossible; all romantic experiments and literary movements were in vain. A force that arises in matter itself was needed to turn the machine's proletarianizing and mentally deadening power into equilibrium. When the printed word no longer had any effect, the burden gradually shifted to architecture.

Regardless of which social system prevails in the world or its parts, a softening human touch is needed to mould societies, cities, buildings, and even the smallest machine-made objects into something positive to the human psyche, without bringing individual freedom and the common good into conflict. These forces have assembled around architecture to such an extent that we can now speak of a new, broader purpose for architecture, encompassing the whole world and its cultural crisis. We might also say: We have now

111. Alajärvi Town Hall and C.L. Engel's church are designs which express the Classical ideal of balance without verbalizing it. Photo: Ingervo.

reached the stage when architecture has regained the status it had in the Classical civilizations of the past.

For architecture to gain authority as a humanizing factor upholding culture, works cast in matter itself are needed – no words can suffice. A monumental force which gives man hope, confidence, and self-discipline is needed. Social awareness and compassion for the human tragedy are called for. Architecture must be deeply rooted in place and circumstance; it requires a delicate sense of form; it must support man's emotional life.

These thoughts, improvised in the solemnity of the moment, may or may not confirm Aalto's assertion that it is easier to solve problems verbally than architecturally, but they do give a fairly good idea of the emotional foundation from which the mature Aalto's architectural 'examples' sprang forth, and of the message he wished to convey with them.

Citizen of the World

During Aalto's 1957 visit to London to receive a gold medal from the Royal Institute of British Architects, *The Times* (April 3), wrote:

"It is remarkable that the Finnish architect Alvar Aalto should have gained a world-wide celebrity in architectural circles on the basis of a number of works that are inaccessible to all but the most assiduous travellers."

The paper was right in that nearly all Aalto buildings at the time (except the Baker House in Cambridge, Massachusetts) were located in remote Finland. Thus it was truly a paradox that since the 1930s he had been one of the leading exponents of modern architecture. There were weighty reasons, however, for the provincial Finn's promotion to the centre of the international stage while his Scandinavian colleagues remained more or less on the periphery.

In Part II of this biography *(The Decisive Years)*, I discussed some of these reasons. One was that during the fighting years of the 1930s, Modernist architectural journals such as *Stein Holz Eisen* in Germany, *Architectural Review and Architectural Record* in Britain, and *Architectural Forum* in the United States published pictures of the relatively few designs in the new style that were actually built, in an attempt to show that the Rationalist utopia had been victorious on all fronts. So much the better if the buildings were in Finland, Czechoslovakia, or Greece; after all, the Rationalist goal was a new international community. In Aalto's case, his bentwood furniture had given him the advantage of having a certain presence in countries where he had built nothing. His career on the international arena had been further boosted by his pavilions at the World's Fairs of Paris in 1937 and New York in 1939.

The primary reason for Aalto's growing reputation, however, was his charismatic personality, which enabled him to recruit uniquely influential supporters. Morton Shand and Sigfried Giedion laid the foundation for his fame, and a chorus of critics, unanimous in their praise, soon followed their lead. Aalto was pampered by the foreign critics who came to Finland and saw the country through his eyes. Moreover, the postwar years saw a real race among the leading architectural journals of the Western world to be the first to publish his latest

112. As sociable personally as he was laconic in letters, Aalto became a living myth to the world around him. Photo: Göran Schildt.

designs. In this bitter journalistic rivalry, Aalto was bombarded with letters year after year from *Architectural Review* and *Architectural Record* in Britain, *Architectural Forum* and *Progressive Architecture* in the United States, *L'Architecture d'Aujourd'hui* in France, *Domus, Casabella,* and *Zodiac* in Italy, *Werk* in *Switzerland, Bauwelt and Bauen und Wohnen* in Germany, and *Cuadernos de Arquitectura* in Spain.

Organizers of architectural exhibitions on three continents were equally eager. The impossibility of accommodating everybody taught Aalto that nonchalance, strict selectivity, and enigmatic behaviour, even towards friends in the field, by no means cooled the media's interest; if anything, it spurred it on. He became accustomed to the thought that critics and exhibitors were not doing him a favour by bringing his name into the limelight, but that, instead, the supplicants were disturbing his work. Thus, on May 27, 1952 when an editor of *Architectural Forum* reminded Aalto in vain of an unanswered inquiry, he responded: "Here is hell. There is about 2,000,000 cubic meters – 60,000,000 cubic feet – mostly official buildings on my desk, so you can see I cannot move around very much!" On New Year's Day, 1959, he wrote to his friend Ernesto Rogers, who was editor of *Casabella* at the time: "There are publishers running after me every day with authors, photographers, bayonets and pistols to have the publicity before you. The new fashion is to publish a house, maybe even before the architect is born. I prefer to publish the houses after they are really ready."

Aalto's lack of interest in what he considered personal publicity appeared in his surprisingly reserved reactions to proposals to write books about him that a series of prominent critics sent him right after the war. Is there another architect who would not have been grateful to receive this letter, dated May 3, 1948, from Sigfried Giedion, chief ideologue of the Modern movement:

113. Sigfried and Carola Giedion visit Alvar and Elissa Aalto in Finland. The hosts on the far right and on the left, with the guests of honour next to them. Photo: Federico Marconi.

"I would like to publish your works in a series I am planning with the Oxford University Press. For I think that it would be useful to both of us if I put my name to a publication of your works in America, which has the biggest market." Aalto did not reject the proposal, and he received Giedion cordially when the author came to Finland to gather material for the book, but despite Giedion's urgent requests, he never took the time to hunt up the necessary documentation and illustrations. The book was postponed year after year, and in 1952 Giedion wrote: "It is now simultaneously too late and too soon to publish a book about you." He evidently felt that the enormous gap in the explication of Aalto's works at the end of the war had been at least partly filled by his long chapter on Aalto in the second edition of his famous book *Space, Time and Architecture* (1949) and his essays for the Zurich (1948) and Paris (1950) exhibition catalogues. Meanwhile, Aalto's new orientation was difficult to assess without a few years' perspective.

In 1948 Morton Shand also expressed interest in filling in the glaring gap in the documentation of Aalto's work. He had a willing publisher, but no more luck than Giedion in obtaining the material he needed from Aalto. Max Bill fared no better, although in 1948 Aalto promised to help him prepare a monograph, being well aware that his usual passivity would thwart the plan. A suggestion made in 1947 by Moholy-Nagy's Chicago publisher Paul Theobald was quite obviously unrealistic: Aalto himself was to write the complete text of a book entitled *Aino and Alvar Aalto, Pioneers in Contemporary Architecture*. Aalto liked the idea in principle, but never found the time to carry it out.

The high regard in which Aalto's works of the 1940s were held, however, made the need for a representative monograph increasingly pressing. Books had been published about all the other pioneers of modern architecture; the question was no longer whether to publish but how to do it. Aalto was aware of the risk of misinterpretation – as Giedion's favourable but simplistic writings had shown. Perhaps Aalto himself should sacrifice some of his time to ensure that the book to be published would do him justice.

His Swiss friends introduced him to Hans Girsberger of Zurich, a very cultivated and serious publisher, whose tiny publishing house had issued excellent books on Le Corbusier, Richard Neutra, and Mies van der Rohe. Aalto placed stringent conditions on his participation: not only would he deliver the illustrations and text ready for printing in German, French, and English but he would also be responsible for the layout. The negotiations and preparations took over ten years and very nearly reduced the publisher to despair. Nonetheless, in 1963 *ALVAR AALTO* (Editions Girsberger) finally came out. That the book was published at all was largely due to Aalto's imperturbable Swiss assistant, Karl Fleig, who helped him write the texts and meet all the perfectionist standards he set himself.

In the meantime, however, two books about Aalto had been published without his sanction. The first of these, published in 1954, was by the Swiss architects Eduard and Claudia Neuenschwander, who had worked at Aalto's office for some years. The second, by Aalto's American friend Frederick Gutheim, was a collection of articles Gutheim had originally written for *Architectural Forum*. Under the circumstances, both books were excellent and, apart from the Girsberger volume, they were the only serious studies published before Aalto's death. Italian architect Leonardo Mosso, who had worked at Aalto's office for several years and was the first to start a serious archival study of his work, was forced in the face of the maestro's negative attitude to abandon an ambitious plan for a richly illustrated study in several volumes by the Milanese publisher Communità.

Aalto's disdain for publicity is explained partly by his fear of the misunderstandings he encountered in so many commentaries on his works. A desire to control and correct what was written was also involved. For the Girsberger book he compiled a relatively restricted selection of his works, omitting, among other things, his entire Neo-Classical youth. Hence the text may overemphasize the Rationalist elements in his architecture.

Aalto evidently felt that in me he had found a relatively sensitive disciple, and that I had interpreted his works correctly in innumerable articles written for various international architectural journals and as arts correspondent of the Stockholm newspaper *Svenska Dagbladet*. When the Girsberger book was coming out, he asked me to write the all-important introduction. But whenever the idea of my writing a book about him came up, he recoiled. "You must write about architecture's problems, not mine!" When it came to the point, this great

114. Hans Girsberger and Karl Fleig, the Swiss team that brought out the first authorized book on Aalto's architecture in 1963.

115. "You must write about problems architecture's, not mine!" Aalto indoctrinating his future biographer Göran Schildt.

actor did not wish to reveal his true self. He wished only to be remembered for the various roles he had played. I have infringed on this shyness by writing this biography, but have done so in the name of my love for the man. I believe that Alvar Aalto was too fascinating and brilliant a personality to be passed over.

This is what Aalto himself wrote on the subject (in a letter, dated October 16, 1961, to Alfred Roth in Zurich):

Personally I do not enjoy publicity. This is not because I am a modest person, but because publicity does not give a correct image of my architecture, and always has journalistic overtones, which is unpleasant . . . You cannot require a person who has more than twenty official building commissions going on simultaneously to have time for a bagatelle like public relations. Seriously, it hurts my capacity for work and rends my soul.

We may thus largely blame – or credit – Aalto himself for his status as a mythical figure bereft of any clear historical frame of reference. This did not prevent him from being most human to his many friends and acquaintances at home and abroad. His global reputation and his many personal contacts around the world made him much more of a citizen of the world during the postwar years than most of his countrymen.

In the next few chapters, I shall try to provide an overview of Aalto's international world, and of his lively contacts with other people in many foreign countries. Let us begin with the countries with which Finland has the closest ties, its Scandinavian neighbours.

Scandinavia

After the disheartening results of his cooperation with Albin Stark, Aalto set aside his hope of building something of importance in Sweden for a long time. Peacetime had opened up the world outside Scandinavia, and the new opportunities there tempted him more than did the idea of working in neighbouring countries. His masterful exhibition pavilion in Hedemora, erected for the town's 400th anniversary, was pulled down after the festivities. The Artek factory in Hedemora flourished in 1948 with the furniture orders for the MIT dormitory and the Harvard library, but when the dream of the Aino Institute and the large sales organization in the United States foundered, sales gradually petered out, and in 1957 Artek Sweden was disbanded.

By then, however, Aalto's new activities had reached such a peak of intensity that he was again tempted to try his luck in slow-moving Sweden. He opened with a small but significant exhibition entitled *Constructive Form* in Stockholm in 1954, where he introduced the X leg for chairs and tables, perhaps his most elegant furniture idea. The following year he took part in the large summer exhibition *H 55* in Helsingborg, where he brought out a prototype for the atrium apartment that formed the basic element of his Interbau building in Berlin.

His renewed interest in Sweden was most obvious, however, in his participation in several major Swedish architectural competitions. In 1955 he won first prize in a competition for a new local government building in Gothenburg. He took this victory to mean that he would be commissioned to design 'Gothenburg's new city hall'. In 1957, before the committees had watered down this proposal and finally rejected it, he took part in another major Gothenburg competition. Drottningtorget, or Queen's Square, and the adjacent railway station are still an unsolved traffic problem and an eyesore in the city today. Aalto's undeniably brilliant winning entry, however, was too bold and far-reaching not to arouse opposition among sticklers for detail.

In 1957 he also won another Swedish competition, which involved building a new, high-class housing area on Kampementsbacken hill in Stockholm's Ladugårdsgärde area. The houses that he spread out over the slope with a sure touch were variants of his highly praised Interbau building in Berlin. The committees responsible for construction of Kampementsbacken made such radical changes to Aalto's plan, though, that of the basic design only a few superficial details remain.

In 1958 Aalto surpassed himself with a marvellous entry for a town hall in Kiruna. Here again, the jury could not refuse him first prize, but it also gave a 'second first prize' to Artur von Schmalensee. The latter's entry, based on a large, covered, heated interior courtyard, was certainly appropriate for the climate, whereas Aalto's had a magnificent exterior with forms borrowed from

116. The fan-shaped leg, introduced by Aalto in Stockholm in 1954, was perhaps his most elegant furniture idea.

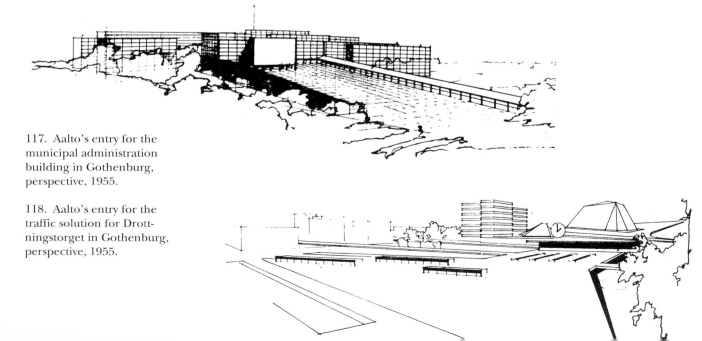

117. Aalto's entry for the municipal administration building in Gothenburg, perspective, 1955.

118. Aalto's entry for the traffic solution for Drottningstorget in Gothenburg, perspective, 1955.

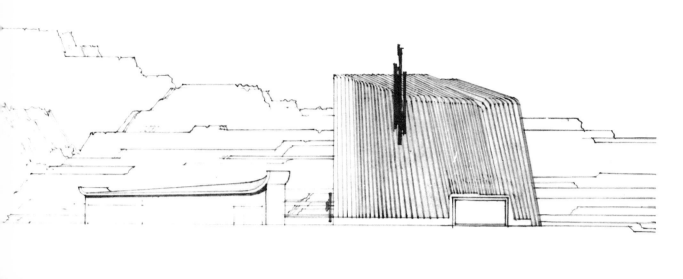

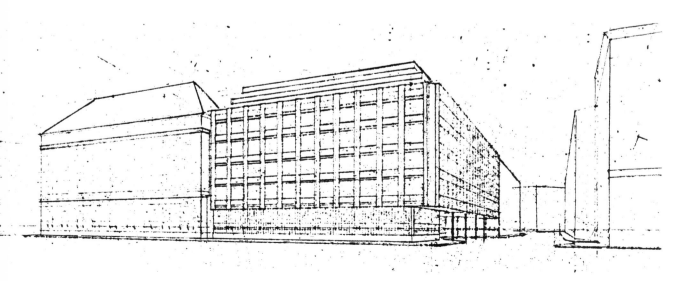

the mounds of slag that surround this old mining community. Schmalensee's architecturally conventional – and cheaper – design was the one that was built. Only with time did it become clear that Kiruna had thus lost a building that could have become as much-admired and frequented as Le Corbusier's church in Ronchamps and Jørn Utzon's Opera House in Sydney.

One must admire Aalto for his tenacity in competing again for a Swedish assignment. This was for an annex to the Stockholms Enskilda Bank head office at Kungsträdgården in Stockholm. His favourable experiences with Finnish business leaders and bankers, who had recently commissioned new office buildings from him for Enso-Gutzeit and the Nordic Union Bank in Helsinki, must have raised the hope that he would find an equally bold entrepreneurial spirit among Sweden's Wallenberg set. At least that is what his entry's motto, 'The Grey Eminence', seems to suggest. He drew a blank, however: Swedish caution won the day. Peter Celsing won first prize, but even he did not get the commission. As built, the bank office was a purely technical exploitation of the site's space quota.

It seems as if Aalto's old friend Gregor Paulsson experienced a pang of conscience on Sweden's behalf after the bank competition. In 1963 he managed to persuade the Västmanland-Dala students' union in Uppsala to commission a new club building from Aalto. The result was another completely unique design that bore no resemblance to any other Aalto building. The basic idea consisted of raising the house on *pilotis* so as to preserve the existing garden and of making the assembly hall divisible with the help of moveable walls sliding into cantilevered 'wings' off the facade. The building was both practical and aesthetically attractive, but the number of enrolled students increased so rapidly during the next few years that the facilities began to show wear and tear,

and additional space was needed. Aalto reluctantly agreed to have some of the empty space under the seemingly airborne building filled up with meeting rooms behind transparent glass walls. The entire lower level, however, was soon converted into a series of lucrative rented shops, completely ruining the building's appearance. Apart from the office building Aalto designed for his dynamic supporter Ernst Sundh, erected in Avesta in 1955, the Uppsala clubhouse is the only Aalto building in Sweden – a meagre reward for his persistence.

After frequent stays in Sweden in the 1950s, Aalto noticeably spaced out his visits in the '60s. Improved flight connections between Finland and the Continent were not the only reason. His setbacks in Sweden had soured him and had also alienated him from his Swedish friends. It is symptomatic that he forbade the inclusion of both his winning entries in the Gothenburg competitions in books on his work – he did not wish to be reminded of them.

In 1960 Pontus Hultén took the initiative for a major exhibition of contemporary Finnish architecture at the Museum of Modern Art in Stockholm, and Aalto promised to speak at the opening. I was living in Stockholm at the time and was among the friends who welcomed Alvar and Elissa upon their arrival. They were staying at the Grand Hotel, as usual, and Elissa was trying hard to keep a tight rein on Aalto until evening, so that his performance would go well – as we know, he always spoke without a text. But some old Swedish friends appeared at lunchtime, and the whole afternoon turned into a symposium, in the classical sense of the word. I remember how nervous we were when half-past seven approached and the expectant listeners queued up from the doors of the Museum of Modern Art all the way to the National Museum.

Alvar was definitely not in good form when we drove him to the field of battle. With the best will in the world, I cannot say that the talk was one of his more memorable ones. It set a record of brevity for him, at around ten minutes; under the circumstances, however, it was a heroic effort, made possible only by the old warhorse's experience. A small sample of the transcript may explain why the public seemed satisfied in spite of everything and greeted the speech with prolonged, warm applause:

I should like to begin by telling you about how Finnish architectural standardization happens. Since you do not understand Finnish, I will give you a translation: "Ring out my bliss! Carefree waves, sing of my joy! Do what you will, girl of Finland! The Finnish summer is short!" This is the basic idea of Finnish architectural standardization, and all the detail follows from it.

Aalto's relationship with Denmark was a little more satisfying, as in that country his work was generally received with sensitive appreciation. His many lectures in Copenhagen, at royal events and at architects' meetings; his intimate friendships with Poul Henningsen, Kay Fisker, Edvard Thomsen, Arne Jacobsen, and Jørn Utzon (who worked at Aalto's office briefly in 1945); his receiving the Sonning Prize in 1962 in Copenhagen – all these indicate a certain affinity between Aalto's work and the Danish temperament. Denmark, a land of

furniture makers, is the world's largest importer of Aalto furniture today, partly because of the furniture's high quality but also because it expresses a cultivated appreciation of nature that is shared by the Danes. Aalto's lamp designs were also well received in Denmark and have been distributed widely by the Louis Poulsen company.

Aino and Alvar Aalto's great 1947 retrospective exhibition in Helsinki was shown the following year in Copenhagen and Oslo, but not in Stockholm. In 1951, a year of crisis for Aalto, he unsuccessfully entered a competition for the design of a hospital in Glostrup; the following year, the plan he sent to the competition for the Lyngby-Taarbaek cemetery was relegated to second place, after considerable wrangling among the jury.

A young Danish architect, Jean-Jacques Baruël, worked at Aalto's office in the mid 1950s. Thomsen's favourite pupil at the Academy, Baruël had been engaged by Aalto on his teacher's recommendation. He came of a French Huguenot family which had sought asylum in Denmark during the Wars of Religion in the seventeenth century; his background appealed strongly to Aalto's feeling for history. Their obvious temperamental similarities soon made them friends, and when Baruël set up as an independent architect in Denmark, following a competition victory in Sweden, Aalto was sorry to see him go. When a competition for an art museum in Aalborg was announced in 1958, Baruël, seized by a desire to work with his former boss once again, suggested a joint venture. Aalto did not really have time for the Aalborg competition, but he had plenty of ideas about how to approach the assignment. Baruël came to Helsinki, and for a few short days they worked on the basic plan, together with Elissa Aalto. She and Baruël later completed the entry in Copenhagen. The result was an undisputed first prize. As usual, however, the road to completion was a long one. Fortunately, Aalborg's city fathers were bolder and more forward-looking

123. Aalto through Danish eyes: portrait by Hans Bendix in *Politiken*.

124. Funeral chapel in Lyngby-Taarbaek competition entry, 1952.

125. North Jutland Art Museum in Aalborg, designed in 1958 but completed in 1972. Photo: Baruël.

than their counterparts in Gothenburg and Kiruna, and in 1966 construction began under Baruël's direction.

Aalto's special feeling for Denmark is rather touchingly illustrated by an episode from his old age. Late in life, he suffered from temporary losses of balance, which naturally led to a certain watchfulness among his nearest and dearest. He was not one, however, to submit meekly to being overprotected, particularly by an anxious wife. One winter's day, he disappeared on his way home from the office. There was great alarm at home and a fruitless search through the streets of Munkkiniemi and in the pubs he frequented. Only late at night were the fears of some tragedy dissolved by a phone call from Copenhagen. Aalto had run away like a schoolboy. He had hopped on a plane and was now sitting with Baruël in his beloved Hôtel d'Angleterre bar, tremendously proud of having proved that he could manage so well on his own.

All his life Aalto had excellent contacts in Norway. His old assistants and friends Harald Wildhagen and Erling Bjertnaes were there; he lectured and exhibited in Trondheim and Oslo, and in later years he had a good Norwegian friend in Arne Korsmo. But for one reason or another there was never any serious talk about an Aalto building in Norway.

In Iceland, however, he had the opportunity to carry out an exquisite design. In 1963 he was commissioned, without competition, to design 'Nordens Hus', the Scandinavian House in Reykjavik. Construction was financed jointly by all of the Nordic countries. He inspected the site in passing on his way to Canada that September, and revisited Reykjavik in spring 1964. I remember his comment on returning: "Iceland must be the most individualistic country I have seen. No two houses are alike there." He liked the Icelanders for their anarchistic willfulness, but found that the Reykjavik townscape had run a little too wild. The Scandinavian House, which includes a library, exhibition facilities, auditorium, newspaper café, and superintendent's flat, is located in a large open area near the city centre, and blends effectively with the landscape. As in his Kiruna town hall plan and in his later design for Rovaniemi Theatre, Aalto modelled the building's silhouette on the surrounding low fells.

Russia

Having discussed Aalto's contacts with Finland's western neighbours, let us turn to his relationship with the great power in the east. This is appropriate not merely to maintain geographical order; Russia was very important to Aalto, though not in a favourable sense.

Remember that Aalto grew up in a subjugated Grand Duchy, that he went to the Czar's prison in his youth and identified strongly with the Jaeger movement, which prepared for Finland's liberation from the Russian Empire. His feelings toward 'our eastern neighbour' remained coloured by these experiences and had little to do with the Communist system. He saw in Russia – regardless of its political system – a potential threat to his native country. His attitude to Russian culture also reflected this fear. He always retained the idea, formed in his early years, that the Russians were a semibarbaric, unbalanced people with no share in the European cultural heritage.

Aalto's attitude toward communism was another matter. As I pointed out earlier, he had left-wing friends even in his student days (*The Early Years,* pp. 89–90), and undertook, without any qualms, to design a workers' clubhouse in Jyväskylä only a few years after the Finnish civil war. In the 1930s, his Communist friends Hans Schmidt and André Lurçat and his Social Democrat friends Markelius, Gropius, and Giedion felt that he shared their views completely. We have seen, however, that in his 1939 plans for the journal *The Human Side* he distanced himself from "Soviet imperialism, which has completely betrayed socialism and has proved to lack all organizational capacity".

We can only conclude that Aalto, as a true liberal, categorically opposed every

kind of political or ideological compulsion and was skeptical of Marxist dogma but respected those who voluntarily embraced left-wing ideas. The consistency of his position is shown by the fact that he joined the newly formed Finnish-Soviet society immediately after the war, and sat on its art committee together with the well-known left-wing extremists Hella Wuolijoki, Hertta Kuusinen, Johan Helo, Reinhold Svento, and Cay Sundström. His participation in the society's activities was minimal, however, and in no way hampered his resumption of contact with the United States.

The most conspicuous result of Aalto's liberalism was his acceptance of the commission to design the Kulttuuritalo, or 'House of Culture', in Helsinki for the Finnish Communist Party. The assignment was greeted with widespread astonishment and even some criticism. How was it possible for an architect who had just returned from America, had worked successfully for Finnish big industry, the Church, and government institutions, to work for Communists in the midst of the Cold War? And how was it possible that the Communists should want a building in the Western Modernist style at a time when the spirit of Stalin still lived and the 'Socialist Realism' he had prescribed dominated architecture in the Soviet Union and in Eastern Europe? The project originated quite by chance, in the encounter between two independent thinkers, Alvar Aalto and Matti Janhunen, who perceived a mutual sympathy when Aalto was starting his work on the National Pensions Institute headquarters. Janhunen, a Communist and former minister of health, was head of the National Pensions Institute for a time and a member of one of the parliamentary committees that oversaw this major building project.

The House of Culture was in many ways a key work for Aalto, who reached the peak of his creative ability in the 1950s. The building consists of a detached, spiral-shaped auditorium and a rectangular office building, welded together in a highly effective way. The contrast between undulating brick walls and a copper-clad cube stemmed from Aalto's MIT student dormitory, in which the restaurant volume breaks out of the main facade. The motif was reinforced in the House of Culture by Aalto's experimental use of custom-made, wedge-shaped bricks, with which he was able to produce sharper curves than he had with the standard bricks he'd used for the dormitory.

He also tested two other 'inventions' in the House of Culture. One was an asymmetrical ground plan for the auditorium, the rear wall of which bulges to one side. With this design, he combined the intimacy of a small room with the spaciousness of a large one, while abolishing the static rigidity of symmetrical spaces. The other experiment was aimed at producing flexible acoustics that could be adjusted for different kinds of events – speeches, recitals, chamber music and large orchestral concerts. Variation is achieved via the sound-absorbing slabs suspended from the side walls. The number of slabs can be increased or reduced as needed; they also function as abstract works of art.

Aalto's House of Culture must surely have aroused the amazement of the many Soviet delegations that visited Finland in the 1950s and listened to the protestations of peace and friendship between the two countries exchanged in the Finnish building. Soviet architects also sent delegations to Finland: one of these came to study the first *Finland Builds* exhibition in 1953. Aalto's Swiss assistant Karl Fleig recounts an amusing story about the reception they met with at Aalto's studio. They were immediately favourably impressed when they discovered that their host spoke passable Russian – having been force-fed the language in his school years in Jyväskylä. After a moment's conversation, Aalto announced: "All the architects in my studio are talented musicians. What would you like to hear? Piano? Violin? A little Rachmaninoff, perhaps? Why not!" He then turned to the young Marja Pöyry, a gifted concert pianist: "Marja, it's your turn today. Would you care to play some Rachmaninoff for our guests?" Which she did with great panache. Need it be said that the Russians were deeply impressed with the artistic talent to be found at Aalto's office?

Here again one finds Aalto adopting the same attitude he displayed during his wartime visit to Germany: poking fun at a disliked opponent in a perfectly unexceptionable way. This attitude brought him new triumphs during a visit to Leningrad and Moscow in 1962, his only visit to the country to which he could never quite reconcile himself.

Before discussing this journey, we should note that around 1960 a change took place in Soviet cultural policy. In 1959, the government building administration, Gosstroi SSSR, invited Aalto to take part in a restricted competition for a model town of 20,000 inhabitants southwest of Moscow. He sent his regrets. The next year, the Museum of Finnish Architecture was invited to present the entire range of modern Finnish architecture at an exhibition in Gorky Park in Moscow. Around that time, the Russians were trying to restore Aalto's famous Viipuri library to its original condition. It had been badly damaged by artillery

128. Aalto's Viipuri Library, damaged in the war, was patchily restored in the 1960s. The broken glass of the skylights was replaced with plastic sheeting. Photo: Göran Schildt 1982.

fire during the war and had lain in ruins for over fifteen years. In the absence of the original drawings and without some of the necessary materials, the restoration was rather unsatisfactory, but the good intentions that underlay it were evident.

After repeated proddings, Aalto could no longer worm his way out of visiting the Soviet Union. In May 1962, he set off with his wife to Leningrad, where he gave a lecture at the Academy of Architecture, and then proceeded to Moscow. He could very well have lectured in Russian, but preferred to speak Finnish. In Leningrad, the interpreter was a girl from Ingria, an area in which a Finnic dialect was once widely spoken, but her knowledge of Finnish was rudimentary. Every time that Aalto spoke of his social goals, she translated them as 'socialist goals'. The climax came when he talked of his church at Vuoksenniska, with its 'social facilities' such as meeting rooms, club rooms, pingpong room, etc. The audience was a little puzzled to hear that the Church of Finland preached socialism.

Another episode occurred when he asked his Muscovite hosts to take him to Prince Kropotkin's house. "My uncle was a good friend of Kropotkin's, who visited him in Finland once." The Russians said they had never heard of such a prince, which Aalto thought was a little much. After a while they returned and said: "We have found Kropotkin's home and will drive you there." When they arrived, Aalto said: "May I give you a piece of advice? Put up a signboard on the house saying: 'KROPOTKIN LIVED HERE'. You will need him one day." (It should, perhaps, be pointed out that the uncle who was Kropotkin's friend was pure invention).

Aalto was obviously a reluctant and uncivil guest in the Soviet Union – which did not prevent the chairman of the Russian architects' association, Professor

129. Alvar and Elissa Aalto in Moscow, May 12, 1962, with hosts A. Sakharov, V. Boutousov, and I. Yaralov.

Nikolas Kolli, from lavishing attention on him and later from sending him polite annual New Year's greetings.

After this journey, Aalto felt that he had done his share and refused to go again, turning down invitations to both the centenary celebration of the Soviet architects' association in 1967 and to an international architects' conference in Moscow in 1975. The indifference he displayed to the honours that the Russians showered on him during the last ten years of his life is almost embarrassing. Soviet architectural journals extolled Aalto. Professor Andrei Gozak wrote an excellent study of his work and assembled a comprehensive collection of his writings. Leading Russian intellectuals, such as Pyotr Kapitsa, head of the Soviet space programme, asked to meet Aalto when they visited Finland.

All to no avail: Aalto remained cold to everything that came from Finland's former motherland.

The Devastated Reich

In Aalto's mind, Germany was in some ways the antithesis of Russia. Whereas he disliked Russia but was tolerant of Marxism, he detested Nazism from its very beginnings but had positive feelings about Germany. Since his youth, German had been the foreign language in which he was most fluent; he read Goethe and Burckhardt in the original and had many personal friends in Germany until Hitler exiled most of them. It was thus natural for him to seek contact with old acquaintances such as Ernst Neufert, Hans Scharoun, and Ernst May, once they reemerged from the ruins of the Third Reich. Both Germany and Austria offered more tempting building assignments than did other countries in these years, and foreign architects were invited to compete for them.

Aalto's first attempt to join the reconstruction of the fallen thousand-year empire was in 1953, when he took part in a competition for the design of a gigantic centre for sports, concerts, congresses, and exhibitions at Vienna's Vogelweidplatz. He won first prize with a plan that was one of his boldest and most beautiful. The technical intricacies of the roof suspended from steel cables, a design later used with success in the United States and elsewhere, worried the cautious Viennese, however. They applauded Aalto's design, but gave the commission to the local architect Roland Rainer, who had designed an utterly conventional hall instead.

When the local architects' association invited Aalto to lecture in Vienna in April 1955, a large and enthusiastic audience gathered in the Brahms-Saal to hear Aalto speak on the subject "Between Humanism und Materialism". He said not a word about his rejected design and merely suggested in passing that architecture is an activity which may call for daring and artistry. One wonders whether the Viennese noticed the implicit message when Aalto said:

130. Sports, concert and congress building at Vienna's Vogelweidplatz, Aalto's prize-winning entry. Photo: Kolmio.

Once I was in Milwaukee with my old friend Frank Lloyd Wright. He gave a lecture that began like this: "Ladies and gentlemen, do you know what a brick is? It is a small, worthless, ordinary object that costs 11 cents, but it has one wonderful property. Give me a brick and I will make it worth its weight in gold." This was the first time that I heard anyone tell an audience so directly and strikingly what architecture is all about. Architecture means transforming a worthless stone into a nugget of gold.

In 1954 Aalto had a better opportunity to make his mark on central European architecture. While East Berlin was building its massive and dreary Stalin Allee, the West Berlin authorities invited fifty-three architects from fourteen capitalist countries to build their versions of another kind of future, characterized by affluence and individual freedom, on a site only a few miles away. The area for which the selected architects were to design blocks of flats was called the Hansaviertel. The district was to be inaugurated in 1957 as part of a large exhibition called *Interbau.* This exhibition pointedly stressed the very tangible rivalry among architectures, cultures, and social systems going on in the shadow of the Cold War.

This gave Aalto, who loved competitions, a welcome opportunity to measure his skill against that of colleagues such as Walter Gropius, Hans Scharoun, Max Taut, Jacob B. Bakema, Oscar Niemeyer, Pierre Vago, F.R.S. Yorke, Arne Jacobsen, and Kay Fisker. There was no direct competition with jury and prizes, but when the buildings were completed in the summer of 1957, many viewers agreed with *Welt am Sonntag,* which ran the following headline in its exhibition issue: VON ALLEN BEWUNDERT: AALTO BAU (Aalto Building Admired by All).

131. Aalto's apartment block in Berlin's Hansaviertel, 1954–57. Photo: Havas.

132. The Essen Opera, designed in 1959, had to wait thirty years to be built.

The subtlety about Aalto's building was its grouping of apartments around balconies that were as large and deep as atriums. He also succeeded in avoiding the boxy impression fatal to so much Rationalist housing, by means of pronounced shifts in the facade itself. This was much more natural than the coloured balconies and other cosmetic tricks to which many of his rivals resorted for the same reasons.

Aalto's success with the Berlin building opened the doors to German competitions, which were usually restricted to a limited number of invited contestants. During the following years, he received eighteen invitations from Germany, accepted ten, and won five competitions. What is more, his winning designs were carried out. The biggest and most important of his German commissions was the Essen Opera, which he designed in 1959. Although the authorities repeatedly gave the go-ahead for construction, it was postponed time after time. First, building a new city hall was more urgent, then Aalto was asked to scale back the plan to cut the price. The years went by, and although the working drawings had been completed by the time that Aalto died, there was still no final decision on when the work would begin. This design, in which Aalto had incorporated some of his boldest and most crucial ideas, and which had filled him with optimism, was one of the greatest disappointments of his old age. But architecture differs significantly from all other art forms. Its monuments can be completed long after the designer is dead and can be more durable than any other human achievement. The fact that the Essen Opera House was built thirty years after its inception will be a mere footnote one hundred years from now.

The slow pace of the Essen project led to unexpected consequences for the capital of Finland. We may say that the Finlandia Hall in Helsinki came about because Aalto tried to save at least the essence of the dormant German project. The Finlandia Hall is, in fact, the little sister of the full-fledged Essen Opera. On the other hand, when the opera house was finally built, the mistakes made in erecting its sister building could be avoided.

The idea of an asymmetrical auditorium, which Aalto had cautiously tried out in his plan for Kuopio Theatre (1951) and had triumphantly implemented in the House of Culture in Helsinki, reaches its fullest expression in the Essen Opera. Three balconies soar above the parterre, with balustrades that give the space a magnificent sculpturesque form akin to that of the New York exhibition pavilion. The Finlandia Hall has only one balcony with a balustrade that follows the basic plan of the auditorium. The staggered balconies of the Essen Opera recur in a mirror image in the adjacent foyer, making it one of Aalto's most fascinating rooms.

The most important similarity between the Finlandia Hall and the Essen Opera, however, is that both employ one of Aalto's most original technical 'inventions', which is based on the idea that an invisible reserve space above the auditorium and separated from it by an acoustically permeable louvred ceiling could give rise to variable acoustics. Variation is achieved using sound-reflecting

133. Aalto's sketch of the
Essen Opera's asymmetrical
auditorium gives expression
to the breathtaking elegance
of his concept.

sliding screens up in the empty loft. Aalto had already tried this device in the
Vienna sports centre design, though without any optical demarcation beneath
the screens.

I shall return in a later chapter to the practical consequences of this
innovation as well as to the decision to use white marble as the cladding for both
the Essen Opera and the Finlandia Hall.

One of Aalto's most expressive buildings is the Wolfsburg Cultural Centre. It
arose out of a 1958 competition design, and houses a small city library, an adult
education institute, and various facilities for cultural activities. Aalto's cherish-
ed fan shape, with wedges jutting into the interior, here takes on a psychological dimension that links it to the very core of his philosophy. He always
said that he sought an artistic synthesis of all the practical and psychological
aspects affecting a project; a union of disparate determinants in a living core.
The five auditoria of the Wolfsburg Cultural Centre form a stepped cluster
in the facade overlooking the piazza and send out wedges inward, a graphic

134. Model built by the Aalto office of the Essen Opera auditorium is still perfect in form. Photo: Ingervo.

135. The Essen Opera was built from 1986 to 1988 by the German architect Harald Deilmann, who followed Aalto's plan to the letter but lacked his mastery of form.

illustration of how studies in the building centre on a humanist core. The closed outer walls of these rooms, clad with a refined mosaic pattern of white and dark blue marble, create an impression at once serious and playful. In fact the idea was borrowed from the campanile and side elevation of the Cathedral of Siena.

136. Wolfsburg Cultural Centre. Photo: Kidder Smith.

Aalto would not have been Aalto if he had not combined this message with a more concrete, social one. This was illustrated by a lecture he gave at an architects' seminar in Jyväskylä in the year that the Wolfsburg complex was completed. On July 8, 1962, *Uusi Suomi* newspaper reported:

Professor Aalto pointed out that today almost everyone is somehow involved in industrial production. In a city such as Wolfsburg, wholly dominated by a single industry, this is particularly evident. Most of the 60,000 inhabitants, mothers and fathers alike, work shifts in the car factory. A significant share of the city's income is allocated to building projects intended to relieve the monotony of the industrial worker's life. The workers' leisure time continues to increase, but paradoxically many do not know what to do with it. Wolfsburg started out with the decision to build a public library, then other elements were added to the building programme: auditoria for music and lectures suggested the idea of an open university. Then exhibition facilities, clubrooms, and studios for instruction in the various arts were added. The cultural centre is only the prelude to a larger building complex. A botanical garden is now in the works, and a theatre and concert hall are to follow. Wolfsburg must be one of Europe's best managed cities administratively. Typically, the mayor is a famous medical specialist, who has selflessly taken on a political role while carrying on with his medical practice.

At the building's inauguration in autumn 1962, Aalto wrote the following lines in the Wolfsburg guest book:

The drawback of machines and industry is the danger of monotony without sufficient

Arbeit an den Maschinen und das industrielle Leben hat als Negativum die Gefahr die Monotonie ohne genügende Variationen. Das neue Haus soll Gegengewicht bilden, aber auch als ein repräsentativer Bau das Stadtbild bestimmen. Das waren die Wünsche der Stadt Wolfsburg in unserer ersten Konferenz. — Klare Worte als Aufgabe für die Architektur in unserer Zeit

137. Siena Cathedral, photographed by Aino Aalto in 1948.

138. Aalto's comments in the City of Wolfsburg visitors' book on the counterbalance necessary to offset the monotony of industrial

variation. The new cultural centre is intended to form a counterbalance, but also to contribute to the townscape. This was the wish expressed by the City of Wolfsburg at our first meeting. A clear expression of the goals of architecture in our era.

After a while, however, he seems to have been seized by doubts about this philosophy. Could meaningful leisure time really outweigh an inhuman routine at work? In a letter to Heinz Nordhoff, head of the Volkswagen works, Aalto modified his position: *The counterbalance to monotony must arise within the work itself and in the factories.*

Aalto's later projects in Wolfsburg did not turn out quite as he had hoped. The city economized by striking the annex to the cultural centre from its budget, and in a competition for the Wolfsburg Theatre he was defeated by Scharoun. He was, however, commissioned to design a parish centre and a striking church there in 1960, and three years later he also designed a church for the nearby community of Detmerode. Both churches represent a remarkable return to his unrealized entries in Finnish church competitions in the 1920s.

The Neue Vahr tower block, built in Bremen in 1958, was much discussed. With his usual braggadocio, Aalto told the Finnish press that he was building "a centre for the whole of modern Bremen". In fact the commission was for one twenty-two-storey apartment block, a rather controversial assignment for a sworn critic of technology to undertake. Aalto elegantly raised the problem to

139. Aalto's sketch for the Wolfsburg Church showing plan, section, side perspective, interior perspective, and view of the bell tower.

140. Neue Vahr high-rise block in Bremen, 1958–62. Photo: Ludwig.

141. The Heilig Geist Church in Wolfsburg, 1960. Exterior photo Göran Schildt. Interior photo: Mosso.

an issue of principle. If high-rise housing is unsuitable for families and generally ill suited for long-term living, such 'housing machines' might still be perfectly acceptable for singles or young couples who wished to live in the city centre for a while. The Neue Vahr complex consists entirely of small apartments with one or two rooms and a kitchenette. The fan-shaped ground plan allows all flats to open up in a wedge to a large window and a balcony; the rear of the house, as in the MIT dormitory, is taken up by lifts, staircases, and common stairways.

Besides the Wolfsburg Theatre and piazza, Aalto's unsuccessful German competition entries included town hall plans for Marl (1957) and Castrop-

142. Aalto in conversation with Federal President Heinemann after receiving the order *Pour le mérite* in 1969. Photo: Bundesbildstelle.

Rauxel (1965), a cultural centre for Leverkusen (1960), and an office building for the BP company in Hamburg (1964). The invitations he turned down or did not have time for included the Freie Universität in Berlin, the university of Bochum, the Karlsruhe city theatre, the city hall of Bonn, a multipurpose centre in Kassel, the renovation of the old city hall of Cologne, a sports and music centre for the Farbwerke Hoechst in Frankfurt, and a combined cultural centre and town hall in Velbert, south of Essen. He would no doubt have been fully employed in Germany for the rest of his life if he had chosen to focus his practice there.

Other hunting grounds beckoned, however, and his work in Finland interested him more. His involvement with German architecture gradually shifted to retrospective exhibitions of his life's work and the acceptance of various tributes. Hans Scharoun, who was head of the Berlin Academy of Arts, arranged a major Aalto exhibition there, which later travelled to Wolfsburg, Hamburg, and Essen. In 1969 he became a member of the order *Pour le Mérite*, which was founded by Frederick the Great. This is the highest cultural accolade awarded in Germany, and can be held by no more than thirty Germans and the same number of foreign citizens at one time. Federal President Heinemann conferred the order upon Aalto at a formal audience in Bonn, and the ceremony was followed by lunches and dinners at which Aalto made the acquaintance of many famous fellow members. He naturally felt quite at home in this company.

Switzerland

143. A contingent of Aalto's 'Swiss Guard', gathered in Zurich in 1968 to celebrate the master's seventieth birthday. Seated next to Alvar and Elissa, from left: Leonardo Mosso, Lisbeth Sachs, and Rudolf Neuenschwander. Standing, left to right: Walter Moser, Annelies Moser, Laura Mosso, Rudolf Brennenstuhl, Marlaine Perrochet, Federico Marconi, Kerttu Fleig, Margrith Moser, Alice Biro, Karl Fleig, Margrith Brennenstuhl, Lorenz Moser, Claudia Neuenschwander, Theo Senn.

Since Aalto's first visit to Zurich, in 1930, Switzerland had been the country outside Scandinavia that he had visited most frequently and with the greatest pleasure. On almost every visit to the Continent he included Zurich on his itinerary, and over time Switzerland became a second homeland to him. This was entirely due to the many close friendships he had formed there. The three generations of architects of the Moser family and their wives were there; so were Hélène de Mandrot, Sigfried Giedion and his wife Carola, and Alfred Roth, all of whom had visited the Aaltos in Finland on at least one occasion. Switzerland also had a growing number of young architects who had worked at Aalto's office. No country was so regularly and numerously represented at his office, from his first Swiss assistant, Walter Custer, who had come to Finland in 1931, to the last, Michele Merckling, who is still working with Elissa Aalto in 1990. I have already written about Paul Bernoulli and Lisbeth Sachs. Among Aalto's postwar assistants, Karl Fleig played an important role in more ways than one. On the occasion of Aalto's seventieth birthday in 1968, his former Swiss assistants arranged a well-attended, cheerful gathering in Zurich with the motto 'Aalto's Swiss Guard'. In this Aalto had of course been anticipated by the popes, who have kept a bodyguard of Swiss soldiers in Rome since the Middle Ages.

Intellectually, Aalto's most important friendship must have been with the Giedions. As he wrote in his obituary for Sigfried in 1968, many important patterns of thought and artistic impulses emerged in conversations under the large plane tree which grew outside the Giedion home in Zurich's Doldertal district. The tree and the house were still standing in spring 1977, when I visited 84-year-old Carola Giedion Welcker to find out what she could tell me about the Giedions' long friendship with Aalto.

The home itself gave an insight into the intellectual atmosphere Aalto had found there. An enormous Kandinsky painting dated 1910 hung in the living room, and an equally large Juan Gris in the bedroom. A sitting woman by Brancusi, several large Max Ernst paintings, Mondrians and Klees, a Schwitters collage, several Arps, and a delightful little Delaunay on sheet metal caught my eye, but there were even more paintings by Léger and Le Corbusier. Art and books filled every nook and cranny of the spacious villa. It turned out that some of these treasures had been purchased during the war, when the artists had needed Swiss francs, but that most of them were gifts. Many artists would stay with the Giedions whenever they were in town and would express their gratitude by leaving works of art.

"Yes", Carola Giedion said to me, "we differed so completely with Aalto on what one should spend on. His home was small and modest, but during his travels he lived like a prince. We travelled modestly, but invested in our home."

Carola Giedion was a close friend of Brancusi's and wrote an important book about him; for many years, she was even closer to James Joyce. "I am happy to have introduced Aalto to Brancusi; they had the greatest admiration for one another. Unfortunately I never had the chance to introduce him to Joyce. They had the same feeling for myth. *Finnegan's Wake* and Aalto's stories were closely related. When we were in Finland in 1962, Aalto told me a lot about the *Kalevala*. That was the kind of thing we talked about, not modern art."

The old lady, who died a few years after our meeting, had an excellent memory and recalled many episodes from the Giedions' meetings with Aalto in Switzerland as well as Greece, the United States, Mexico, and Finland. Carola characterized the hospitality Aalto had shown her and Sigfried during their visit to Finland as 'Homeric'. Her farewell to me was: "What Aalto gave us was a new relationship with nature, something sorely needed in our technological era. We have a wooden country house designed by Aalto's pupil Neuenschwander. Sigfried always said, 'I find it so much easier to write in the woods.' It was Aalto who gave wood back to us. My experience of his spaces is always connected with wood, both in its growing form and as a constructive medium."

Aalto and Sigfried Giedion had more important things in common than merely an appreciation of wood, however. Going back to the roots of Aalto's architectural credo, we find that two Bauhaus representatives, Gropius and Moholy-Nagy, influenced him significantly around 1930. But it was Giedion who later was intellectually closest to him.

Whether it was Giedion who influenced Aalto or vice versa at the time when the two friends began to oppose the simplistic goals of early Rationalism is moot. Aalto seems to have enjoyed a considerable lead on a practical level, at least considering that Giedion virtually ignored him in the first edition of his epochal *Space, Time and Architecture,* published in 1941, but in the second edition he devoted more space to Aalto than to his former heroes Le Corbusier, Gropius, and Mies van der Rohe. The reason was that only then had Giedion discovered that Aalto had found an exemplary means of reconciling the call for social justice, technological advances, and the benefits of tradition within the bounds of nature's great chain of being. Both men saw striving for this synthesis as humanity's only possible salvation.

Many of Aalto's visits to Switzerland were for practical reasons. Exhibitions of his work were held there in 1948, 1957, 1959, and 1964. He had to supervise the printing of the Girsberger monograph and the book *Synopsis,* containing architectural sketches, oil paintings, and philosophical texts by Aalto and published by the Zurich Polytechnic in 1967. He received an honorary doctorate from that institution in 1963. He lectured at universities, conferences, and associations on such topics as "How Badly May We Build?" and "Art Is the Only Way to Harmonize 1,000 Conflicting Factors".

In 1964 a Finnish newspaper related a plausible anecdote that was probably invented by Aalto himself. One day he got on the afternoon flight from Helsinki to Zurich, where he was to deliver a lecture. The plane's take-off was delayed by a snowstorm, and by the time he got to Zurich he was running late. He took a taxi to the congress hall, where a large audience was waiting. He immediately walked up to the podium and started to speak. The audience was puzzled at first, but was soon completely captivated. Every point he made was greeted with waves of laughter and applause, and when he concluded a good hour later, an

Alvar Aalto
Arkkitehti
Munkkiniemi
Riihitie 20 puh. 480123

endless ovation ensued. Then one worthy gentleman stood up, thanked him for the instructive presentation, and added: "I wonder if you are aware that this is a medical congress. The architects are meeting one floor up."

Most of Aalto's trips to Switzerland were not for business, however. From the early 1950s on, he made a habit of spending a winter holiday at one of the Swiss resorts. Sankt Anton, Davos, Crans-sur-Sierre, Cademario, and Arosa were some of the places the Aaltos visited, always staying at the best hotels. Elissa, the girl from Lapland, learned the foreign art of slalom at the ski resorts; Alvar contented himself with cross-country skiing.

Aalto had no ambition to build in Switzerland, and hence was surprised to find himself involved in no less than three Swiss architectural projects in 1964. The first came to him through Alfred Roth and consisted of a sixteen-storey apartment block in Lucerne's lakeside district of Schönbühl. The design attracted considerable interest in Switzerland, as it gave Aalto the chance to apply his pet idea of *flexible standardization*. Prefabricated construction as such was quite highly developed in Switzerland. Units weighing up to 4,000 kilos were made using a method called *Preton Verfahren*. These units could be installed in eight to ten minutes, but had been used up to that time only for

145. The brilliant orator who never spoke from notes. Here at a Nordic planning conference in Helsinki in 1965. Photo: Saarinen.

146. Occasionally Aalto jotted down a few "props" for his speeches. Here are some of the themes he served up for the Finnish Cultural Foundation's celebration in 1962.

147. Elissa and Alvar on a winter holiday in Switzerland, 1964.

148. Schönbühl high-rise block, Lucerne, built of prefabricated units. Photo: Pfeiffer.

monotonous, rectangular houses with strip windows. Aalto showed that they could also be used to assemble what the newspapers called "biologically formed houses, in which the rooms open up like flowers toward the windows and view". The *Neue Zürcher Zeitung* wrote that the use of prefabricated units had made the Schönbühl house incredibly inexpensive to build, resulting in low rents. All of the apartments were rented long before the building was completed in 1967.

Aalto's second Swiss project emerged out of an invitational competition for the design of an evangelical church in the Altstetten district of Zurich. The basic design, a symmetrical basilica, contained an asymmetrically differentiated interior with diagonal pews. Aalto's entry won first prize, but the Swiss democratic system, which calls for referendums even on municipal building projects, proved an insuperable barrier to his newfangled ideas.

His third Swiss design was for an international cultural centre in Beatenberg in the Berner Oberland. This project was initiated by the Danish interior designer Kai Dessau, but the financing arrangements fell through. Aalto had had his doubts about the plan from the start and drew only a perspective sketch of an institute in a fairytale alpine setting. The sketch decorated a flyer sent to prospective donors.

149. Model of Altstetten Church, Zurich. Photo: Michael Bernadotte.

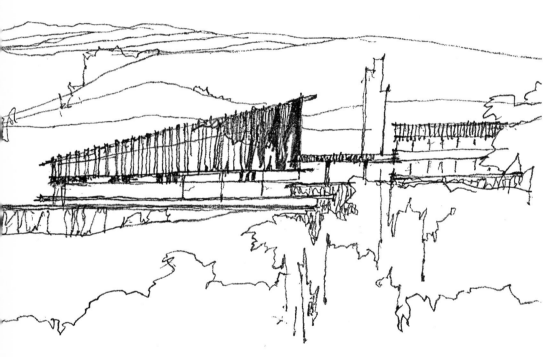

150. Sketch of the unbuilt culture centre in Beatenberg, drawn by Aalto for the fundraising prospectus.

The Middle East

The seemingly arbitrary jump from Switzerland to the Middle East is justified by the fact that Switzerland was the springboard that made it possible for Aalto to work with clients in several countries in that part of the world, an unknown quantity for Finns at the time. The Swiss had international business experience and were able to provide useful advice. When negotiations in Baghdad and Teheran got under way, the language skills and knowledgeability of Aalto's Swiss assistants proved invaluable.

It all started in 1954 when Aalto received an invitation to take part in a competition for the headquarters of the National Bank of Iraq in Baghdad. He visited the city and sent in an entry, but was defeated by the Swiss architect William Dunkel. He was in excellent company, however: Peter Celsing of Sweden and Gio Ponti of Italy were also among the losers. For Aalto, however,

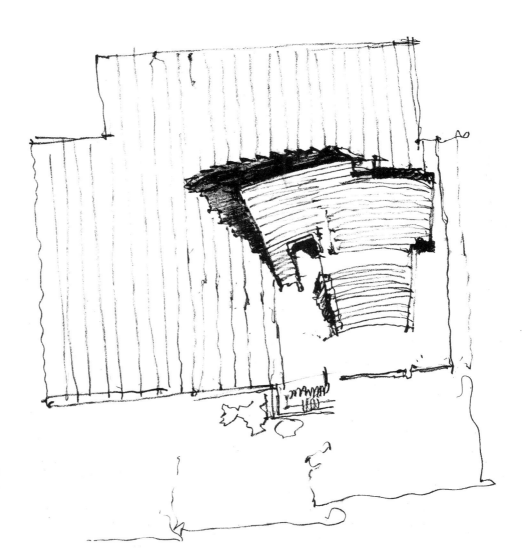

151. Roof and open-air auditorium of Baghdad Art Museum, sketch from 1957.

this was only an exercise in planning for Islamic countries. In June 1958 he was *urgently* invited by the Iraqi Minister of Development to present himself in Baghdad for a truly comprehensive commission that was to be awarded to him without competition.

This time there was no need for Aalto to exaggerate when he came back and told the Finnish press about the assignment. King Faisal of Iraq had suddenly decided to give his capital a modern, Western-style centre, and the enormous task had been divided into three parts. Le Corbusier was to design sports facilities and a stadium, Frank Lloyd Wright a theatre, and Aalto an art museum and 'ministerial palace' (actually the general post office) in the heart of the city. *Hufvudstadsbladet,* Helsinki's Swedish-language newspaper, quoted Aalto (September 9, 1958):

It is comparable to building Senate Square in Helsinki . . . While working in Baghdad, one of the world's hottest cities, I am also working in Kiruna, where the problem is cold and snow. In both cases, the important thing is not to forget 'the little man', not to succumb to aesthetic formalism or overdone technology. I intend to minimize the use of air conditioning in Baghdad and rely on Mother Earth instead by making the building heavy – part of the soil, as it were. The roof will consist of a double parasol of louvres, and the walls will be clad with ceramic tiles in the local tradition. The entire project calls for great tact, so as not to destroy the character of the city.

As we see, Aalto had already worked out the main features of his museum plan when he returned home. The plan was clean-drawn in record time, but the drawings had barely been completed when King Faisal was assassinated. The entire power configuration in Baghdad changed, and plans for the new centre were shelved.

Back in 1954, when Aalto was preparing for the national bank competition in Baghdad, he had suggested a partnership to his old friend Alfred Roth, who had experience in working in the Arab world. Roth refused, as "Aalto was too much of a bohemian to do business with" (interview with the author, April 29, 1977).

Roth's dilemma was that he understood administration but was short in architectural invention. When Roth was contacted in 1964 by a Lebanese banker, Madame Lucienne Sabbagh, asking him to design a complicated multipurpose building on a large but difficult site in Beirut, he decided, despite his reservations, to try a partnership with Aalto. All went well in the beginning. Aalto discussed the project with the client at a conference in Geneva and drew sketches, but when the lady was slow to pay his fee, he backed out. Alfred Roth is therefore credited as the sole architect of Beirut's Sabbagh Centre, which contains a bank, cinema, shops, and housing.

The next year Roth again tried to interest Aalto in a joint project. This involved an annex to the University of Beirut, and they agreed to meet in that city. But when Roth came to the hotel he found Aalto in the worst possible condition, lying on the bed in his room, surrounded by a battery of empty bottles, oblivious to the world. Madame Sabbagh had invited them for dinner

152. Alfred Roth vacationing with the Aaltos in Ischia, 1962.

the next day with the President of Lebanon and the ambassadors of Finland and Switzerland. Aalto did not want to meet any of them or talk with the university representatives. Only after a doctor had been called in to treat the patient could the incapacitated master be sent back to Finland, his mission unaccomplished. That is what could happen abroad when Elissa was not with him.

Small wonder that Roth felt that their collaboration was problematic and suggested a strict division of labour when they tackled the demanding Schönbühl district project in Lucerne. Aalto was solely responsible for the apartment block, and Roth designed the adjacent shopping centre.

Aalto's last Moslem adventure also originated in Switzerland. The owner of Zurich's Galérie Semika Huber was a friend of Farah Diba. Through her Aalto received an unofficial inquiry as to whether he was interested in designing a museum in Iran. The queen had studied architecture in Europe before her marriage, and had an expert's appreciation for the Finnish master. This first, tentative contact was soon followed by an official invitation to visit Teheran, signed by Dr. K.P. Bahadori, head private secretary of Her Imperial Majesty, the Shachbanou of Iran. Accompanied by Elissa and Karl Fleig, Aalto set off on October 2, 1969 on another quest to capture a desert mirage.

The following account is based on an interview with Fleig on April 30, 1977:

During the first audience in Teheran, the queen explained her wishes. She had selected a site in the old city of Shiraz for which she wanted Aalto to design a museum of modern art as part of her husband's efforts to modernize Iran. They then set off for the building site, accompanied by a senator who was also an architect and by court officials. The site was a hilltop above the historic city

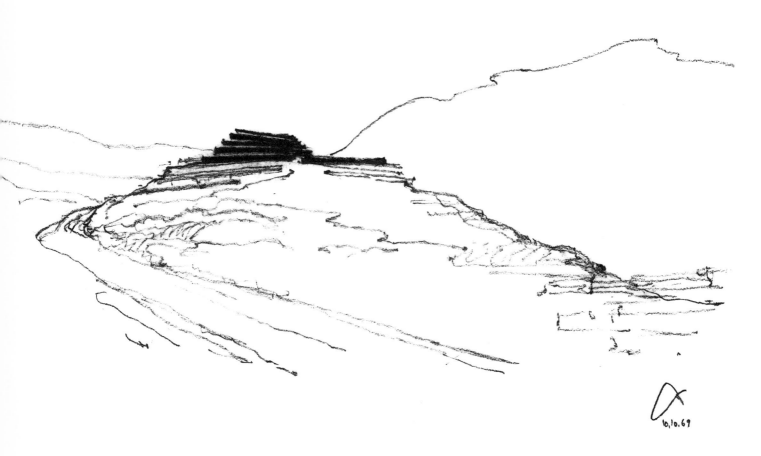

of Shiraz, in a magnificent landscape of mountains and terraces. Aalto immediately saw what the museum should look like: an accumulation of rising terrace forms.

On the way back, the company spent a night in Isfahan, where the senator presided over a sumptuous dinner at which wine and even vodka were served. Elissa watched with concern as her husband downed one schnapps after the other, solicitously served by an attentive waiter. Fleig was able to reassure her, however: he had instructed the waiter to fill the master's glass with water, which Aalto fortunately did not notice. On returning to Teheran, he immediately began to draw a sketch of the museum. The hosts wanted to take him sightseeing, but he was completely uninterested. Only out of politeness did he

153. Aalto immediately visualized his art museum in the landscape near Shiraz. From his sketchbook, October 10, 1969.

154. The Aaltos sightseeing in Isfahan.

155. The Aaltos sightseeing in Persepolis.

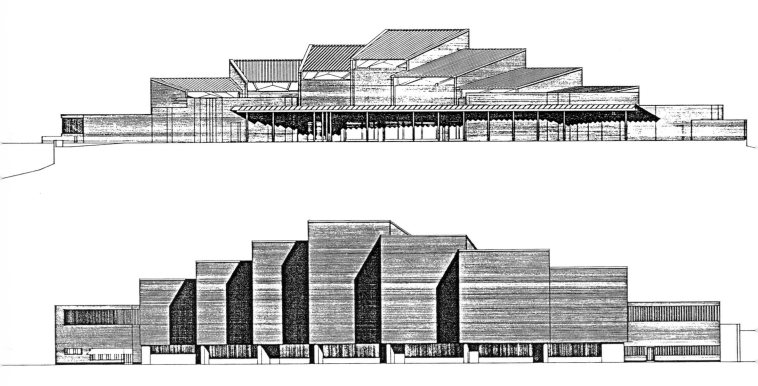

go to see some mosques, contenting himself with viewing them from the outside. However, he was fascinated with the problem of restoration and rehabilitation in the old parts of Teheran. He also gave a lecture to the architecture students at the university.

He wanted to have a finished sketch of the museum to show Farah Diba before leaving. He did this at a second audience, for which he prepared by abstaining from alcoholic beverages for a whole day. The queen was most impressed by the design and declared that it should be used as the basis for construction.

The authorities then proceeded to draw up a contract that restricted Aalto's power to the planning stages only. He refused and demanded control over construction as well. This was of course inappropriate in a country where all business was based on commissions, secret agreements, and various kinds of machinations. He heard no more of the museum for several years. In 1972, however, a London engineering office contacted him after having been asked to do the structural drawings for the museum. An agreement on collaboration was reached, but then a new, more serious obstacle appeared: the Iranian revolution swept the Shah and Farah Diba aside and, with them, Aalto's modern museum in Shiraz.

156. Shiraz Art Museum. Front and rear elevation.

Carefree Days on the Nile

As we have seen, Aalto was almost shockingly indifferent to tourist attractions. In his old age, he was also unwilling to go to the theatre or to art exhibitions, or even to read new books. "Do you think I am receptive?" he would ask ironically if his presence was wanted at some cultural event. He kept to his old favourite books and to matters directly connected with his current projects. He was like a plant that can assimilate food only for its own growth. He scoffed at indiscriminate 'culture consumption'; fads did not interest him.

Thus it was little short of incredible that in 1954, when I and my wife headed up the Nile in our little yacht the *Daphne*, he agreed to sail with us for some ten days. In a newspaper interview, he said that after a year and a half of uninterrupted work he needed to rest his brain and was therefore going to relax with friends on the Nile.

After a visit to Baghdad in preparation for the national bank competition, Alvar and Elissa arrived just before Christmas in Luxor, where the *Daphne* was moored below the Art Nouveau facade of the old Winter Palace Hotel. They stayed at the hotel for a week, while we made a fairly thorough study of the temples and graves on both sides of the river. We spent Christmas Eve in the *Daphne*'s cramped but cosy cabin, and on December 29 set out south on our adventurous voyage. The idea of sailing 1,100 miles up the Nile and back in a boat with a keel was actually mad, as the river is full of moving sand bars. We struck bottom repeatedly and unexpectedly, and the swift current would then threaten to push the boat even higher aground. The very first day of our sail with the Aaltos, we had a series of such mishaps, followed by efforts to set ourselves free and find a better route. Alvar sketched a map of the *Daphne*'s progress that

157. Christmas Eve 1954 in the cabin of the *Daphne.* Left to right: Mona Schildt, Alvar Aalto, Astri Morales, Göran Schildt, Juan Morales, Elissa Aalto, and our Nubian travel companion Idris. Timed-release photo.

VANSTER

ISNA

HÖGER

158. From Alvar's sketch-book for the Nile voyage. The *Daphne's* groundings and route are drawn on the map of the Nile in the left margin. Above, a cargo sailing vessel; below, the skipper's lady peering out of the cabin hatch.

159. Happy New Year 1955. Alvar waking up on January 1.

DAPHNE.
LUXOR ~ ISNA ~ EDFU.

ELISSA   ALVAR.
             1 JAN. 1955

160. Sketch in the *Daphne* visitors' book.

day, during which we did, however, have a brisk following wind from the north to speed us along when we were not stuck. On December 30 we reached the little town of Esna. I quote from the yacht's log:

Passed through a lock with ten aiasas (sailing cargo ships) *or so, and put in next to Esna's main street. A police car took us to the temple. Silt from the Nile has raised the ground some 6–7 metres since antiquity, and the ruin is in a pit right in the middle of the town. Only the hypostyle hall and a forest of columns is left, a late Egyptian but highly evocative monument. Alvar said that his fingers itched to make a town plan for Esna with a terraced plaza and the temple as a portal to a community centre with offices, museum, etc.*

Left at one, after buying fruit and a few bottles of vermouth on the pleasant street along the waterfront – the town was quite attractive for all its primitiveness. Weak wind, warm, almost hot. Mostly used the motor. Alvar sat in his shorts, drawing views in his sketchbook. "We haven't seen any bad architecture all afternoon!" He admires the way the villages are built. The adobe bricks give rise to spontaneous pylon forms, and the horizontal lines are broken beautifully by vaults, cupolas, towers. All the houses are the colour of clay, in varied hues. Construction is flexible in Alvar's sense: rooms can be added or vacated as needed.

At sunset we heard a whistle from the far shore, where we had previously caught sight of the El Kula pyramid with our binoculars. We steered toward it and were welcomed by two policemen sent by the mayor of Esna to protect us. An evening's walk to the pyramid, an archaeologically inexplicable structure, a stepped pyramid built of small cubic blocks using clay for the joints. Perhaps an archaistic tomb from a late period? Walked along the riverfront with our police escort to see the richest man in the region, sheik Tourist (that really is his name), who received us graciously in his columned house and treated us to blaring gramophone music and tea under a blinding photogen lamp in a dreary reception room. Alvar conversed politely with the sheik, who turned out to be a former M.P. Back in the darkness to our pleasant cabin, where to celebrate New Year's Eve Mona laid out a luxurious meal of tinned ham, tinned peas, and chips. Drinks, schnapps, and some real Chianti bought by Alvar were imbibed to excess, which is why we could not stay awake for the arrival of the New Year, but allowed the gentle lapping of the Nile against the side of our boat to lull us to sleep by eleven o'clock.

The trip was a pleasant but hardly sensational experience. Imagine my surprise twenty-two years later when Carola Giedion told me that Aalto had returned from Egypt with the most extraordinary stories of his voyage up the Nile. Unfortunately she could not recall any of the details, and I am still ignorant of how Alvar transformed our days on the Nile into a Homeric epic.

Italy

In my mind there is always a journey to Italy: it may be a past journey that still lives on in my memory; it may be a journey I am making or perhaps a journey I am planning. Be this as it may, such a journey is a conditio sine qua non for my architectural work.

This lyrical and revealing declaration Aalto made in a 1954 article for the journal *Casabella*. It brings back the memory of his first, unforgettable trip to Italy, his honeymoon with Aino in 1924, which confirmed his dream of the

cultivated vitality of the Renaissance and of classical antiquity. It also bears witness to his lifelong dependence on Italy as a source of inspiration and as a confirmation that his view of life was rooted in reality. Of course one might say that this was an illusion: he saw what he wished to see in Italy. In any case, the reality he found there matched his expectations closely enough to draw him back time and again.

We have noted that he was fond of Switzerland because he had good,

161. Aalto captured the Italy he loved on film in 1947: the piazza in Bergamo and Brunelleschi's Capella Pazzi.

214

dependable friends there. In Italy, by comparison, his love of the country made him many friends. One of these was Ignazio Gardella, a fellow member of CIAM who resumed their contact, broken off by the war, by writing to Aalto in 1946. Gardella reported that their mutual friend Pagano, an architect known for his left-wing sympathies, had died in a concentration camp. Aalto's reply claimed, with typical exaggeration, that eleven of his assistants had been killed in the war.

In 1947 CIAM held meetings in Bergamo and Milan, providing Aino and Alvar with many joyful reunions with old friends. At the time, perhaps his closest Italian friend was the young Ernesto Rogers, a partner of Gianluigi Banfi, Ludovico Belgioioso, and Enrico Peressuti in the famous Italian office BBPR.

162. Sketch from Italy, 1948: towers of San Gimignano.

163. The offensive neon sign on Säynätsalo Town Hall.

In 1947 Rogers, who was editor of the journal *Domus,* managed to elicit from Aalto what is perhaps his most interesting essay, the much-quoted "The Trout and the Stream" (*The Decisive Years,* pp. 222–223). In later years they kept in touch. Rogers visited Aalto in Finland in 1954, and witnessed the curious drama inspired by a neon sign that had been set up by Säynätsalo's local savings bank on the facade of the newly inaugurated town hall. Aalto found it so disfiguring that, before Rogers's eyes, he smashed it by throwing stones at it. The action was

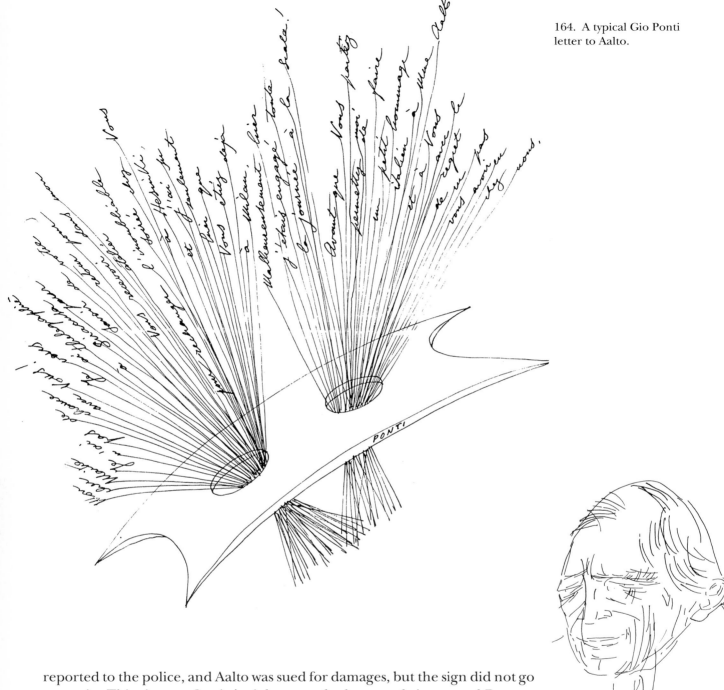

164. A typical Gio Ponti letter to Aalto.

reported to the police, and Aalto was sued for damages, but the sign did not go up again. This victory of artist's rights over the law greatly impressed Rogers.

Other Italian architects with whom Aalto enjoyed friendly, though not terribly intimate, relationships included Bruno Zevi, the leader of the 'organic school of architecture' in Rome, the Milanese universalist Gio Ponti, and those masters of precision Franco Albini and Carlo Scarpa. Aalto had a very different kind of friendship with painter and designer Roberto Sambonet of Milan. Sambonet visited me in Finland in 1952, and we went together to see Aalto,

165. The maestro captured by Roberto Sambonet's pen.

216

whom I had previously met only in passing. Thus my friendship with Aalto stemmed, paradoxically, from the seduction that Italy held for him. Roberto and I published an aesthetically hyperrefined, illustrated volume entitled *Medelhav* (The Mediterranean) in 1955, and dedicated it to Alvar. Roberto later made some very lifelike oil and ink portraits of Alvar, who in turn drew up plans for an unusual villa for Roberto.

Aalto's important Italian contacts also included some of the architects who worked at his office. The most active of these was Leonardo Mosso of Turin, who began studying the maestro's extensive but chaotic drawing archives during his years in Finland and attempted to assemble a complete catalogue with descriptions of all of his projects. Another Italian assistant Aalto valued highly was Federico Marconi of Udine, a relative of the great radio pioneer.

It was thus natural for Aalto to be the focus of the kind of event at which the Italians, with their flair for stage design, excel: a truly spectacular exhibition. After the war, the city of Florence had already exhibited, in the magnificent Palazzo Strozzi, the complete works of Frank Lloyd Wright and Le Corbusier. On the initiative of Carlo L. Ragghianti, perhaps Italy's most influential architecture critic, Aalto was invited in autumn 1965 to fill the palace with his life's work. In his excitement at appearing in the city of Giotto and Brunelleschi, he discounted the effort of assembling the exhibition as well as the costs always associated with the uncertainly funded cultural events in Italy. He filled seventeen large rooms in the palace with models, photographs, drawings, sketches, paintings, and design objects to create one of the largest displays ever of his work.

166. The official opening of Aalto's Florentine exhibition in the Palazzo della Signoria, November 12, 1965. Photo: Levi.

I was in Florence with Alvar and Elissa when the exhibits were installed and also took part in the official opening on November 12, 1965. The event culminated in a city reception in the Palazzo della Signoria for all the dignitaries (and freeloaders) in town. Even for those of us who thought we knew Aalto's work, the exhibition was dazzling and full of surprises. This was the first time that Aalto's architectural sketches and pencil drawings on thin paper were shown in public; they provided a completely new insight into his 'synthetic architecture', his effort to fuse all architectural motifs into a whole. In an article on the exhibition (published March 4, 1966 in *Svenska Dagbladet*), I wrote:

Style is an ambiguous term that can be used simply to indicate a recurrent form scheme in an artistic era or in an individual artist. Aalto reminds us of the deeper significance of the word, the connection of style with the ingredients of a philosophy of life. Aalto's style takes its distinctive character from his working method, which is best understood by studying his architectural sketches and oil paintings, both well-represented in the Florence show. The sketches are surprisingly reminiscent of Chinese virtuoso ink drawings contemplating nature. The reason is the simultaneously intuitively receptive and boldly creative attitude, the extraordinary sensitivity to the dictates of the unique task at hand, to all the concurrent forces that use the draughtsman's full personality as a reactive medium and are channelled in seemingly simple forms with a strong aura of reality and 'naturalness' that derives from the complicated riches those forms encompass and

167. Kiruna Town Hall taking shape on Aalto's drawing board. Sketch from 1958.

218

condense. Nothing here is incidental, since form and structure are determined with the inevitability and complexity of the roundness of a fruit or the appearance of a landscape. We might speak of a sense of reality, a will to accept all the forces that affect the human condition in order to bring them into equilibrium.

In his opening speech Carlo Ragghianti extolled Aalto as a new Francis of Assisi, a man who was a friend of both the elements and the wild beasts, a redeemer and an apostle of the love of life. This comparison may seem rather high-flown to sober northerners, but it does contain a kernel of truth. Aalto did not seek anything that we do not possess; he found the harmony in that which we already have. It is refreshing to meet such assured faith and ability in a world whose equilibrium is always threatened.

What Aalto sought in Italy was not primarily honours, such as his exhibition in the Palazzo Strozzi, his membership in the Venice Art Academy (1958), or his honorary doctorate from Milan's technical university (1964). There were two other reasons for his frequent trips to Italy.

168. Sketch from 1953 journey to Greece: city gate of Mycenae.

The first was to enjoy some rest and recreation during his holidays. On a few occasions he exchanged the Swiss winter resorts for Italian ones, such as Bardonecchia in 1964 and Sestriere in 1965; but more often it was his need to prolong the short Nordic summer that drew him to Italy. His all-but-manic zeal for work made it impossible for him to take the rest he increasingly needed as years went by, so his holidays in the south never lasted longer than ten days, and often were combined with working conferences or lectures.

In the 1950s, just after his marriage, he extended his holiday destinations to include Sicily (1952 and 1953) and even Greece (1953). A little later he went to Capri and Ischia (1958 and 1962), and to Ronchi near Massa Carrara, where the daughter of his Swiss friends Werner and Silvia Moser ran a small *pensione* by the sea. In his old age, however, he almost always headed for the city that both reinvigorated him physically and took him back to his first visit to Italy, Venice. His fixed holiday address was the Excelsior Palace Hotel on the Lido. There he could engage in the mornings in his favourite sport, long- distance swimming along the shore, and spend the afternoons at the Piazza San Marco or on strolls through the architectural setting he loved.

Aalto's second goal in Italy was to build something on its hallowed ground. This turned out to be quite difficult to accomplish. His pursuit of Italian building assignments was almost as disappointing as similar efforts in Islamic countries. Time and again the fata morgana of shimmering palaces and dancing fountains loomed before him, only to vanish into thin air when he approached.

His first Italian disappointment occurred in 1955, when our mutual friend Roberto Sambonet told Aalto that he was thinking of founding an artists' colony at Malpensa near Milan with some like-minded friends. Could Aalto

169. Alvar Aalto and Göran Schildt on the Lido, 1956.

170. Aalto with his friends Louisa and Roberto Sambonet on the Lido, 1956, Photo: Göran Schildt.

possibly design a small house for him with this in mind? Since I was familiar with the facts, and knew that Roberto's father was not likely to be willing to pay for this whim and, moreover, that the site for the colony had not yet even been found, I tried to moderate Aalto's enthusiasm. Architectural ideas had started to spawn in his fertile mind, however, and he lovingly designed a truly ravishing little studio villa, based on the circular, conical *trulli* houses of Calabria. When Roberto asked Alvar what he owed him for the plan, the reply was, "Between colleagues, you can give me one of your paintings." Young Sambonet was not even considered a saleable painter on the art market in those days.

The unbuilt Sambonet house could have been a useful lesson to Aalto concerning the Italian tendency to realize their dreams only verbally. He did not heed the warning, however, because he himself had so many imaginary exploits to his credit. Instead, he nibbled at one treacherous bait after another.

This is not the place for a detailed discussion of the many Italian projects that never went beyond talk or preliminary sketches. One of these was the renovation of parts of the centre of Catania, an idea that an adventurous construction company dangled before Aalto and veteran architect Pier Luigi Nervi in 1958. Another was a hotel project in Turin, for which no less a personage than Fiat director Giovanni Agnelli requested sketches, even though he did not yet even own the plot on which the hotel was to be built. There was a church with seating for 1,500 of which the brothers of the Madonna della Mercedes monastery in San Remo dreamed but had no money to build. There was the vision of a type building for the Ferrero company, to be duplicated like a trademark along all the Italian *autostrade,* suggested to Aalto by the company's ingenious director in 1966. And there was an offer with which an unauthorized representative of the city lured him in 1973, according to which a museum dedicated to Aalto's life's work would be built in the garden of the Villa Strozzi near Florence.

More serious offers that led to plans and drawings were also legion. One was made by a major landowner in 1966 and involved the construction of a satellite town called Patrizia near Pavia. It was to include housing for 11,000 inhabitants, two churches, a shopping centre, and more. Aalto's plan was based on long, serpentine housing volumes in a park setting. It was much admired at a large press conference in Pavia's city hall in 1968, where the prefect, bishop, mayor, and other notabilities also gathered to listen to his eloquent presentation. To read the newspapers, one would have thought the new town was almost built, which did not prevent it from coming to nothing.

Aalto's brilliant plan for a concert hall and open-air arena for cultural events in Siena met with the same ignominious fate. The city council commissioned him to integrate the old, abandoned fortified area, La Fortezza, with modern activities. Aalto was all aflame: a worthy counterpart to Siena's two historic squares, the cathedral piazza and Il Campo, which stemmed from a Classical

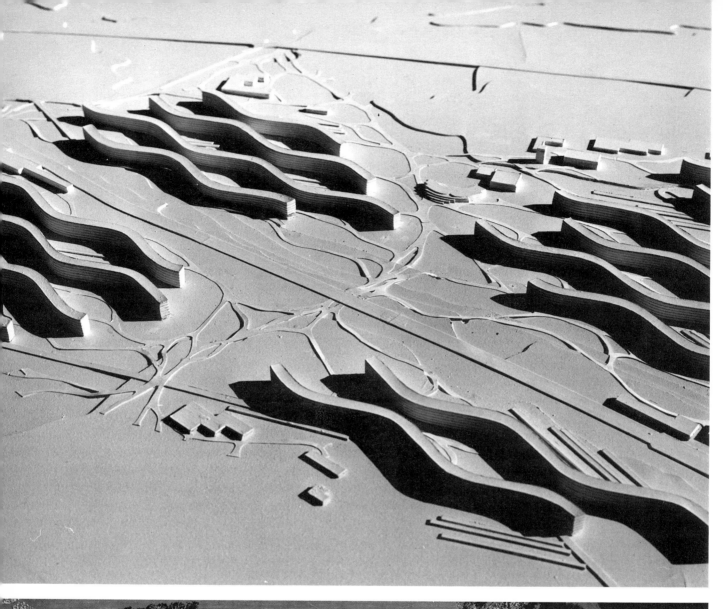

171. The serpentine apartment building designed by Aalto for Pavia's satellite town Patrizia.

theatre cavea, would rise here like an acropolis within the city walls. His design was enthusiastically applauded and admired by both the clients and the public at Aalto's architectural exhibitions, where the model of the Siena Fortezza held a place of honour. The Siena authorities never got around to making the decision to start construction; it was always postponed by a new election or a budget cut.

Aalto came quite close to hitting the jackpot in the Italian lottery in 1969, when Adriano Olivetti's niece Erica, who was married to university professor Marino Bin, asked him to design a villa in a hillside park area only eight minutes' drive from the centre of Turin. The clients' 'wish list' on what the house was to contain makes for an interesting sociological document. They stated that they did not want a large and ostentatious house, only a sort of forest cabin. In addition to a living room communicating with an enormous indoor swimming pool, the lower floor of the house was to contain a large library and a dining room, and the upper floor the owners' bedroom with a closet, exercise room and bathroom, a bedroom and playroom for their five-year-old daughter Debora, a series of guest rooms, and a room for the daughter's governess. The spouses also each needed a smaller study, since "both worked at home". Accommodations for three servants, five saddle horses, and a dairy cow(!) were to be provided in a separate building, if possible. The garage needed space for only four cars.

Aalto had to design the whole villa three times over before the clients were satisfied. Unfortunately they were divorced just as construction was about to begin.

Of Aalto's Italian clients, Cardinal Giacomo Lercaro of Bologna had the most serious intentions. He was an ardent champion of the ecumenical movement, and had invited Aalto to a conference on the theme *Architettura Sacra* back in

172. Siena's Fortezza with Aalto's concert hall and open-air auditorium, model from 1966. Photo: Ingervo.

173. Fourth version of the Villa Erica near Turin, 1969.

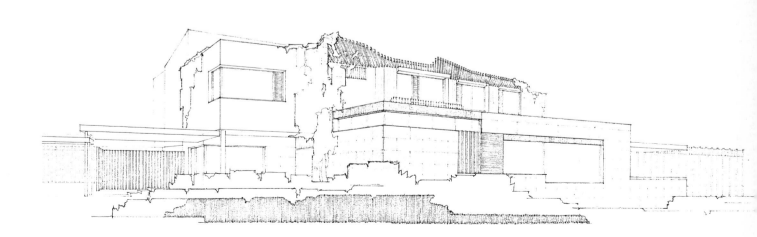

1955. In the early 1960s he had commissioned a church from Le Corbusier and, a little later, one from Kenzo Tange, both to be built within his diocese. Having admired Aalto's exhibition in the Palazzo Strozzi, he wanted an Aalto church within his domain. In January 1966 he took the Aaltos with him to the small village of Riola di Vergato in the mountains above Bologna. Was this a site they would consider? Aalto was able to show him the preliminary sketches that spring. The church in Riola is unlike any of Aalto's previous religious buildings. It is lighted by a series of stepped clerestory windows in the vaulted roof, which is supported from within by concrete arches reminiscent of the frames of his bentwood furniture.

Cardinal Lercaro was an extremely pleasant and liberal-minded man, and Aalto got along with him very well. The only problem was that for financing Riola had to rely on Providence: as the village was too poor to afford the church, construction had to be postponed. Aalto was convinced that this plan would meet with the same fate as his other Italian projects. But the cardinal had better contacts with Providence than could have been expected. The city authorities of Bologna had to vote on some major municipal projects desired by the Grandi Lavori construction company, and the outcome hinged on the decisions of a handful of devout council members. A discreet agreement was reached: if Grandi Lavori would build the church in Riola for free, the pious citizens would trust the company's morals and support its projects. A few weeks before his death, Aalto received the incredible news that construction in Riola had begun.

The church was consecrated in 1978, but at that time the bell tower, which was

175. The interior of Riola
Church before the pews were
installed.

176. Without the campanile,
the church looks a truncated.

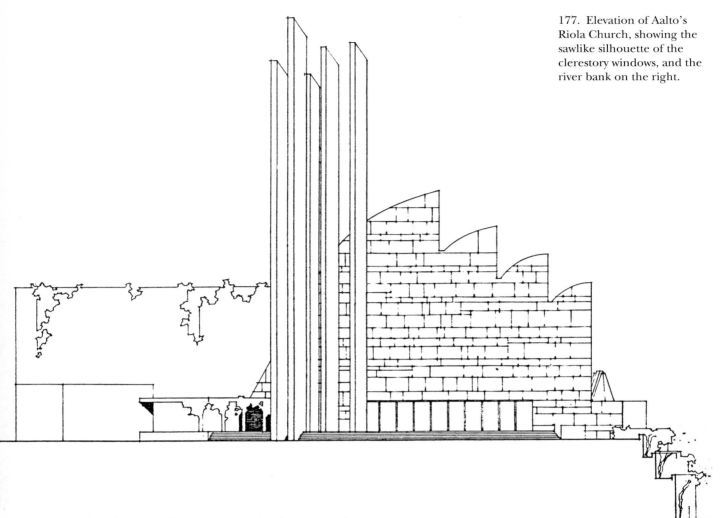

crucial to the overall impression, had not even been started. It turned out that Grandi Lavori, having won its contracts, considered that this assignment was not part of the agreement with Providence. Therefore the only Aalto building erected on Italian initiative today stands in a regrettably truncated and unsatisfactory form.

Italy does, however, possess one complete Aalto work, built in 1956. Its construction was entirely the result of Nordic determination. In 1956 Maire Gullichsen persuaded Aalto to design a Finnish pavilion for the exhibition area of the Venice Biennale. Made of light timber units at the Ahlström works in Varkaus, it was transported by road to Italy. Aalto's idea was that the pavilion could be dismantled between exhibitions. It would be "like the brave soldier Schweik's field altar, easy to set up and easy to fold up until it was needed again".

Unfortunately the concept was spoiled by carelessness at the factory. In assembly, the units could not be bolted together and had to be fastened irreversibly with nails. This did not show from outside, however, and so did not significantly disturb our enjoyment when we erected the pavilion under Alvar's and Elissa's direction amid the Giardini's fresh early summer verdure. The newspapers were enthusiastic. The stern professor of architecture Bruno Zevi wrote in *La Stampa:* "A simple and smart solution, without pretensions, anti-monumental, and very attractive after the structuralist exercises in which the newer buildings of the Biennale excelled."

178. Opening of the Venice exhibition pavilion in 1956. Photo: Göran Schildt.

179. Denise René, Maire Gullichsen, Mona Schildt, and Elissa Aalto on the Lido beach at the time the Venice pavilion was erected. Photo: Göran Schildt.

In my memory the assembly and inauguration of the Venice pavilion is bathed in the glorified light that surrounded Alvar and Elissa, still newlyweds, and the friends gathered about them. Alvar had a pavilion-type beach hut out on the Excelsior Hotel's beach on the Lido. We gathered there in the afternoons, cooled ourselves in the lazy surf, laughed at Alvar's stories. Maire Gullichsen was there with her children and their spouses. Artists such as the Swede Kurt Jungstedt and the Danes Richard Mortensen and Egill Jakobsen, art dealers Denise René and Louis Carré, Italian friends like Paolo Venini and Roberto Sambonet, all now either grey-haired or dead, stand before my mind's eye in all the freshness of youth against a background of colourful huts and milling crowds along the Lido.

But let us return to the setbacks Alvar suffered in his efforts to build something on Italian soil. I have sometimes wondered whether this might be one of the reasons why he started using Italian marble in his Northern buildings in the 1960s. The marriage he sought between his architecture and Italy could take place in Finland, if need be. Marble, after all, is not merely physically quarried in Italy: it is a symbol of the Classical heritage.

Even when he started planning the main building of the University of Technology in Otaniemi in the 1950s, he believed that the architecture department should be built of marble for pedagogical reasons: it would give budding architects a feeling for quality. He also intended to erect a number of Classical columns in the courtyard. "My friends in Italy can surely find suitable columns, and the authorities will grant an export permit when they hear what the purpose is", he explained when I wondered how he would manage the bureaucratic formalities. It goes without saying that no Classical columns were ever erected in Otaniemi.

In 1960 he visited the Carrara quarry to examine the various grades of marble and to find out about export possibilities. He had hit upon the idea of facing his monumental buildings with marble veneer, partly because it was attractive but also because he thought it would be economical. Were not the higher construction costs offset many times over by the elimination of all later painting or maintenance? Aalto buildings that are wholly or partly clad in marble include the Enso-Gutzeit offices, the Academic Bookshop and the Finlandia Hall in Helsinki, and the savings bank in Ekenäs. Today, after nearly thirty years of experience, only the last of these buildings has more or less lived up to expectations, presumably because Ekenäs is a rural idyll. Quite simply, marble has turned out to be unsuitable for use in a big city. It cannot withstand the combined effects of air pollution and cold climate: it buckles and curls like bacon in a frying pan. Aalto believed that architecture cannot make progress unless architects are allowed to experiment. Those who are obliged to replace the disintegrating marble cladding of his buildings today may feel that they are paying a rather high price for Aalto's desire to bring about a marriage between Italy and the North.

A happier fulfilment of his dream remains to be mentioned. Shortly after

180. Ekenäs Savings Bank, with its still intact marble facing. Photo: Holmström.

181. Alvar and Aino Aalto's grave in old Hietaniemi graveyard in Helsinki. Photo: Marconi.

Aalto's death, Elissa decided to erect a Classical marble column on his grave, or at least to acquire an authentic capital for the purpose. This was easier said than done, however. The ban on the exportation of antiquities was insurmountable even for the highest placed officials who took up the matter. Finally, Federico Marconi found an eighteenth-century capital that could plausibly be considered modern and thus exportable. It is today the main element of Aalto's tomb, and a beautiful reminder of his indissoluble ties with Italy.

France

The strong French bourgeois tradition led to a strange, schizophrenic attitude to the arts in the years between the wars. Literary modernism such as that produced by Mallarmé, Proust, and Jarry was quickly accepted, since it did not in any way intrude on the safe milieu of the bourgeois home. Music by Poulenc or ballets by Satie could also be swallowed; even a painting by Matisse or Picasso could be smuggled in to reside among the period furniture and velvet drapes. But how many Frenchmen were willing to live in interiors designed by André Lurçat or Le Corbusier?

The highly successful Parisian art dealer Louis Carré, whom I had the honour of visiting in 1957, also lived in a suburban villa with perfectly conventional furniture, but filled with bold modern paintings by Matisse, Bonnard, Léger, etc. Because he also traded in New York, however, he began to realize that the modern art that had made him so wealthy also had an architectural dimension. His 'stables' also included Calder and Léger, who told him of their miraculous friend Aalto. They also reassured him that Aalto did not necessarily build houses with flat roofs, but would surely consider a pitched slate roof of the kind Carré wanted over his head.

This was the background for the letter that Aalto received from Louis Carré in 1955, inquiring if he was willing to discuss a villa project. Aalto suggested that they should meet the following summer in Venice, where they both had business – Carré as an art dealer, Aalto to erect his pavilion. Their meeting was a success, and that summer Carré visited Finland, saw the Villa Mairea and

182. Monsieur and Madame Carré with Elissa Aalto and Finnish President Kekkonen during his state visit to France. Photo: Iris.

183. Maison Carré under construction in July 1958 and after completion in autumn 1959.

succumbed to Aalto's magic. Alvar and Elissa then went to France and were taken to the intended site in the village of Bazoches-sur-Guyonne, quite close to Versailles. The hilltop site overlooks a landscape of deciduous groves, vineyards, and small villages stretching out into the distance. It is in the midst of 'la douce France', as depicted by Cézanne, Pissarro, and Monet. The pitched slate roof Carré desired was the obvious solution here: it echoed the rhythm of the landscape, as the silhouettes of Aalto's buildings so often do.

Carré was a very demanding and authoritarian gentleman, but his profession had taught him to respect the artist's sovereignty in creative matters. Aalto was therefore given relative freedom in designing the art dealer's villa – which Aalto jokingly dubbed the Maison Carré after the Classical temple in Nîmes, which from time immemorial has been called *la maison carrée*, 'the square house'.

The drawings were finally completed in autumn 1957, and construction began. Elissa was the site architect in charge and was able to improve her already good French during long stays in France. The most demanding detail, the free-form hall ceiling, was built by Finnish carpenters sent to France for the purpose. In the summer of 1958, Carré revisited Finland to select furnishing details. New furniture variants were designed, including a new chair type with legs made up of thin, spaghetti-like wooden rods. This chair was never mass-produced.

After being completed in 1959, the house was inaugurated with a reception for 359 invited guests. The list of invitations includes all of Aalto's friends on either side of the Atlantic, but not many of these were prepared to travel to France only for a cocktail from California, Boston, or Scandinavia. The Parisians were more responsive. Among those who celebrated Aalto's achievement were Braque, Calder, Cocteau, Le Corbusier, Charlotte Perriand, Arp, Giacometti, Jacques Villon, and Christian Zervos, not to mention ministers such as Jean Monnet and Claudius Petit and old friends like Maire Gullichsen and the Giedions. Léger and Brancusi had a legitimate excuse for missing the festivities – they were no longer among the living.

Aalto's later trips to France were sporadic, consisting mainly of short visits to friends. In 1972, the French Academy of Architecture awarded him its gold medal. By that time he was so worn out that he was unable to make one of his usual improvised, witty speeches, and contented himself with a few formal words of thanks.

England

Aalto's contacts with England were formal rather than practical. He never had the chance to build anything there, but the British showered him with honours. The most flattering of these, without a doubt, was the gold medal of the Royal Institute of British Architects, conferred upon him in 1957 by Her Majesty Queen Elizabeth. When word of the coming distinction reached Aalto's old friend Morton Shand, who was living quietly in retirement in Cambridge, he immediately wrote to congratulate Aalto. The letter was in German, the language they had spoken together in their youth:

Dear Aalto, You (Sie) have been famous for so long that I no longer dare address you familiarly as Du. Nor do I know if I dare disturb you with such an unimportant matter as congratulations for the RIBA medal. I shall, however, try to do so with all due humility, though no less cordially, especially as the ceremony, tiresome as it will no doubt be for you, may give us the chance to meet again.

My God, how remote seem the days when, to the amazement of my countrymen, sunk deep in the slumber of tradition, I published your Turun Sanomat Building! Or the time we arranged our little exhibition of your 'naked' furniture at Fortnum & Mason's, with which the Finmar company then astounded Londoners. I still see in my mind's eye how the higher RIBA animals smiled superciliously and shook their heads when I appeared as a prophet and soothsayer. Today we have come so (apparently) far that I suspect that the

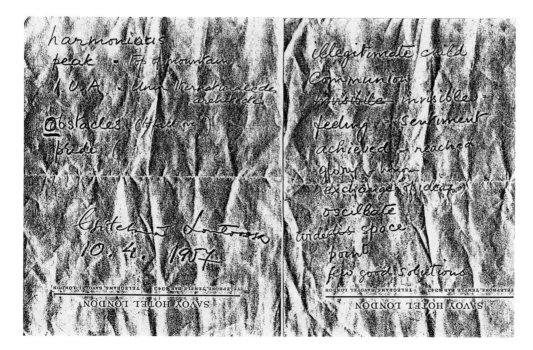

184. This crumpled piece of paper was Aalto's only prop for his 'discourse' to the Royal Institute of British Architects on April 10, 1957.

185. First page of Aalto's 'discourse' as printed in the *RIBA Journal*.

The R.I.B.A. Annual Discourse, 1957
by Professor Alvar Aalto H.C.M. (Finland)
given at the R.I.B.A. on 10 April

Professor J. Leslie Martin, Vice-President R.I.B.A., in the Chair

Professor Leslie Martin: The programme of lectures given by this Institute, and given usually to a specialist audience, is, of course, quite well known. But it has occurred to the Public Relations Committee that a great Institute of this kind could well support a lecture of a different kind and with a different aim. This lecture, which is to be given annually, is to be called a Discourse: This, I think, is an appropriate word. It suggests that the lecture will involve not merely statements, but that it should be also an assessment.

By some miracle of timing, this first Discourse coincides with the award of the Gold Medal to Alvar Aalto. I think this is important, because when this Institute makes its highest award we ourselves are faced with some kind of assessment. We look again at the work of the holder of the Medal. It is brought before us in the form of exhibitions, and again we re-assess it. This is actually taking place. The comparisons between the work of all the great masters, all the great leaders of architecture will again be made. The barriers will be drawn between them; the partitions will be erected.

Now these distinctions between the work of great architects are interesting, but these divisions do not occur to me as the important ones. If I drew any line at all, the line which I would draw would be horizontal and not vertical. Above this horizontal line I would choose to place the creative work of these great designers, and below it the rest. And the thing which would strike me, I think, when I look again at the work of Alvar Aalto, is a different series of distinctions. They would be distinctions between architecture of his kind, which is ordered, controlled, worked for, and not just accidental; between the detail of his kind which is the result of the completeness of a great idea and not just a trivial end in itself; between his kind of architecture, which cannot easily be drawn but rests in the building itself, and that which looks well only on the drawing board.

It is these things that I think we should assess. I do not know whether Alvar Aalto can explain the secret of these positive qualities of his work, but it is because his work contains them in such powerful abundance that we sit, this evening, at his feet.

THE DISCOURSE

I AM DEEPLY IMPRESSED by Dr. Martin's words, and especially by the correct and crystallised wording 'horizontal line'. The main thing is not to make a difference of different personalities, different countries and different conditions. There is still that old thing—good and ill, good and bad. Our time is full of enthusiasm for, and interest in, architecture because of the architectural revolution which is taking place during these last decades.

There is a very, very small percentage of good and human construction in the world today. The title of the exhibition upstairs is 'Architecture in Finland'. It represents, of course, only a small percentage of Finnish building activity. The civilised, cultural creation is too small in every country, and not only in my own country. I think that the percentage is the same in all the countries of Europe.

I think that probably Dr. Martin's words will go down in history as describing the way in which the activities of the architect should be pushed on the side of increasing the amount of minimum good, reasonably good, construction and planning for humanity—for more than 2 or 3 per cent per country.

The architectural revolution is still going on, but it is like all revolutions: it starts with enthusiasm and it stops with some sort of dictatorship. It runs out of the track. There is one good thing that we still have today; we have all over the world, maybe in Uruguay, maybe in Scandinavia, maybe in England, maybe in South Africa—in all these countries—well-organised groups of creative people calling themselves architects, with a new, real—what should I say?—direction for the world. Slowly, from being formal artists, they have moved over into a new field; today they are the *garde d'honneur*, the hard-fighting squadron for humanising technique in our time. With a client in Paris, a few days ago, I had a discussion about just such a simple thing as ventilation. He said, 'Technique *sans esprit* is the worst thing in the world'—which it is.

Let us see how we do this work. Are we doing it rightly? Let us take two poles. If I step down from New York Central Station, or a station in Chicago, and some of the young architects are there, the first question—if they do not know me—is, 'Are you old-fashioned or modern?' I have heard this question in all civilised languages and lastly in Portuguese, in Estoril. I think this is probably the most naïve but the most used formula—'Are you old-fashioned or modern?' If we look deeper into this question, we see just why it is nonsense and nothing more.

There are only two things in art: humanity or not. The mere form, some detail in itself does not create a good humanity. We have today enough of superficial and rather bad architecture which is modern. It would be hard to find any architect able to design a Gothic or a Georgian detail today.

Let us take some capital of entertainment—Hollywood, for instance. Of course, all the houses are modern. You can find very few houses which really give human beings the spirit of the real physical life.

Let us take the other pole. A few months ago an Indian architect went to snow-covered Finland—I think he was from Bombay or New Delhi—and he had a book in which he had written all the questions which are the most important in the building art. Sitting down, he asked the first thing, after saying 'How do you do?'—What is the module of this office?' I did not answer him, because I did not know that. One of my chief lieutenants was sitting on my right. He answered. He said, 'One millimetre or less.'

These are two poles which demonstrate first the pendulum of the most popular forms of discussion, and then this last one, this nonsense number two—the seeking of a module which should cover all the world. This represents at the same time the dictatorship which finishes the revolution, the slavery of human beings to technical futilities which in themselves do not contain any piece of real humanity.

How should we carry on our fight? In what way? What should be the real intercommunion between all the architects of the world, and what should we tell the people? I think we should go back to Dr. Martin's horizontal line. The Institute of Finnish Architects, a few days ago, left at the Secretariat General of the International Union of Architects in Paris, a suggestion that we should state the obstacles which keep the good product back, why so few cities are well planned, why so many good city plans are turned down, why there is so small a percentage of good housing, and why in our time we almost lack official buildings which are symbols of the social life, symbols of what may be called democracy—the building owned by everybody.

The reasons which really stop culture at the line of 2 per cent, 4 per cent or 5 per cent of the whole are, of course, deep and very difficult to analyse. That is the question of our time; it is a question of the deeper meaning of civilisation and culture, a question of the movement over from, let *young people look on you more as a reactionary, whereas the surviving high RIBA animals of the Thirties will applaud loudest at the ceremony. Time's revenges, time's revenges!*

As for the silly medal itself, you need not make any further studies. Le Corbusier, ever the fine gentleman, made the relevant inquiries 2–3 years ago to establish whether the medal was worth his trouble to accept. It actually turned out to be real gold. If there is no longer any free space among the jingling decorations on the front of your tailcoat, you can get rid of it by giving it to a doorman as a modest tip or even by slipping it in the collection box at some church service.

But I should have written more briefly, as I know that your incoming letters are always used, unopened, to light the fire. May fortune always shine upon you, Morton Shand.

Aalto's reply contained the line: "We are the last surviving soldiers of the Salvation Army from those years." He hoped that Shand would come to the award ceremony in London from April 8 to 12. It turned out, however, that his friend could not afford to leave his Cambridge home – the war and old age had finally ruined him.

Aalto's stay in London was rather strenuous, including as it did opening a large exhibition of Finnish architecture and attending a series of official lunches and dinners. Such burdens never irked him, however. After the festivities, he and Elissa were more than ready to accompany RIBA's vice-chairman J. Leslie Martin, who had presided over the ceremony, to his home in Cambridge. There he was also reunited with Shand over a bottle of excellent wine, "as behooves old friends". After returning home, Aalto sent Shand one of his new X leg chairs as a gift, a melancholy finishing touch to the tale of the two friends' diverging paths. Shand died soon after this meeting.

Martin was the new British associate on whom Aalto now concentrated. Martin came to Finland with his wife Sadie in 1961, and Aalto gave them his usual 'Homeric' reception. Alvar and Elissa again visited the Martins in Cambridge the following year, and were introduced to their neighbour Henry Moore. These frequent meetings were based on plans for mutual benefit. Aalto wished to recruit Martin, who was famous for his Royal Festival Hall in London, as the acoustics expert for his concert hall in Helsinki, and Martin was eager to find a suitable building assignment for Aalto in England. Unfortunately, all their efforts came to nothing. The Finlandia Hall's acoustics are what they are, and Cambridge had to do without a university building by Aalto.

Aalto did, however, obtain an assignment indirectly through Britain. A British-Finnish company manufacturing paper machines had sold one to the Pakistani Ministry of Industry for installation in Chittagong (Chandraghona) in what is now Bangladesh. The company had recommended Aalto as architect for the mill. This resulted in a meeting in London between Aalto and a Pakistani ministry official by the name of Khursheed Ali. The clients originally asked for complete plans for the entire industrial area, until Aalto calculated that his design fee would be $15,500. He wound up doing just the floor plans for the mill for $1,500. The Chittagong paper mill is one of the few buildings Aalto designed without visiting the site. Nor did he go to

186. Sir Leslie Martin, Alvar's new English friend.

the opening ceremony in 1951, for which he had reason to congratulate himself. If we are to believe his account, savages from the forest attacked and mowed down the entire company.

Brazil

In 1953, the Brazilian architects' association named Aalto, Le Corbusier, Ernesto Rogers, Max Bill, Josep Lluis Sert, and Lucio Costa members of the jury that was to choose the recipient of the Materazzo Prize at a large architects' conference in São Paulo. Tourists were a rarity in Brazil in those days, and to obtain visas Hugo Alvar Henrik Aalto, 54, as well as his wife Elsa Kaisa, 31, had to present medical certificates stating that they were neither alcoholics nor drug addicts.

The congress ran from January 17 to 24, 1954 – in the middle of summer. It was hot and rainy in São Paulo, and the programme of incessant official lunches and dinners was exhausting. The jury unanimously awarded the prize to Gropius, and he and Aalto were named honorary members of the Brazilian architects' association. Upon receiving this tribute, Aalto improvised a speech which vividly illustrated his basic approach to architecture. Brazilian architecture was widely criticized at the time for its excessive aestheticism and formalism. Aalto saw it in another light:

I am deeply impressed by your architecture as a whole. It is very interesting for me, being from a country in so many ways contrasting with Brazilian conditions, to notice that Brazilian architecture to a very large extent takes its motifs from the climate and special conditions of the country. I have never seen such a large interest to build houses so to say on a biological basis. The 'skin' of your houses has found its own forms which in deeper meaning seems to be to protect the human being from the pressure of the climate. This way Brazilian architecture can be understood as an important step toward the humanizing of the art of building. I think this is the right country to say discussions of only styles, modern or old-fashioned, are useless and bring people to some kind of 'makeup' or 'cosmetics' of architecture.

From São Paulo the Aaltos went on to Rio de Janeiro, where they rested for a week at the Copacabana Palace Hotel and socialized with Oscar Niemeyer. Elissa characterized him in a report to the office as "a charming person, although they have around 20 cats, 1 parrot, and 1 dog in their home". She also wrote that during a swim along the Copacabana Alvar had been knocked down by a giant wave, but had been saved by a lifeguard. He was taken to hospital with a dislocated shoulder, an injury that would frequently recur in less dramatic circumstances.

In an interview with a local newspaper, Aalto made some comments on Niemeyer's home that further developed his ideas about 'biological architecture':

187. Aalto and the donor's wife Jolanda Materazzo in São Paulo, 1954.

188. Gropius's speech upon receiving the Materazzo Prize in São Paulo, 1954.

189. Oscar Niemeyer's house near Rio de Janeiro. Note the house plan above the photograph. From the book *Oscar Niemeyer: Works in Progress*.

Talking with Lucio Costa, we started discussing flowers that cannot be transplanted and that are beautiful only in their own habitat. Oscar Niemeyer's house is such a flower. It must be seen in its own beautiful valley. It cannot be photographed, as its multidimensional forms call for an art that simultaneously captures the whole valley and the interior and exterior of the house. It is an exquisite flower which grows in an enchanted setting.

After returning home, Aalto wrote to Niemeyer:

I think very positively of the tropical flowers of your architecture. For me it represents a gay and sweet comparison to Corbu's often repeated words: La vie est difficile et l'architecture aussi (Life is hard and so is architecture). *It is very important to rail in our art on the right track.*

Aalto later had the good fortune to be represented in Brazil by a work of his own. When the Finnish Embassy in the new capital, Brasília, was being planned, he was asked to design two of its reception rooms and a bentwood wall sculpture.

The United States

We already know that Aalto had left the United States in December 1948 in utter panic upon hearing of Aino's critical condition. His attitude to that country remained distant throughout the '50s, marked by an aversion that resembled fear. The United States, after all, was linked with the agonizing turn his life had taken with Aino's death and his shipwrecked dream of Artek's global triumph.

Conversely, the United States also seemed to reject Aalto. The rivalry between Gropius and himself, between Bauhaus Rationalism and 'organic' architecture, that he had discussed when Harvard offered him a professorship, had ended in victory for the Bauhaus line. Gropius and Mies, closely followed by their American disciples, built geometric skyscrapers for American big business. The International Style dominated the market.

Aalto had no desire to go to the United States in order to play second fiddle. Despite MIT's generosity in keeping him on its directory as "absent on leave", and despite his friend Wurster's efforts in 1954 to bring him to teach at Berkeley, he wrote off any thoughts of continuous involvement with an American university. Some entirely unrelated concerns induced him to set foot upon American soil again, tentatively at first and supported by his young wife.

He first returned to the United States for a few days on the way home from Brazil in 1954, wanting to show Elissa what kind of city New York really was. Two years later he received a letter from his old friend Wallace K. Harrison, the Rockefellers' brother-in-law, who had helped Aalto build the Finnish pavilion in New York in 1939 (*The Decisive Years*, p. 172). Harrison now came up with a tempting offer concerning the future Lincoln Center in New York, for which he had been commissioned to develop plans. Would Aalto come over to the Plaza Hotel for a couple of weeks and help him draw up a plan for the area?

The temptation was strong, since Aalto at once optimistically assumed that one of the monumental buildings to be built, perhaps the opera or the theatre, would fall to him. In October 1956, he and Elissa spent ten pleasant days in New York as Wallace and Ellen Harrison's guests. The two men sketched together diligently at Harrison's office, and on returning Aalto wrote Harrison that he would be glad to continue on his own with some part of the project. Harrison sent a diplomatic reply. It started with thanks for "the inspiration that you were to us", but then continued: "In the meantime we are going to develop the plans from the point where we left them at the end of our wonderful meeting. The Corporation cannot assume any further obligations before we have raised funds for this project."

Only now did Aalto realize what was going on behind his back: Harrison would build the whole opera house on his own, just as, with the help of his relatives, he had built most of the Rockefeller Center between 1931 and 1940. All he had been looking for was the stimulation of Aalto's ingenuity and daring.

240

190. Wallace K. Harrison and Alvar Aalto in New York in the 1940s. Photo: Aino Aalto.

There were no problems with funding the project, as the Rockefellers had bought up the whole run-down neighbourhood in good time, and the value of the property was spectacularly on the rise.

Aalto took the episode in his stride, however. His work on the Lincoln Center opera house had inspired him to develop his vision of a large, asymmetrical auditorium with balconies forming an undulating plane. This vision he was able to bring out fresh and unused when he entered the Essen Opera competition in 1959. More important, his stay in New York had broken the evil spell: working in the United States was possible again.

Americans also seemed ready to revise their attitude toward Aalto. A major exhibition, *20th-Century Architecture*, arranged by the American Federation of Arts in Washington in spring 1959 and later shown at New York's Metropolitan Museum of Art and in other cities, was a significant turning point. It was based on a strict ranking order between the five older masters Wright, Gropius, Mies, Le Corbusier, Aalto and the younger masters, including Breuer, Harrison, Philip Johnson, Neutra, Eero Saarinen, Edward D. Stone, Buckminster Fuller, and the office of Skidmore, Owings & Merrill. In October that year, *Time* magazine published a long article on Aalto, saying that after the war, with the victory of Mies and the glass facade, Aalto seemed to have become "architecture's forgotten man", but that with his use of traditional materials and the unforgettable town hall in Säynätsalo, he had now become the most timely of all architects. The magazine quotes Eero Saarinen:

In the postwar decade Aalto seemed headed away from the mainstream of architecture – until now. The development of the last few years has proved him right. Architecture, while maintaining its gain in technology, is turning to Aalto's treatment of natural materials.

Such comments were welcome, of course, even though the emphasis on materials seemed to miss Aalto's main point. He could only resign himself to the impossibility of making himself understood. When John Burchard, his old friend from MIT, pestered him to contribute to the Daedalus journal's survey on architecture as a form of art, he finally replied with this telegram:

JUST UNABLE TO PRODUCE ENOUGH ARCHITECTURAL PHILOSOPHY YOU MAY PUBLISH THIS TELEGRAMLETTER AS A SUBSTITUTE STOP SIBELIUS SAID IF YOU PUBLISH THREE WORDS OF EXPLAINING MUSIC AT LEAST TWO WORDS ARE WRONG THIS MAY BE TRUE ALSO IN MY ARCHITECTURAL PHILOSOPHY STOP IN ORDINARY DISCUSSIONS IN RECENT DECADES THE IMITATION OF TRADITION HAS BEEN POINTED OUT AS MAIN ENEMY OF ART I THINK HOWEVER THE NUMBER ONE ENEMY IS MODERN FORMALISM WHERE INHUMAN ELEMENTS ARE DOMINATING STOP TRUE ARCHITECTURE AND THE REAL THING IS ONLY WHERE MAN STANDS IN CENTRE BEST REGARDS ALVAR.

With the resumption of contact with the United States, Aalto also began to spend more time with his American friends. In 1957 Wurster brought his whole family to Finland to meet Aalto. In 1958 Calder wrote to propose some kind of collaboration, and in 1959 James and Laura Sweeney visited Finland. He was also the object of an increasing flow of official honours, which, however, can be of no great interest to any but the person concerned. Suffice it to say that he went to the convention of the American Institute of Architects in Miami in 1963 to receive the country's highest architectural honour, the institute's gold medal. The following year Columbia University in New York awarded him an

191. Sandy and Louisa Calder flanking Maire Gullichsen and Alvar Aalto on a 1950 excursion to the Finnish lakeland.

192. George F. Kennan making Alvar Aalto an honorary member of the American Academy of Arts and Letters at a ceremony in Helsinki on August 12, 1968. Photo: Lehtikuva.

honorary doctorate, and in 1967 he received the newly established Thomas Jefferson Medal at Jefferson's home Monticello in Virginia. (The only previous recipient had been Mies.) In 1968 Aalto was made an honorary member of the American Academy of Arts and Letters. This was a particularly spectacular occasion. Since Aalto was unable to travel to the United States to receive the award owing to ill health, the academy's president George F. Kennan came to Helsinki and conferred the insignia on Aalto at a highly publicized ceremony at the U.S. Embassy.

Of more note is the fact that in the autumn of his life Aalto was able to carry out two new, though perhaps not fully successful, designs in the United States. The first was an office suite for the Institute of International Education (IIE) in New York. This rather complex assignment made him a frequent transatlantic flyer again; its background and implementation deserve a closer look.

In spring 1961 Aalto accompanied two directors of the Finnish department store Stockmann to the United States to study department stores in Chicago, Detroit, Pittsburgh, and New York, in preparation for the company's new building project in Helsinki. On this occasion he naturally contacted his old friend Edgar Kaufmann Jr., whose father had become a millionaire in the department store business. At that time Kaufmann spent weekends in his world-famous house Fallingwater at Bear Run, designed by Frank Lloyd Wright. During Aalto's visit, Kaufmann had what he thought an excellent idea. After all, Aalto had designed one of his greatest works, the Finnish pavilion at the New York World's Fair of 1939, in an ordinary, ready-made unit building, upon which Wright himself had declared: "Aalto is a genius!" Kaufmann had just donated a considerable part of his inherited wealth to a foundation that bore his parents' name. This foundation, intended to promote culture, would get off to a good start, he believed, if it gave the IIE, a specialized U.N. agency that trained teachers in developing countries, a headquarters worthy of its mission. This was obviously a cultural purpose, and the purchase of the top floor of the skyscraper his friend Wallace Harrison was building across the street from U.N. headquarters in New York was thus a justifiable expense. And if he should commission Aalto to turn this suite into an architectural masterpiece, both the foundation's cultural contribution and its prestige would, naturally, be enormously increased. He immediately asked Aalto's opinion.

For Aalto, the inquiry came at an opportune moment. Since Finland, as one of the countries defeated in World War II, had not been a member of the world organization when the U.N. headquarters was built, Aalto had not had the chance to design any of the meeting rooms in this new Tower of Babel. The work had gone instead to his friend Markelius and to several other less distinguished colleagues. Suddenly, here was a chance for revenge. Aalto promised to think about it.

In September 1961 Aalto and Kaufmann met at the Danieli Hotel in Venice for further discussions. The following spring Aalto sent a detailed description of a floor plan to Kaufmann. Within the shell of Harrison's building Aalto

193. Edgar Kaufmann Jr. receiving the Aalto family at Fallingwater, 1940. Photo: Aino Aalto.

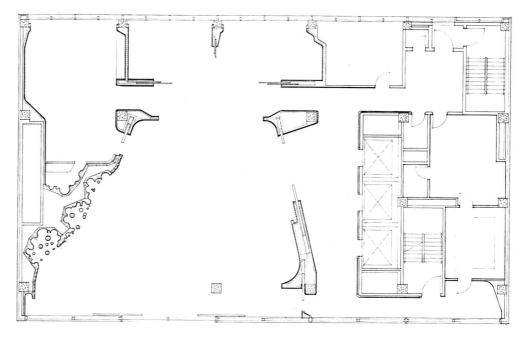

194. Plan from 1962 for the Kaufmann suite in New York, showing wood-covered walls with a gigantic 'forest sculpture' on the left side wall of the main room.

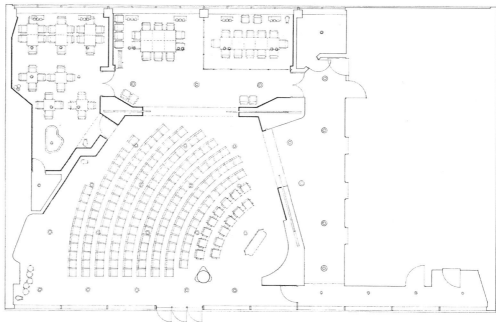

195. The Kaufmann suite as it was built in 1963–64. The sculpture has shrunk to a small, flat relief; the walls are whitewashed.

imagined a large reception and conference room, high and wide on the facade side and with a lower inner side connected with some smaller meeting rooms and offices. The reception room would be completely clad in wood; the floor would be smooth, of course, using various kinds of wood "in a flowing system"; the ceiling would have an undulating form; and the walls "made as a wooden sculpture, sometimes very deep, like a forest, sometimes with thinner profiles

245

and forms". For the work to have "the precision and quality of a musical instrument", the fittings should be built in Finland and shipped in parts to New York.

Aalto's description filled Kaufmann with joy: this was just the kind of thing he had hoped for. It came, therefore, as a great disappointment to him that the final result was so far from the original plan. We can trace the unfolding drama through a series of letters which also leave us feeling disappointed with Aalto for not wanting or being able to give free rein, just this once, to his lifelong inclination for abstract sculpture that he always stopped short of realizing completely.

There were two main obstacles to this. First, New York City's fire code turned out to permit only a very limited use of wood in interiors, and the material had to be chemically fireproofed. This treatment destroyed the natural play of colours in the wood. Second, Aalto had only limited time and strength. A giant sculpture of the kind he had envisioned would have taken months, perhaps years to complete. A glance at the works on his desk in the years 1962–64 shows why he could not make of the IIE suite the gem he had imagined. Projects such as the Helsinki centre plan and the Finlandia Hall, the Helsinki University of Technology main building, the Stockmann department store and Academic Bookshop in Helsinki, the Essen Opera, Rovaniemi City Hall, Seinäjoki Library and Theatre, Detmerode Church, the Enskilda Banken in Stockholm, the student club in Uppsala, the Kivenlahti master plan, and any number of minor assignments were on his desk simultaneously. How could he have devoted himself to the finer nuances involved in making a 'forest sculpture'?

When Kaufmann received the finished drawings in February 1963, he minced no words: *I am unable to accept the drawing. The wood sculpture wall in the white plaster interior will be abrupt in comparison to the firm crescendo of the all-wood interiors. Many spaces and details in the last drawings seem to me to look a bit neglected, a bit offhand. What we want is a small jewel.*

Aalto replied: *In my original sketch is a little too much wood, the whole thing getting too monotonous without counterpoint and cadence enough.* So much the better for Aalto if he managed to make himself believe this argument. Kaufmann let this pass, but came back with various complaints as work continued. In summer 1964, he wrote: *If we can only be average, why bother you? Time and money will be wasted if we get only routine details. Please protect our hopes!*

Aalto's reputation was so solidly established, however, that when the IIE facilities were officially opened in the presence of a large attendance, New York's most feared critic, Ada Louise Huxtable, wrote in the *New York Times: A landmark is gained . . . The most beautiful and distinguished interior that New York has seen in many years . . . Deceptive simplicity belies a most sophisticated style . . . Alvar Aalto still leads the field of design.*

Seeing the IIE suite today, however, one can hardly help feeling that Kaufmann was right. The rather flat, small relief with its fireproof bentwood rods is pretty enough, but it does not give the interior the unique, overpowering

246

196. Main wall of the Kaufmann room with simplified
relief. Photo: Ingervo.

artistic impact of Aalto's 'Northern Lights' wall in the 1939 World's Fair
pavilion.

In 1963, Aalto finally felt strong enough to face the painful past. He revisited
MIT and Boston. Together with Elissa, he made a brief visit to the school, talked
to the students, and finally saw his dormitory in its completed form. But when
the Kennedy family invited him to act as a consultant, along with some other
architectural celebrities, in the planning of the John F. Kennedy Memorial

Library in Boston, he begged off. He did not have the time to attend the meeting in Senator Edward Kennedy's home and sent a letter expressing his opinion: *The assignment should be given to an American architect.* The library was eventually designed by the Chinese architect I.M. Pei, who had by then become completely Americanized.

In autumn 1963, Aalto went to the annual congress of the Union Internationale des Architectes in Mexico City, lecturing at the opening of a large exhibition of modern Finnish architecture. The title of his lecture was "The Enemies of Architecture", and it began with well-calculated effect: *According to Karl Marx, there have been few wars in the world in which more than three enemies have fought one another. Architecture, however, has more than three thousand enemies simultaneously trying to conquer the field.*

The Giedions also were at the conference. Carola Giedion told me that after the congress the participants made a very interesting excursion to the Yucatán, but Aalto preferred swimming and sunning on the beach in Acapulco. "He was not interested in sightseeing."

During these years Aalto received a variety of offers or inquiries almost daily. Most were from students of architecture in remote countries who wished to train with him or from magazine editors, asking for material, but there were also a great variety of building proposals. Among these was one from a Finnish-American lady, Anne S. Lind, in Detroit, who in 1960 sent a site map and a hundred-dollar bill as a fee for drawings for a villa in Californian style (she intended to move to Santa Monica). The boys at the office set up an internal competition to see who could produce the most Californian design. Anne S. Lind was so delighted with the final plan that she sent Aalto a dozen embroidered handkerchiefs as a gratuity.

In 1964 Aalto received a letter from the Benedictine abbey of Mount Angel in Oregon, inquiring whether he would design a library for the monks. He told his secretary to turn down the request as politely as possible by replying that such an assignment could be negotiated only in a personal meeting – say, at the Hotel Eden au Lac in Zurich, where Aalto would be staying the following month. Imagine his surprise when at the appointed hour a tall monk in a magnificent white cowl approached him in the lobby of the luxury hotel and introduced himself as Father Barnabas from Mount Angel. Aalto always had a weakness for ecclesiastics, perhaps because of his own obsession with role playing. Despite his total lack of interest in religion, he had worked frequently and without problems with God's representatives on earth, and so it was to be once again. First, the two of them agreed how providential it was that Aalto lived in an area called Munkkiniemi (Monk's Cape!), where monks – perhaps even the Benedictines – must have lived once. They then turned to practical matters, including the question of the architect's fee. Here again they were in agreement, so upon returning home Aalto set out to fit a magnificent library onto the contour map given him. He harboured no great illusions about the likelihood of the project's being carried out, but the challenge interested him: the steeply sloping building site gave him the chance to produce a completely new variant of his previous libraries, which had all been built on level ground. He also made a beautiful model of the Mount Angel library, which was shown at the 1965 exhibition in the Palazzo Strozzi.

From his brief meeting with Father Barnabas, however, Aalto could have gained no idea who the man under the cowl had been before his calling took him to the abbey – and who he became again, in the 1980s, after leaving the abbey for unknown reasons. When I interviewed him in 1986, he was a

197. The Mount Angel library interior goes down three storeys from the main level. Photo: Morley Baer.

prosperous real estate agent, though he still had close ties with Providence and the True Order of the World. It cannot have been too difficult for him, in 1967, to find among his closest acquaintances the anonymous donor who suddenly made the project possible.

It was not easy to manage such a large construction project at such a distance. Aalto saw the site only once, in 1967, during his last visit to the United States, but as luck would have it, the Finnish-born architect Erik Vartiainen, who had studied at Berkeley, was working in Aalto's office at the time. Vartiainen agreed to act as site architect in Oregon, and an old MIT colleague, Vernon de Mars, a professor at Berkeley at the time, agreed to solve the attendant legal problems by taking nominal credit for the design. The library was dedicated in May 1970 in the presence of numerous invited guests (but in the absence of Aalto). The programme included a speech by the Abbot Primate of the Order of St. Benedict, who had come from Rome for the purpose, and a jazz concert by a friend of the abbey, Duke Ellington.

The Mount Angel Library is an unusually poetic Aalto work: it gave him the chance to expand on the theme of the 'library pit' that recurs in almost all of

198. The 'book pit', as designed by Aalto for the Rovaniemi Library in 1961. Photo: Rista.

his library designs from the Viipuri Library on. Sunk below the main floor level, the design gives the visitor the feeling that he is descending into the books' own world, which lies on a deeper level than the everyday world. Was it the proximity of the dramatic, roaring Pacific surf that inspired Aalto to apprehend the world of books as an endless ocean that invites the reader to descend into its depths?

The weakness of the Mount Angel library is that it was never subjected to the improvements and new ideas during actual construction that give Aalto's best work its incomparable quality. Vartiainen's anxious letters from the construction site went unanswered, and he had to solve the many problems that arose to the best of his ability. However skilfully he did so, he could not take responsibility for the radical redesign which might have made better use of the view from the acropolis site or given the details a richer modulation.

All the same, Aalto's faithful admirer Ada Louise Huxtable, who was present at the inauguration, wrote in the *New York Times* (May 13, 1970): *Aalto's architecture continues to teach basic truths about space, light and function. We can find the essential lessons here . . . principles that must be applied whatever new sociological role the architect defines for himself in a troubled world.*

Aalto's last visit to the United States in 1967 struck a melancholy note. It was the last time he met his old friends and colleagues William Wurster and Gardner Dayley, in San Francisco. Wurster had recently lost his wife and was confined to a wheelchair, suffering from severe Parkinson's disease. How remote seemed the happy days of the 1930s and '40s! Dayley was suffering from brain cancer and a few months later jumped to his death from the Golden Gate Bridge.

After returning to Finland, Aalto wrote to Wurster: *Dear Bill, what a wonderful thing it was to see you again . . . I met you in a wonderful spirit, which I am admiring,* (you are) *still the same chief of architecture in California and the USA. I was thinking about your words: WE ALL HAVE OUR TRAGEDIES, BUT STILL OUR LIFE AND WORK IS SERVING IN THE REAL HUMAN SENSE.*

The Academy of Finland:
the Bubble that Burst

The Academy of Finland, chartered by the Finnish Parliament on September 16, 1947, could have sprung forth out of Aalto's patriotic spirit and his obsession with Antiquity. Actually, though, he was not among those who dreamed up the Academy, or even among those cited as possible members at the time. With his reputation as an unreliable, protean character and radical critic of the Establishment, Aalto would certainly not have been welcome among the earnest souls who assumed responsibility for high culture in Finland.

The Academy of Finland was not born without a struggle and many curious twists of fate. Resistance to the project did not follow party lines; it had more to do with some individuals' well-founded doubts about the whole idea. The would-be academicians included two of my former teachers at the University of Helsinki: Eino Kaila, an internationally renowned professor of philosophy; and Onni Okkonen, a locally well-known professor of art history. Another aspirant was the rather traditional National Romantic sculptor Wäinö Aaltonen, who had decorated the Parliament chamber with allegorical nude figures.

At the height of the controversy, the pro-Academy faction invited top government officials and the press to Wäinö Aaltonen's studio to hear two lectures. Professor Okkonen declared, with all the authority of a specialist, that Wäinö Aaltonen was a genius on the same order as the greatest sculptors of the Italian Renaissance; founding an academy would thus turn Finland into a new Florence, shedding its light over the whole world. Professor Kaila then provided a rousing description of Classical Greece and the Athens of Pericles, which had had only one hundredth of Finland's population, but by investing generously in culture had become a beacon for mankind. Clearly, we need look no further for one of the main reasons for founding the Academy: the war, and with it the dream of a greater Finland, had ended in bitter disillusionment, and a new outlet had to be found for national ambitions. Whereas the more realistic of the defeated countries had pursued a course aimed at economic revanche, little

Finland sought, rather touchingly, to win honour and recognition as a cultural pioneer.

The official arguments in favour of the Academy were more matter-of-fact, of course. There was a risk that the leading Finnish scientists would emigrate if foreign countries could offer them better working conditions; creative talents needed to be able to concentrate on their work without being weighed down by teaching duties or financial worries; the ambitious should have a goal to strive for. A 1947 Act of Parliament set up a special committee charged with nominating worthy Academy candidates from among both scientists and artists. As with other nominations, the President of the Republic would have a certain freedom of choice in confirming the candidates. The Academy would have twelve members, to be addressed as "Mr. Academician" (the possibility of a woman's being elected was not even discussed), and the members' pay would be on a par with that of cabinet ministers. No joint projects were specified: each member would carry on with his work in his own field, and the members' common duties would be restricted to attending occasional meetings.

Under its longtime president, biologist A.I. Virtanen, the only Finnish scientist to have won a Nobel Prize, the Academy functioned to the satisfaction of the elect, at any rate. The public accepted it also: it lent a certain glamour to the grey reality of the Republic. It was always exciting to read, after one of the twelve academicians had been pensioned off at age 70, who had been nominated to replace him.

As for Aalto, the spectacular success he had enjoyed at home, and especially abroad, in the late 1940s could not be ignored for long. In autumn 1950, a committee of experts placed him at the head of the list submitted to the President for the next nomination. The incumbent, however, was none other than J.K. Paasikivi, whose enmity with Aalto's father (and, subsequently, with Aalto himself) was mentioned in part I of this biography (pp. 41–42). This antipathy was strong enough to induce Paasikivi to break all precedent by leaving the vacancy unfilled. In 1953 his suspicions of Aalto were confirmed by SAFA's refusal to cooperate with Jussi Lappi-Seppälä, whom the President had just appointed head of the National Board of Building. Paasikivi tantalized Aalto that year by awarding him the Commander's Cross of the Order of the Finnish Lion and inviting him to the annual Independence Day reception at the President's Palace, but withheld the Academy appointment. In response, Aalto ignored the invitation and refused the decoration. In his autobiography, Lappi-Seppälä gleefully writes that in 1954 the President summoned Aalto for a private talk, whereupon Aalto, convinced that his nomination had finally been accepted, sent for a case of champagne to celebrate. But during the talk, the President instead told him off for the architects' actions against the Board of Building. Aalto then declared that he refused to accept the Commander's Cross from the President.

In the end, however, it was Aalto who had the last laugh. The newspapers started commenting on the strange circumstance that the Finnish artist who enjoyed by far the highest international reputation was not good enough for the Finnish Academy. In April 1955, the irascible old man in the President's Palace bowed to the inevitable and made Aalto an academician, even though the struggle between SAFA and the Board of Building still smouldered.

For a scientist, an appointment to the Academy meant a rather radical change, as it required him to quit any professorship or other occupation in which he was engaged. For Aalto, work went on exactly as usual. *It's really only my mother who draws a sigh of relief,* he said when I congratulated him. *Now I'll have a pension when I'm old, just like my father.*

His academician's role fit him like a glove, and clearly contributed to his postwar transformation from puckish bohemian into stately gentleman. On excellent terms with his fellow academicians, he was elected president of the Academy in 1963. Aalto took his presidency as another spectacular role to play, another honour conferred upon him. In his plan for the new centre of Helsinki, he reserved the site just across from the Parliament House for the seat of the Academy.

The idyll, however, was more fragile than it seemed. Behind the scenes lurked a threat that suddenly leaped out into the open. One of the items submitted for President Urho Kekkonen's approval on December 11, 1964 was the nomination of artist Sam Vanni to the Academy. The President accepted the nomination, but dictated for the record a fateful statement which began:

The Academy of Finland, founded seventeen years ago, has not fulfilled the hopes attached to it as a college of academicians. It has not developed into a leading institution for scientific and artistic activity that could contribute with its authority to the development of our intellectual life. Its chances of generally advancing scientific research were small to begin with, and little use has been made of what chances there were.

199. Aalto with fellow academician Rolf Nevanlinna in Jyväskylä in the 1960s.

254

200. Urho Kekkonen and Alvar Aalto in confidential discussion during the President's state visit to France. Photo: Iris.

The President continued with the heretical thought that the contributions of the academicians would have been just as significant even if the Academy had never been founded, a claim that can hardly be refuted in Aalto's case, at any rate. He concluded:

I therefore consider that the Act on the Academy of Finland should be repealed and the resources thus released used more purposefully to promote scientific research and creative art.

The Academy's president took this rebuke as little short of a personal affront. Why had not the President come to him for a confidential talk between gentlemen, instead of unilaterally declaring that the Academy should be abolished? Were not he and Kekkonen old friends? Had he not accompanied the President on a state visit to France and showed him his newly-built Maison Carré? Had not Kekkonen and he met de Gaulle, the occasion on which Aalto had said: "I am also for a Europe of Europeans!"

Their mutual regard and understanding was not quite as deep as Aalto had imagined, however. The power-loving Kekkonen distrusted Aalto, whom he could never bring into a position of dependence, and likewise distrusted the whole Academy, which was too independent for his taste. True, Kekkonen had managed to infiltrate the Academy through his satellite, folklorist and cultural policymaker Kustaa Vilkuna, whom he had made an academician; but the first president of the Academy had disliked Kekkonen's Soviet policy, and compliance with the demands of realpolitik was generally low among this circle of freethinkers.

Only a week after the President's challenge, the Ministry of Education sent the Academy a request for a statement. The academicians' first reaction was to admit that the President was partly right. The Academy had had insufficient resources from the beginning, and its members had simply carried on with their earlier work. The Academy therefore needed greater resources to enable it to support junior researchers, set up its own institutions, and assume greater responsibility in establishing correct language usage, for example. The Academy also suggested that the number of members be increased to eighteen, to permit representation of a greater scientific and artistic range.

The daily press enthusiastically joined the fray, as did the cultural institutions – the Ministry of Education, the universities, the scientific societies. The president of the Academy, lacking experience with Finnish universities and having no idea of how the various institutions functioned, soon found himself skating on thin ice. In his plight, he turned to a fellow academician, Georg Henrik von Wright, who had been professor of philosophy at the University of Helsinki for many years, was a member of numerous learned societies, and also had international academic experience, having succeeded no less a man than Ludwig Wittgenstein as professor of philosophy at Cambridge. Aalto and von Wright had great sympathy for one another, and held similar views on many subjects. Both distrusted a one-sidedly technological civilization and strove to stand up for a classical humanist cultural heritage.

The debate over the Academy's fate raged for five years. The members soon realized that there could be no question of extending their power and that instead they must concentrate on warding off the threat of complete annihila-

201. Meeting of the Academy of Finland on January 15, 1968, the last during Alvar Aalto's presidency. Left to right: composer Joonas Kokkonen, philosopher G.H. von Wright, folklorist Martti Haavio, meteorologist Erik Palmén (acting chairman), author Mika Waltari, ethnologist Kustaa Vilkuna, Academy secretary Lauri Saxén, linguist Erkki Itkonen, and artist Sam Vanni. Aalto himself was ill at the time. Photo: Kaulia.

tion. In the need to find a compromise, the onus fell increasingly on von Wright, who worked out a judicious and realistic proposal together with fellow academician Rolf Nevanlinna, a mathematician. Von Wright, who was elected president of the Academy in 1968, led the last battle, and through tenacious discussions with Kekkonen managed, against all odds, to reach a solution that saved the erstwhile Olympians' face and preserved the institution's name as an honourable memory.

The first Academy of Finland was dissolved in 1969, but the old academicians were allowed to keep both their titles and their salaries, while new, purely honorary titles of academician, without financial benefits, continued to be awarded. Unfortunately, in its present form the honour seems to carry rather little weight. The public has small interest today in who has the right to call himself an academician. The Academy itself has turned into an administrative body that directs advanced research and distributes financial assistance among projects recommended by various science committees.

Aalto retired from the Academy in 1968 and from that time until his death received the pension on which his mother had set such store.

The Practical Foundation

Brilliant ideas are of course important elements of an architect's work. They can never come into their own, however, without the foundation provided by an office of skilful, like-minded associates. And an office cannot function without balancing its accounts. We should therefore take a look at these two aspects of Aalto's architectural achievement: the administrative machinery that made it possible for his visions to come true, and the cash flow that kept the machinery going.

What struck me most, during years of observation and in innumerable discussions with Aalto's assistants, was that all of them seem to have experienced their time with Aalto as a wonderfully exciting adventure. They did not try to hide the difficulties involved with such an exceptional employer. The master could be brutal and unreasonable on occasion, though such instances were rare. Worse were their irregular working hours and the financial insecurity that plagued the office for so long.

In principle, working hours were up to an employee: he could come and go as he pleased and make a note of his own hours. But since Aalto was often occupied with meetings and social duties during the day, it could happen that he did not have time for drawing until nine o'clock at night. He would then call the office manager and ask him to muster a suitable group for night duty. One of his long-term Swiss assistants, Paul Bernoulli, told me that this could go on for weeks on end. Around 1 a.m., the housekeeper, Alli, would serve hot chocolate in the studio, and around five the exhausted boys and girls could take taxis home, paid by the office. They could then sleep until evening. Needless to say, though, they had hardly any time for a private life. Bernoulli married a Finnish girl who delivered an ultimatum on the day after the wedding: "Either Aalto or me!" She won the battle but lost the war: after working for a while at another, more conventional office, Bernoulli returned to the old combination of self-torture and joy.

Aalto's foreign assistants saw their stay under this singular employer in the exotic North with all the particular sharpness of the stranger's eye and were adept at expressing their impressions in words. That is why I have quoted them

202. The most faithful
associate – Elissa Aalto, as seen
by her husband in the 1950s.

more frequently, in proportion to their numbers, than the more taciturn Finns.
In fact the majority of the architects at Aalto's office were always Finns; they also
made the most significant contributions as office managers and project directors. Many worked at the office for dozens of years: the most faithful member
of the team, Elsa Kaisa Mäkiniemi – Elissa Aalto – recently celebrated her
fortieth anniversary as an Aalto architect. Part IV of this biography will contain
a list of the employees who can be traced in the archives – some 350 all told –
with details of the dates they worked for the office.

Before the war the office usually had from ten to twelve employees; this
number approximately doubled during the busy postwar years. Most of the
assistants were fully trained architects, but there were some students, too. The
foreign contingent was already considerable in the 1930s, with Swiss and Italian
assistants especially favoured. The enormous number of people who wished to
work with Aalto was always a problem. His secretary spent much time answering,
in six languages, the hundreds of entreaties, frequently quite moving, that
poured in year after year from the United States, Japan, India, Turkey, Africa,
and virtually all the European countries. The fact that they were always
answered, in contrast to the many other letters received, shows Aalto's concern
for his young colleagues. After becoming an academician, Aalto called his
office "my academy". More appropriate would have been "my workshop", since

for hundreds of young architects, a stay of two or three years at Aalto's office was an important stepping-stone in their training, just as working in the studio of one of the great Renaissance masters once was for aspiring artists.

There was no waiting list. The surest way of being accepted was to be the son, daughter, or protégé of one of Aalto's old friends or colleagues. Harry Gullichsen's son Kristian, Werner Moser's son Lorenz, and Giedion's protégé Eduard Neuenschwander were obvious choices. Otherwise, chance was the determining factor. The young Danish architect Erhard Lorenz happened to meet Aalto on a beach in Munkkiniemi one summer's morning in 1938. In the course of a lively discussion, Lorenz followed Aalto to the studio and was told to sit down without further ado to make a clean copy of a sketch that was needed just then. By the end of the month, the secretary had placed him on the payroll.

The adventure of working for Aalto also entailed a certain insecurity about the location of one's job. Before the war, the office would sometimes rent rooms in a pilot's house on the lonely island of Hogland, in the middle of the Gulf of Finland, which had neither electricity nor shops. The year that the Viipuri Library was completed, the staff stayed in a seashore villa on the Karelian Isthmus. Lorenz Moser mentioned a summer in the 1950s when the office took a "working holiday" at Säynätsalo, drawing in the open air on desks they'd brought with them. In the winter, they worked at Aalto's home on Riihitie or in rented offices in the Engineers' Building Aalto had designed. Aalto's new office building in Munkkiniemi, completed in 1955, met an important need, since the practice had grown beyond the capacities of its office facilities.

203. Danish architect Erhard Lorenz has just met Aalto at the beach and is about to land an unexpected job.

204. The master's own office in the 1955 office building, with a curving window wall facing the courtyard theatre cavea. Photo: Havas.

But the firm's unconventional lifestyle continued. In an amusing interview in the Munich paper *Abendzeitung* (November 20, 1957), Aalto described his office as deep in the Finnish forest and said that he and his assistants skied to work every day. *Some thirty pairs of skis stand against the walls of the house, as my assistants usually take a tour of the woods at lunchtime.* If readers familiar with conditions in Munkkiniemi today have difficulty reconciling this description with reality, it does give an idea of how Aalto himself thought of his work setting. The interview continues with a story of how he would spend one day in Baghdad, where he was building a cultural centre, the next day in Gothenburg, where he was responsible for the city hall, the next in Paris, where he had designed a private villa, and the next in Lapland, where a "model town" was under construction. *But in summer I stay in my house on the island of Muuratsalo, where there is no telephone and where I can work completely undisturbed, between swims.* Small wonder that the impressed interviewer concludes: *And so, like child's play, the numerous buildings and monuments bearing the signature of Alvar Aalto go up throughout the world.*

The interviewer was closer to the truth than he probably realized. Joy, play and anarchic freedom set the basic tone of Aalto's working environment. *I had never seen anything like it in Switzerland,* said Lorenz Moser, who was, after all, a scion of one of the most successful Swiss families of architects. *When we drew, all thoughts of time and home vanished; betweentimes, we just enjoyed ourselves. I can never forget the creative power that radiated from Aalto and affected everyone, even the pure technicians. What impressed me particularly was that Aalto himself would always draw the most important plans.* Moser also observed with amazement that the master worked without any visible fatigue. *He used to sing while he drew. Usually they were naughty songs that made us laugh.*

Thus one of the basic elements of the working climate was established: total freedom from inhibiting conventions. The second basic ingredient was the high intellectual and cultural tone set by Aalto's constant allusions to Antiquity and to the Renaissance. These periods furnished him with comparisons and the substance of his reasoning. When he presented his plan for Jyväskylä University, he evoked not the Anglo-Saxon campus system but the Palatine. He called the area around Säynätsalo Town Hall the Acropolis, intended to model the squares of Ekenäs on those of Siena, and cited Venice's example in separating pedestrians from motor traffic in his town plans. It is thus hardly surprising that classical references comprised the mottos of most of the plans he sent to various competitions.

205. Conference with one of the working groups at the office. Left to right: Elissa Aalto, Heikki Tarkka, Heimo Paanajärvi, Alvar Aalto, Jaakko Suihkonen, Kale Leppänen, and Ilona Lehtinen. Photo: Lehtikuva.

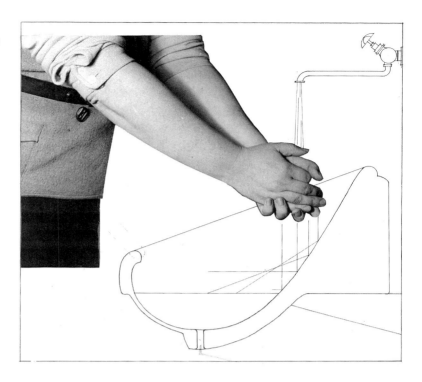

206. The splash-free wash-stand for the patients' rooms in Paimio Sanatorium, 1929.

Aalto's ability to involve his assistants in genuinely creative work contributed significantly to their positive attitude. They were never subjected to a dictatorship, but enjoyed a remarkable degree of independence. Karl Fleig testified to how willingly Aalto would listen to his assistants' suggestions. In Switzerland, Fleig had been accustomed to the employer's unilateral decisions: this is how it shall be done. Aalto said, *Muss gibt es nicht, das einzige was man muss ist sterben.* ("There is no must, the only thing one must do is die.") Instead, *Man könnte so und so machen.* ("This is how it could be done.") If one of his assistants came up with a suggestion that seemed sensible, it was given serious consideration.

Aalto never insisted on having the last word: this he left to time and its effect on the completed building. The realization that architecture is an inherently tentative activity, an effort to master both present and future construction problems with the greatest possible penetration and all available ingenuity, lay at the core of the philosophy that governed work at his office.

Aalto's career was in fact an unbroken series of innovations, discoveries, and experiments, which sometimes turned out to be valid, and occasionally – wholly in accord with the spirit of experiment – ended in failure. His successful innovations include his bentwood furniture, many lamp designs, barrel-shaped skylights sunk in the roof, the asymmetrical auditorium, the open V form, and a series of other solutions that have been generally adopted since. Other inventions have turned out to be technically workable, but unnecessary in practice. These include the splash-free washstand, the flexible stair, the triangular brick, and the single-level intersection for continuous traffic. Others required further improvements in order to work: the tiny balconies intended to provide the workers at Sunila with pleasant outdoor spaces were gradually developed into the atrium apartments of the Hansaviertel building in Berlin.

One of Aalto's favourite experiments was his effort to make an auditorium with flexible acoustics by building an 'echo chamber' with revolving sound reflectors above the main space. The experiment failed miserably in the Finlandia Hall in Helsinki, but seems to work in the empirically improved version of the Essen Opera.

Of course, completely failed experiments must also be cited. A rather minor one was the idea of building houses without foundations on boulders, as Aalto did with parts of his summer home in Muuratsalo. As a result, the doors and windows move with the seasons. Much more fateful was his previously mentioned decision to use Italian marble as cladding for his monumental

207. Early version of the Finlandia Hall's system for variable acoustics: cupped and visible ceiling elements that can be moved with a hoist in the ceiling. The solution probably would have worked better than the one that was built.

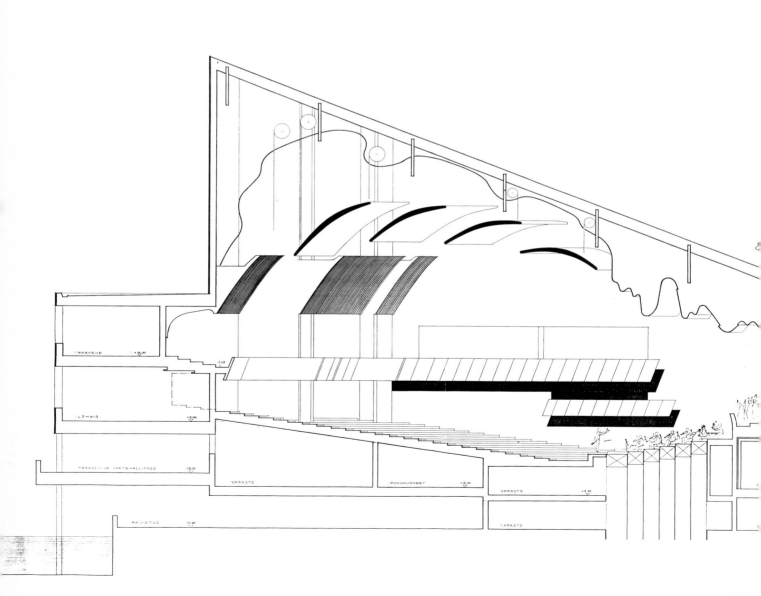

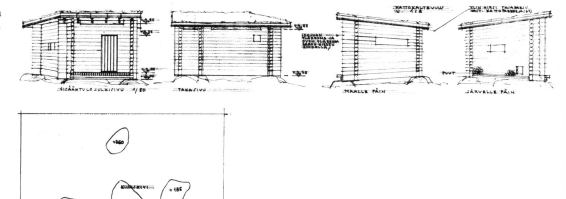

208. The Muuratsalo sauna is built on boulders with no foundation.

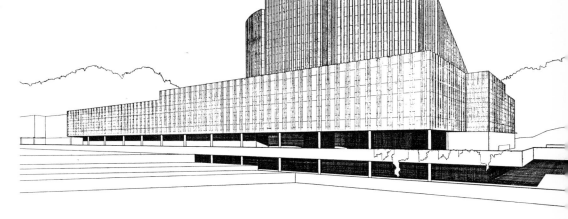

209. The 1964 version of the Finlandia Hall facade, with much more durable wall treatment than in the final version.

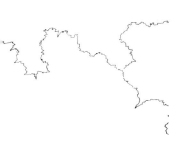

buildings. Aalto could have defended this by pointing out that the ancient Greeks made the same mistake when they built the temples on the Acropolis in the middle of the future metropolis Athens.

For consistency's sake, we should, perhaps, note another category of experiments: those which were never tested in practice. One of these was the magnificent plan for a sports hall in Vienna, its roof borne up by suspended steel cables. It is a pity, of course, that this dizzyingly beautiful building was never built, but one can hardly blame the city fathers for not daring to take the enormous financial risk the project involved. Aalto generally tried to limit the risk to clients by trying out only one or two new ideas at a time. When he built his own summer house at Muuratsalo, he was able to give himself free rein. He called it his 'Experimental House', and intended to carry out a whole series of radical innovations there, including heating the house in the winter with solar

265

energy or with a heat pump storing heat from the lake water, a completely untried idea at the time. (The tax authorities, however, put a stop to such extravagance.)

One thing is certain: few architectural practices have offered such an exciting and stimulating environment for young architects as Aalto's. And few have been so effective at implementing their directors' creative ideas.

I shall now turn to the no less important question of Aalto's attitude toward economic realities.

His nonchalance about money has been mentioned frequently and makes up a recurrent theme in many of the anecdotes about him. Typical are the stories of how he could keep a taxicab waiting, meter running, for days on end, or how he called home from Rome to ask what time it was – he never carried a watch. We also remember, from the second volume of this biography, the story of his Norwegian assistant Erling Bjertnaes about how at the Turku office the wages of his employees sometimes were paid. They might wait for weeks, but after winning a competition Aalto would come storming in, prize money in hand, pick up a few drawing pins, and fasten the cash to the door: "Here's money, boys!"

When the office moved to Helsinki in the 1930s, there was apparently little change. Paul Bernoulli praised Kaarina Saarnivaara, Aalto's secretary at the time: *She could imitate Aalto's signature wonderfully. Her* Alvar Aalto *could be found on many bills of exchange. She made sure that work could go on and that the assistants stayed on. Aalto would have gone bankrupt more than once without her.*

Bernoulli also gave a plausible, though only partial, explanation for the sorry state of Aalto's finances. The constant competitions took a great deal of working time, often for no reward. The office was continually working on projects that no one had commissioned or paid for. Aalto produced the many variants of the AA system, for example, entirely on his own initiative. Add to this his expensive lifestyle: he was constantly flying between continents and major cities, sometimes on business, but often on holidays or visits to friends. He stayed at the best hotels and spent his holidays in fashionable resorts. Back home, he frequented restaurants daily and always gave foreign guests a 'Homeric' reception, which included banquets as well as cab rides to Paimio, Imatra, Säynätsalo, and other Aalto sites. When he sent his assistants on business trips, they too received the royal treatment. When Kaarlo Leppänen went to Paris to confer with Aalto, he was put up at the Hôtel Crillon, and when Hans Slangus was sent to Stockholm he stayed at the Grand Hotel.

The reason was Aalto's unshakeable conviction that he was no worse a man than the councillors, bank directors, and rich heirs who were his clients and for whom this way of life was normal. Was he not making an equal, if not more important, contribution to society than they were? Why on earth should he be content to scrimp and save? The money supply would simply have to adapt; he would not.

The office received many major public and private commissions from the early 1950s on, from the National Pensions Institute and the University of Technology to expansion schemes for big industry. Thus the office declared an annual budget of 29,445,344 marks in 1953. Aalto listed 4,173,791 marks as 'travel expenses' (without verification), and 1,118,964 marks as 'entertainment'. For his summer villa, the 'Experimental House', he claimed a deduction of 2,956,955 marks. He considered the entire project to be a technical laboratory for the office, 'expenditure for earning income'.

In view of this, it is not altogether surprising that in 1955 the tax authorities decided to undertake a complete inspection of his income and expenditures from 1948 to 1953, and instructed all his clients, both public and private, to report all payments made to Aalto. He himself had a very vague idea of what he had received and spent, and the accounts, kept by several different people, were in chaos. After much wrangling with the revenue office, appeals to various assessment boards and so forth, he was eventually charged with having received 10,693,032 marks in unreported income and the Experimental House was declared an ordinary summer villa, resulting in a total sum due of 6,037,025 marks in back taxes. This was to be paid in a lump sum at the end of 1956. Only when a distrain officer arrived at Aalto's office with a notice of bankruptcy did he take action. He managed to obtain a large bank loan, but had to give temporary notice to almost half of his staff. This was a slap in the face for many employees, but Aalto was incurable: the very next year, upon receiving his fee for the apartment house in Berlin, he spent it on a Mercedes.

Thus we understand that he could not afford to be as indifferent about his income as he was about his expenses. The high opinion he had of the value of his work also prevented him from underselling himself. In fact he was capable of charging very high fees on occasion.

His rate scale was quite flexible. When Anni Argillander, his housekeeper of many years, left his service to get married, she received drawings for an attractive single-family home as a wedding present. When his favourite chauffeur, Alvi Hirvonen, asked Aalto to design a house for him, he was allowed to decide for himself how long he would let Aalto use his taxi for free to settle the account. When Aalto designed houses for fellow academician Joonas Kokkonen and for me, we received his personal contributions as gifts, but paid by the hour for the drawing work at the office. His eagerness to tackle a task that attracted him sometimes led him to work for clients who either would not or could not pay. Typical examples of this were his plans for the Kainula adult education institute in Kajaani (1956), a youth centre in Munkkiniemi (1958), and the Halonen Art Museum in Lapinlahti (1973).

His major public and private commissions were priced according to SAFA rates, based on construction costs. There were always unitemized expenses, however, – advance payments not deducted from the final invoice, charges for redesign necessitated by the client's changed requirements, travel expenses, per diems, etc. In most cases the mayors, office managers, industrialists, and

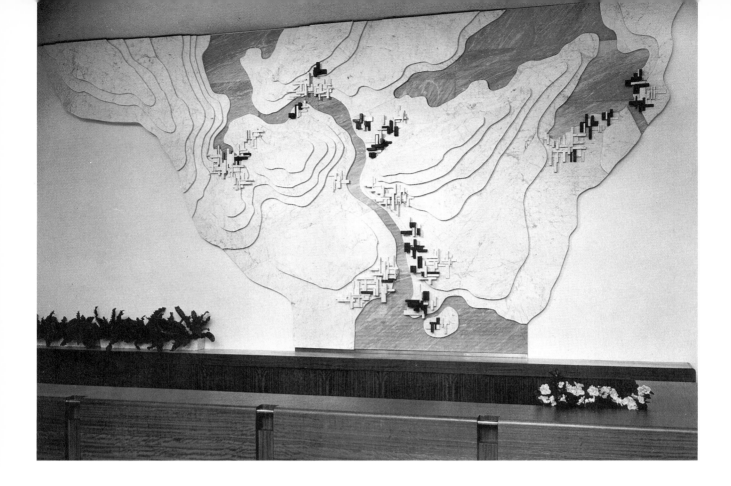

others who were Aalto's clients were such good personal friends of his that, as part of this transaction 'between gentlemen', they overlooked minor surprises in the bill. When Edgar Kaufmann discovered what his foundation owed for the design of the IIE suite in New York, he was astonished and wrote in a letter to Aalto that he thought it "well above American architects' rates", but concluded with the comment: "A difference of a few thousand dollars is not a sum that can spoil an old friendship such as ours." Göran Ehrnrooth, director of the Nordic Union Bank, responded similarly when he heard that Aalto's office had taken 2,276 and one half hours to design a small marble relief in the bank's head office.

Obviously Aalto took in significant sums of money during his long and successful career, but it all vanished as soon as it came. Apart from his home at Riihitie, the Muuratsalo summer house, the office building, and his share of Artek, he left little to his heirs when he died.

210. The fruit of 2,276 hours of architect's work: the marble relief depicting Kymenlaakso industries at the Nordic Union Bank trust department in Helsinki.

Nature, Man, Technology

Aalto entered the architectural debate of his day as "an untheoretical practitioner", a man who answered questions of ideology with the words: "What an
architect says does not mean a damned thing, what counts is what he does"
(lecture to the British Architectural Association, 1950). Yet he obviously built
up a very conscious architectural philosophy over time, formulated it clearly on
many occasions, and sought to apply it consistently in all his works. His
philosophy was based on a few key words that are worth considering.

The central terms were *nature, man,* and *technology.* The first of these is also the
vaguest: it has possessed extremely varied meanings at different times and been
used in different ways by different people. To Aalto, it primarily meant the
complicated system of checks and balances that supports biological life on

211. The ancient coordi-
nation of nature, man, and
technology. From Aalto's
sketchbook for his journey
to Greece, 1953.

earth – a system in which all the components affect one another, man being but one component. Nature is not unchangeable. Man can improve his living conditions, but he must do it in harmony with nature. "Nature is the symbol of freedom", Aalto said (in his 1949 lecture "National Planning and the Aims of Our Civilization"). He did not say, "Nature gives or guarantees freedom"; this would have gone too far. He meant that the increased freedom for which man strives can be achieved only within nature's biological system.

A disturbed balance in man's relationship with nature can very easily result in setbacks, which necessitate some very difficult choices. We see this on an individual level in the form of illness or poverty, but we can also see it on a larger, historical scale. The freedom of choice and well-being achieved incrementally over uncounted generations has often been reversed by backlashes or unexpected disasters brought about by disturbances in the great system of equilibrium.

Aalto believed that the extensive and precipitate changes in the environment wrought during his lifetime had put man in a predicament. Of course he saw these changes in such drastic terms partly because he had grown up in a country that was still fairly isolated. In a 1972 speech (at the Helsinki University of Technology) he said:

The first time I saw a car was when I moved to Jyväskylä as a schoolboy. The time of change in which we live is no older than that. The entire new technological and economic system has established itself during our lifetime. Everything has changed.

Aalto was far from alone in seeing the technological revolution as a challenge. Men like Ruskin, Camillo Sitte, and Frank Lloyd Wright, from countries with much more experience of the darker side of industrialism, had sounded the alarm and advocated a retreat to preindustrial conditions, a society based on handicraft, an agricultural economy, and 'soft' environmental values. Aalto's reaction was different. Too deeply marked by an inbred optimism and faith in the value of technology to reject it, he saw industrialism as the gateway to necessary social reform and a means of providing more tolerable living conditions for all. To his mind, the only problem lay in the indiscriminate haste with which the gifts of technology had been applied. He expressed this belief in a speech at the centenary of his old school, the Jyväskylä Lyceum, in 1958:

After having made the new, happier society possible, industrialism now threatens to suppress its own goal. I still cannot believe that technology and mechanization are intrinsically incompatible with civilization. There must be a way to humanize technology.

What, then, were the dangers Aalto saw in technological progress; which of its aspects did he wish to reform in order to steer developments into a better course? For our generation, worried about global overpopulation and problems of subsistence, seeing alarming signs of the total collapse of the ecological system, and living under the threat of a nuclear disaster, a study of Aalto's concerns is instructive. He was aware of air pollution, he took an interest in traffic planning, and sought acceptable forms of urbanization, but the issue he thought most pressing was the mental effect of industrialization on people, the

212. The master in the lap of nature. Photo: Göran Schildt.

robotization to which the pursuit of efficiency leads, the dissolution of individual personality and social ties for which the fashionable term is alienation. "We have escaped the material slum in our cities, but today we are building a psychological slum", he said in 1965 at an architects' seminar in Jyväskylä. He refused to accept this as a reasonable price to pay for material progress. He felt that the pernicious effects of technology could be avoided. Remedies for evils exist; an important one is a better architectural environment, for which he fought with inexhaustible energy.

We are already familiar with part of his recipe. It included fighting monotony and mediocrity with flexible standardization, building on a human scale, decentralizing cities, industries, and production methods. Above all, he insisted that nature's presence should always be felt. This is possible through the use of natural materials, often wood, for house construction and interior design. It can also be done by using forms, structures, and composition principles borrowed from nature. Most importantly, it can be done by blending living nature with the manmade environment in various ways. Aalto liked ornamental

213. The *Nemo Propheta* with
the Greek flag in the prow.
Photo: Göran Schildt.

plants indoors, windows with views of nature; he added gardens to his housing
where possible and included parks, recreation areas, and bodies of water in his
town plans. A Danish reporter wrote (*Berlingske Aftenavis,* August 28, 1957):

> *When one talks with Aalto about what a city should be like, he spreads his fingers: "Look
> at my hand. The fingers are housing areas, the area between is nature. Unfortunately that
> is not how it works in reality. Our cities stand on a foundation that cannot bear the new
> ways of life brought by industrialism. You should not be able to go from home to work
> without passing through a forest."*

This explains why Aalto paid special attention to recreational opportunities,
both athletic and cultural, in his town plans. Residential areas and places of
work have become so artificial these days that leisure activities are needed to
offset them. Here we might recall Aalto's exchange of views with Volkswagen
director Heinz Nordhoff.

So Aalto never tired of reminding his audiences that industrialization is not
an end in itself but a manmade tool to improve living conditions or, as he
preferred to say, to increase freedom. The quality of life, not the quantity of

manufactured goods or capital, must therefore be the decisive factor. As he put it in a lecture to the Vienna architects' association in 1955: *We say that we are the masters of our machines; in fact we are their slaves. This conflict constitutes one of the great problems of architecture, an increasingly pressing task we face now that we have left formalist Modernism behind . . . Architects today have a very clear challenge: to humanize the mechanical forms of matter.*

One of the questions Aalto would take up in his lectures in those years was: Who are the enemies of architecture? His answer: The client's various unilateral demands on the plan. The most frequent demand is that the building should bring in a profit for the owner, who tends to forget that "the most inhuman house is naturally also the cheapest" (Aalto's lecture at the Royal Institute of British Architects in 1957). Sometimes technical considerations, such as traffic flow, are allowed to determine the plan; sometimes aesthetic effect predominates. According to Aalto, considering various demands one at a time is useless when designing a building or an area. *Architectural planning involves simultaneously solving all functions, traffic, social issues, housing, production facilities, aesthetic and commercial problems, etc., so as to bind them into a coherent network,* he said (in a 1950 lecture at the tenth anniversary of the Finnish Cultural Foundation).

He discussed the forms this simultaneous problem-solving took in his own work in the famous essay "The Trout and the Stream", quoted in Part II of this biography (pp. 222–223). First he would familiarize himself thoroughly with all the substantial requirements of an assignment. This done, he would let them sink into his subconscious, where they encountered his previous architectural experience, values, and ingenuity. With luck, a solution would rise to the surface of consciousness in a form that was at once both completely rational and fully coordinated. Aalto associated this creative process both with nature, in which innumerable factors contribute to each individual solution, and with the origins of a work of art in the artist's psyche. He said (in a 1940 article for the American journal *Technological Review*):

In recent decades, architecture has often been compared with science, and some have tried to make its methods more scientific, even to transform it into pure science. But architecture is not a science. It is still the same great synthetic process, a conglomeration of thousands of significant human functions, and it will stay that way. Its essence can never become purely analytical. Architectural study always involves a moment of art and instinct. Its purpose is still to bring the world of matter into harmony with human life.

His contribution to an international architects' conference in Jyväskylä fifteen years later shows how firmly rooted this attitude was:

Modern society is characterized by an exaggerated worship of theory, an attitude that reflects the human predicament and insecurity. We think that in it we can find salvation from the threat of chaos. But we must realize that pure theory without feeling cannot create anything. You cannot set up series of methods applicable to the most varied circumstances; only intuition can help here. Let me put it this way: theory and methodology should form a basis for an intuitive working method. The question is not which dominates the other, but how to coordinate them. Method is not the antithesis of art, not its enemy but its prerequisite (summary from *Hufvudstadsbladet,* July 5, 1965).

After this sketch of Aalto's approach to nature, man, and technology, let us turn to a test case which shows his preferences especially clearly. It is reasonable to suppose that he sought to carry out his ideal to the fullest when he built his own summer villa on virgin soil, on the island of Muuratsalo, unfettered by the expectations of others.

The conventional Finnish wisdom is that the untouched wilderness is the ideal setting – the place to be. This preference may seem surprising, considering that the Finns have not suffered significantly from the damage done by industrialism to the environment in central Europe, leading its inhabitants to idealize the sublime Alps of Switzerland, the fjords of Norway, and the wild Highlands of Scotland since the nineteenth century. There must be other reasons for the lure of the wilds for the Finn; perhaps his newness to the plethora of human contact that the country's delayed urbanization so suddenly imposed. He seeks relief, in the quiet forests, from unaccustomed duties.

Aalto was an unusual Finn, sociable and urbane to the marrow. He discovered his ideal landscape in 1924 when he first visited Tuscany. Small towns climbing up hillsides, forests, vineyards, mountains, and the sea; a landscape marked through and through by its people, and the people marked by the landscape:

214. From Aalto's sketchbook: Fell scenery in Lapland, 1940s.

215. Aalto's 'wilderness studio' in Muuratsalo stands like a monastery on the rocky shore. Photo: Göran Schildt.

this was the homeland of humanism. Had he been an ordinary Finn, he would have built an outwardly primitive hut using logs from dry standing trees – a hideaway for a refugee from civilization – when he purchased a beautiful plot on Lake Päijänne in 1952. Instead, he built something reminiscent of a monastery on the forested cliffs of Mount Athos, a proud declaration of the presence of civilized man as the dominant element in nature.

We also find here a whole series of enigmatic references to man's gradual conquest of nature. What was the invention that first raised man above the level

216. The open hearth of the Muuratsalo courtyard. Photo: Martinero.

of the animals and gave him a new, more varied diet? It was the taming of fire, the building of a hearth where meat and vegetables could be cooked. The heart of the Muuratsalo home is a pit in the middle of the open courtyard, a fireplace to gather around for warmth in the chilly evenings. Other inventions, perhaps older than the art of building houses, include the terracing of land and staircases made of turf and cloven tree trunks. We have already come upon one such staircase in the courtyard pattern of Säynätsalo Town Hall. We find a

217. The atrium court of the Muuratsalo villa has characteristics of an inhabited ruin. Photo: Mäkinen.

NEMO PROPHETA IN PATRIA

similar one at the entrance to the summer house. The house itself is made of a material of a more civilized age – burnt brick, one of the first industrially made commodities, and one which has perfectly served man's urban needs for millennia. The attractively curved pantile roofing reinforces the civilized impression and brings a whiff of small-town idyll, of Jyväskylä at the turn of the century. According to the original plans the house was to include a studio wing, to allow Aalto and his assistants to combine work and good cheer during their summer visits.

The most evocative element of the house is the large atrium court, overgrown with ivy, which looks like a roofless ruin. Here the theme of the interaction between man and nature takes on a truly poetic dimension. It tells of how nature can take back what it has given man, yet leave him the possibility of moving back in among the fragments of his past, as Rome's inhabitants once did in the ruins of the former world capital.

Naturally, modern technology is also present at Muuratsalo, but only in the subordinate role Aalto wished to grant it. On the shore in its own small cove lies the speedboat *Nemo Propheta In Patria* (the name was given in the aftermath of the shattered-neon-sign episode in Säynätsalo). The boat's hull, reminiscent of an amphibian, is a typical Aalto 'invention'; its function, to bring none but friends to the master's Shangri-La. My own modest contribution was a flag for the *Nemo Propheta*'s prow. In it, the blue and white fields of the Finnish flag are reversed, making it a Greek flag.

277

Planning

Aalto's desire to give form to a complex environment that would be close to nature and conducive to man's personal development was expressed in all his work; no clear line can be drawn between his interior details, his building design, and his planning. Since he always saw his buildings as components of a natural or urban landscape, one might even say that planning was the primary task for him. Crucial though this aspect of his work was to Aalto himself, commentators and critics have given short shrift to it, perhaps because it is easier to write about furniture, glass objects, and buildings than about structuring landscapes. The main reason for their silence, however, is that virtually none of his major plans were carried out. In this chapter we shall take a look at some of his more ambitious planning projects in an attempt to determine why they met such a harsh fate.

The list of Aalto's master plans is long. It goes all the way back to the 1926 plan for the Sammallahti industrial estate, which was a young architect's spontaneous declaration of principles rather than an actual commission from the factory owner. The most impressive aspect of the plan is Aalto's social orientation, his preoccupation with workers' housing, allotment gardens, and recreation areas. Obviously he had been influenced as much by Sweden's social programmes as by Camillo Sitte's eye for the picturesque qualities of a landscape.

Aalto's truly pioneering contribution in planning came with his wartime regional plan for the Kokemäenjoki river valley, described in a previous chapter. The war years also saw his plan for the Oulu "river rapids centre", with an extension of the city's cultural centre placed on the islands that formed in the river's former rapids when a hydroelectric plant was built. The plan called for costly dredging and reclamation and was abandoned.

Immediately after the war, Aalto and three colleagues were commissioned to draw up a reconstruction plan for the decimated capital of Lapland. Aalto's town plan for Rovaniemi came to be called the "reindeer horn plan", partly because the main traffic arteries branched out through the town rather like the antlers of a reindeer, but also because one of the districts had hexagonal plots grouped around a branched street network.

The plan looked very attractive on paper, and architectural journals made it world-famous. The branched street network turned out to have unexpected

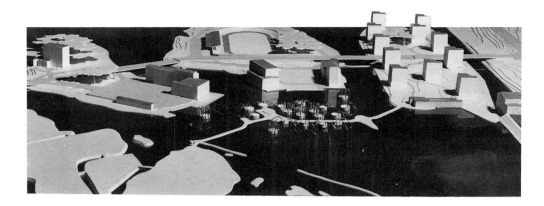

219. Oulu 'river rapids centre' in Aalto's 1941 competition entry.

220. 'Reindeer horn' plan for Rovaniemi, 1945.

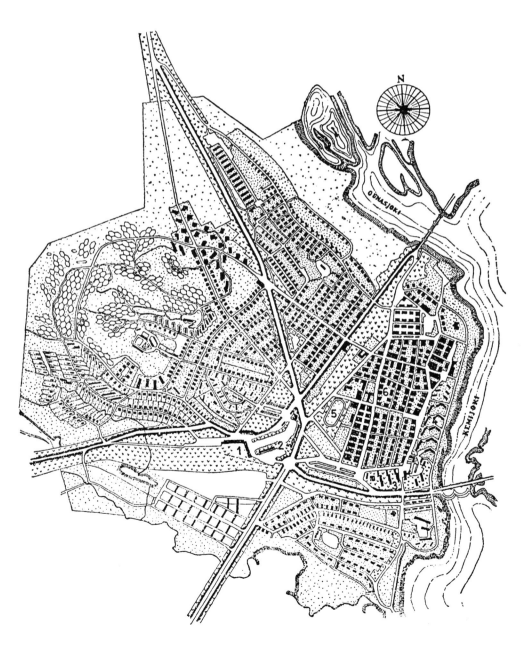

practical drawbacks, however. Part of the problem was that the housing built in Rovaniemi was not as varied as Aalto had hoped; in fact, it was confusingly uniform. But the many irregular branch streets also produced such a labyrinth that residents had difficulty in finding their own homes and taxi drivers never appeared at the addresses their customers specified. Moreover, Aalto's plan of a gradual return to growing wooden houses, which the inhabitants themselves could enlarge with new rooms, was unrealistic. The city, largely rebuilt according to the old plot subdivision with massive, identical concrete apartment blocks, much like other urban areas in the country, never became the intended model of town planning.

In 1951 Aalto was assigned to coordinate the planning of Lapland's river valleys, where large hydroelectric power projects were under preparation. The component plans he drew up for a series of municipalities, however, paid more attention to the livelihood of the local population and to sensitive environmental issues than to the power companies' plans for enormous dams and significant raising of the water level. Aalto recommended building many small power plants rather than a few large ones. He also drew up plans for an experimental village that applied modern farming methods in an effort to keep the rural population from leaving. All this was seen as uncalled for, and the commission was withdrawn in 1957.

Space does not permit a detailed discussion of the numerous and varied planning projects Aalto worked on from the 1940s on, from the industrial village of Säynätsalo, on an island of Lake Päijänne, to the Strömberg industrial and residential area in Vaasa, from the Otaniemi master plan to the Typpi Oy industrial estate in Oulu and the plan for Karhusaari island in Espoo, let alone the more specific plans such as those for the centres of Seinäjoki and Jyväskylä. I shall confine myself to a few brief comments on two planning assignments completed by Aalto for the state-owned pulp company Enso-Gutzeit. The first was for the market town of Imatra, the second for the industrial village of Summa between Kotka and Hamina. I shall go into more detail on three extensive and important assignments which show Aalto at his best as a planner: the master plans for the residential suburbs of Kivenlahti and Gammelbacka, and the plan for Helsinki's monumental centre.

The Imatra plan arose out of the territorial concessions made to Russia under the 1944 peace treaty. Aalto's assignment involved a narrow strip of land twenty miles long but only a couple of miles wide in places, sandwiched between the new border and Lake Saimaa. On this strip he had to combine three villages, relatively far apart, into a new, functional unit. Aalto believed he could turn this liability into an asset. He wanted to design "a unique forest town" in which the landscape would predominate over a series of small, individual clusters. New groups of houses would be built between the old villages, with the entire 'string of pearls' embedded in parklike forests and fields, and furnished with a new centre comprising a town hall, a theatre, a library, and so on. Unfortunately the town plan raised the price of the privately owned land between the villages, with

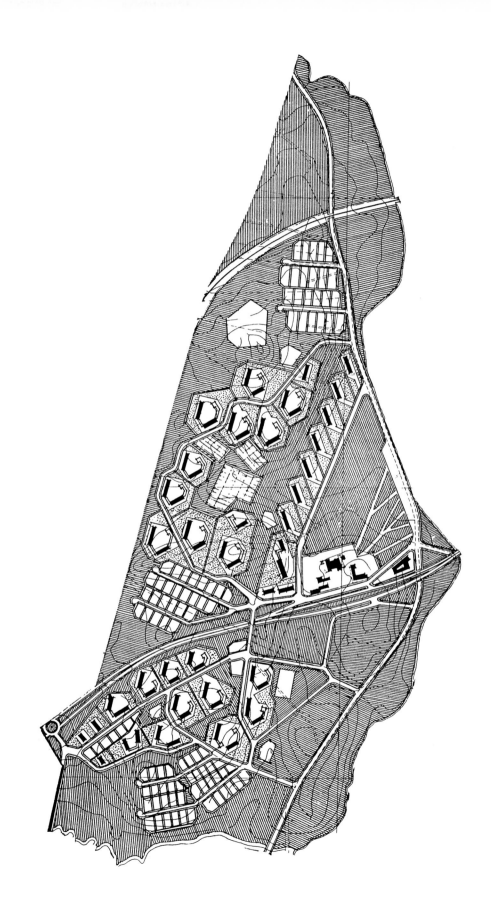

221. The middle section of
Aalto's town plan for Imatra,
with the administrative
complex left of centre.
The main goal is balanced
coordination between built-
up areas, arable land, and
undisturbed nature.

the result that new construction spread amorphously to the periphery. The new centre also turned out to be too expensive to build. Imatra today has little more to show than the remarkable church commonly known as Vuoksenniska Church, designed by Aalto and consecrated in 1958. Fortunately, the meticulous master plan for Imatra has been published in a typographically excellent book entitled *Imatra. Kauppalan yleisasemakaava* (Imatra master plan; 1957), with exhaustive comments in Finnish and English.

Another consequence of Finland's loss of territory at the end of the war was the decision to build a new industrial site, with a pulp mill and shipping port at Summa, not far from the new border. I remember Aalto's enthusiasm when he was commissioned in 1955 to design the mill and housing areas and to produce a master plan for the new village. He felt that here was his chance to surpass his famous prewar model industrial village Sunila.

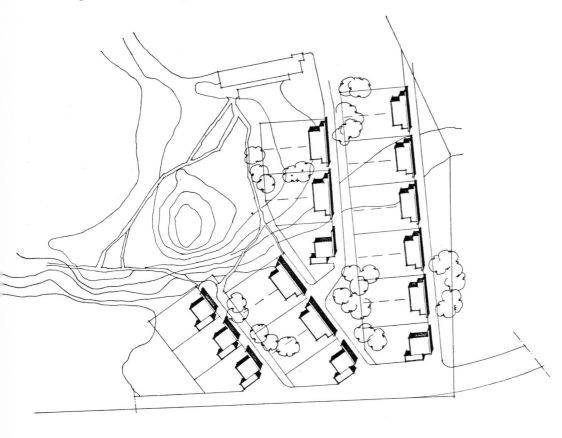

222. One of the Summa housing areas in a sparse pine forest with linking fences between houses. Plan and frontal view.

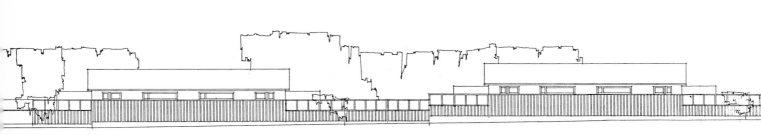

He was partly successful. The low wooden single-family homes forming sparsely built 'town blocks' linked by plank fences in the pine forest have none of the cheap look of earlier workers' housing and would be appropriate in any fashionable city suburb. The relatively modest, well-proportioned managers' villas, beautifully adapted to the steep slope of the site, show the relaxed mastery Aalto had reached in the 1950s. Taken as a whole, however, Summa is an uneven, half-finished work that lacks the coordination that was Sunila's stamp. In these years Aalto probably received too many other, more interesting assignments, and somewhat neglected the development of Summa.

Aalto's regional planning work culminated in two major designs of his last period – two visions which could have shown the way for those carrying out the still-continuing development of the south coast of Finland, but were undone by his contemporaries' complete blindness for environmental values.

To all appearances, both plans had auspicious beginnings. Finland was beginning to recover from the hardships of war and the heavy war reparations paid to Russia in the 1950s. A new optimism was expressed in a desire to build housing areas which would show the wealth, high quality of life, and aesthetic values Finns had been obliged to do without for so long. Around this period a series of model suburbs were built around Helsinki: Lauttasaari, Pohjois-Haaga, and of course the much-vaunted Tapiola. This last project, for which many of the country's best young architects were recruited, was sponsored by Heikki von Hertzen, who set up a foundation called Asuntosäätiö for the purpose. It may seem surprising that Aalto was not invited to take part, but this may have been due to a justifiable fear that he would have monopolized the task.

By 1964 the situation had changed. The restructuring of the former agricultural country into an urbanized society of industry and services had accelerated, bringing rural depopulation, and the pressure of migration on the capital region was growing. A handful of small, carefully crafted suburbs for the wealthy middle class no longer sufficed: housing and services had to be provided for 100,000, even 200,000, new residents near Helsinki. The actual forecasts were vague, but there was no mistaking the urgent need.

Asuntosäätiö had bought up the extensive lands of the old country manor of Stensvik on Espoonlahti bay, west of Helsinki; the city of Espoo owned the adjacent unbuilt lands. The municipality of Kirkkonummi owned the shore across the bay. Heikki von Hertzen saw his opportunity: backed by Aalto's authority, he hoped to persuade all of the landowners to join in a truly far-reaching venture, planning and building a fairly large town on either side of the bay and at its mouth.

Aalto was recruited in 1964 and immediately produced a magnificent preliminary sketch showing a bridge between the two shores. Soon, however, prospective clients started backing out, until only the city of Espoo and Asuntosäätiö were left, along with the construction companies Keskus-Sato and

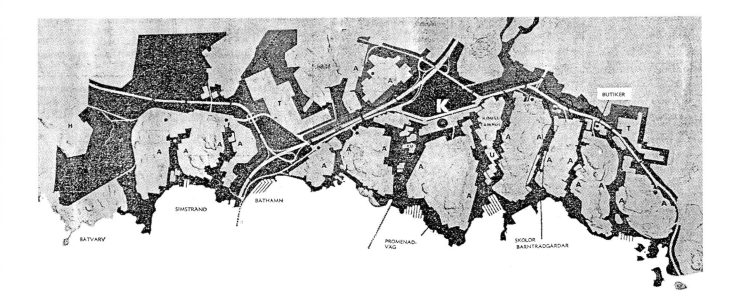

223. New satellite town
of Helsinki on southwest
coast as presented by Aalto
in 1966. The shaded areas
indicate parks and green-
belts between the built-up
hills. The curving coastline
below is reserved for
recreational purposes.

Polaris, both of which owned land on the east side of the bay. The plan presented by Aalto in 1966 was still labelled "Finland's largest single building project" in the press. It was to provide housing, jobs, and services for 85,000 people.

According to Aalto, the area had unique topographic potential. The headlands and bays of the meandering coast gave way inland to a series of forested cliffs at right angles to the shore, interspersed with fields and meadows. Aalto's plan left the entire shore free for public use, with beaches, numerous piers, and facilities for sailing boats and motorboats. The residential zone was placed further inland, with relatively compact groups of buildings on the ridge slopes, tower blocks at the top and lower buildings below, all with an unobstructed view of the sea or the green valleys. The traffic solution was exemplary. A comblike system of walkways led from the beach to all houses, while a similar system for automobile traffic, never intersecting with the walkways, extended to the houses from the highway beyond. Small- scale industry, car repair shops, etc., were placed in a separate zone near the main road which leads to Helsinki, ten miles away. The housing complexes had their own schools and small shops, and a common monumental centre – comprising offices, a conference centre, exhibition facilities, library, theatre, department store, and a church with seating for 1,600 – was placed near the shore northeast of Larsvik.

The reasons why this plan was ground down little by little until not even the details remained were many, but foremost seems to have been a change in the construction climate. A streamlining of traffic capacity, of prefabricated construction, of profitability, and of red tape was considered necessary. In his previously cited thesis, Jussi Rautsi enumerates some of the tangible obstacles that toppled Aalto's plan: 1) the sector plans for the road network were based purely on technical considerations with no reference to the overall plan, and consequently a large motorway without crossings cut the community in two; 2) the prefabricated technology chosen by the developers lent itself to rigid, massive buildings; 3) to financially justify the choice of technology, buildings had to be large; 4) the terms for building loans encouraged the construction of large quantities of inferior housing. We thus find here a combination of all the drawbacks Aalto had in mind when he condemned the type of analytical planning that treats individual factors in isolation.

As it was built, Kivenlahti has none of the special qualities Aalto had hoped to give it. The Elanto newspaper reported in 1972 on the appearance of Soukka, a part of the area which was 90 per cent complete at the time. Attempts had been made to liven up the monotonous lamellar blocks with red, blue, and green balconies; most of the housing was in ten-storey high-rises, with twelve-storey blocks in the business centre. The placing of Aalto's monumental centre was considered mistaken. It was actually never built: the use of an American method analysing the buying habits of driving customers and hence potential business for shopping centres, combined with forecasts of car density and the development of buying power, led to the conclusion that the commercial and administrative centre should be nearer the main traffic arteries – that is, next to the motorway. Rautsi remarks, aptly: "Aalto's premises, such as the importance of the topography and natural conditions arisen over millions of years, were thought to be little more than annoying planning problems giving rise to additional costs. The new generation of architects considered Otaniemi, which was under construction at the time the Kivenlahti plan was drafted, to be 'Stone Age planning'."

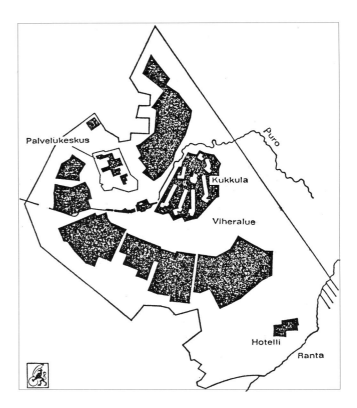

224. Gammelbacka district. The shaded areas stand for housing surrounded by lower-lying green zones. The framed area in the upper left-hand sector is a service centre. The sea begins at lower right. On the shore is a hotel.

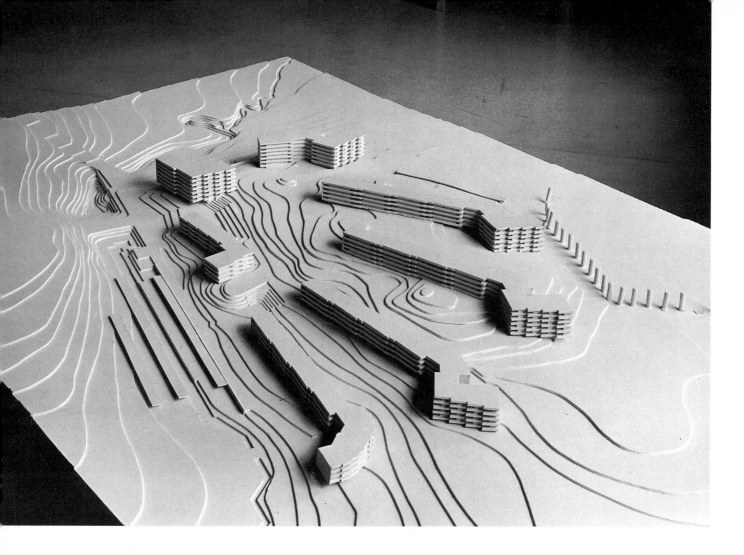

Away with the old reactionary's whims! Kivenlahti had a modern planner, known as Market Forces.

Aalto's second major planning achievement in the 1960s was Gammelbacka. Here the client was a large construction company called Haka, which owned an unbuilt area of 250 acres near the coast in the Porvoo rural municipality, only two miles from the small mediaeval town of Porvoo. The project involved construction of housing for some 10,000 people. As a condition for accepting the assignment, Aalto had demanded complete freedom to experiment with flexible standardization, the subject that had occupied his thoughts for so long. Haka accepted, and the authorities agreed to dispense with the current building standards.

The site topography was both like and unlike that of Kivenlahti. A round, forested hill stood a hundred yards from the shore. On top of the hill Aalto placed seven fairly tall buildings in a fan formation, providing all the apartments with a sea view. To compensate for the lack of ground contact, he gave each apartment a large atrium balcony that could, through glazing, be conver-

225. Model of variable standard housing for Gammelbacka. Photo: Hakli.

ted into a wintergarden. The blocks were sensitively placed in the uneven terrain, forming a vital core for the area. On the slope facing the shore he arranged smaller buildings in an arch pattern; a hotel was the only building that encroached on the shoreline. Green areas between the houses, walkways and roads kept separate, crèches, schools, sports halls, club buildings, and a shopping centre rounded off the plan.

All of the buildings were individually designed by Aalto to be built of standard concrete units put together in different ways. The idea was to make use of the experience gained during the first phase of construction at later stages, and thus make the experiment really worthwhile. *When construction is accompanied by sufficient variation and uses elements suited to the landscape, the conditions for an organically well-formed town are met,* Aalto wrote in a press release dated October 26, 1966.

It all seemed very promising. The only thing lacking was actual construction. This time only a small stone was enough to bring the whole project crashing down. On July 27, 1970 the municipal board wrote to Aalto to point out that his plan for Gammelbacka did not meet the requirements of the governmental housing loan system and the area would thus have to be built to current standards. Aalto replied that in that case Haka should take over the planning.

Kivenlahti and Gammelbacka today appear just as mediocre and depressing as most Finnish housing construction of the last thirty years. A number of questions spring to mind: Would the people who live here be happier, healthier, less alienated, if Aalto's plan had been followed? Or would the area merely have been taken over by wealthier, and therefore less alienated, people who could afford to pay higher prices for quality? One wonders, too, whether these two masterly 'examples', born of Aalto's humane intuition, would have had the effect of improving later Finnish planning.

The Heart of Free Finland

Three preconditions must be met for the making of an architectural master-piece. The first is a need for it within the society that must pay for it. The second is having the right person to do it. The third is that the timing should be right; in other words, psychological and economic factors must be favourable. These harsh preconditions set architecture apart from other forms of human endeavour. Van Gogh and Kafka could work in obscurity to create momentous works, works that no one wanted initially. Einstein in his study and Fleming in

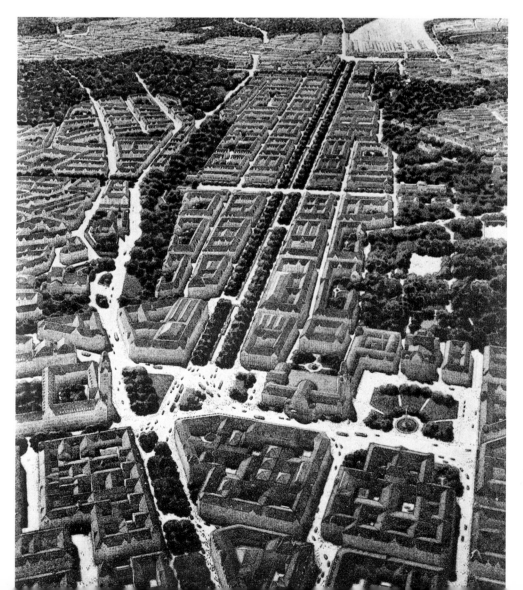

226. Eliel Saarinen's 1918 plan for the centre of Helsinki. The Railway Station, Rautatientori (Railway Square), and National Theatre in the lower part of the central swath are readily recognizable. The twisting, tree-lined stretch beginning at the bottom edge is present-day Mannerheimintie. The ruler-straight street planted with trees is the Avenue of Freedom, intended to run across the reclaimed Töölö Bay.

his laboratory made discoveries that much later would change the world. The architect's consolation is that his work is more durable than that of other creative artists. The problem lies in knowing how to guide it through the eye of the needle of the three preconditions.

When Aalto was asked by the Helsinki City Council, in August 1959, to work out a plan for the new centre of the city, the prospects for a happy end seemed unusually favourable.

As for the need for such a plan, it had had an unusually long time to develop. Its history is briefly as follows. Back in 1918, Eliel Saarinen had laid out a grandiose plan to extend the old centre of Helsinki, the Senate Square designed by Carl Ludwig Engel during the early years of Russian rule. Saarinen's plan called for an Avenue of Freedom (also called King's Avenue), 100 yards wide and modelled on the Champs Elysées of Paris, which would cross the filled-in Töölö Bay from the north and meet the existing streets Esplanadi and Bulevardi in an area which was increasingly becoming the locus of city life. The Parliament House, inaugurated in 1931, further accentuated the shift to a previously peripheral area, the site of the chaotic railway yard built during the Czarist period. The view from the Parliament steps consisted of endless rows of parked railroad cars and dilapidated warehouses and was increasingly unacceptable. New plans for a stately centre were commissioned, and the question of whether Töölö Bay should be reclaimed became increasingly crucial. This former sea inlet, which had already been cut off by the embankment leading up to Saarinen's magnificent railway station, met with no favour from Oiva Kallio, who ruthlessly erased it in his 1924 centre plan, based on the same metropolitan ambitions as Saarinen's vision. A new centre plan, submitted by the Helsinki City Planning Office in 1932, called for partial preservation of the bay.

The war put a stop to further developments, but in 1948 Yrjö Lindegren and Erik Kråkström won a competition for a new centre plan. They managed to preserve the idyllic bay by turning Saarinen's Avenue of Freedom into a simple traffic ramp along the side of the railway. Typically for the spirit of the times, motor traffic from the new Vapaudenkatu (Freedom Street) and from Mannerheimintie was to converge right at the foot of the Parliament steps, in proof of Finland's prosperity and modernity.

Too many diverging interests, however, turned the Lindegren-Kråkström plan into a Gordian knot, which the city fathers called upon Aalto to sever with a brisk blow worthy of Alexander.

Aalto's credentials were unquestionable. One might even say that all his previous work had been systematic preparation for this assignment. The patriotic feeling needed to correctly design the new heart of the capital – the symbol of free Finland – he had clearly shown that he possessed in his two national pavilions at World's Fairs, and in other works. His ability to create the kind of monumental buildings required for a fine city centre was well documented, as was his commitment to social justice and his generally modern

227. Alvar Aalto at the apex of his career, in front of the just completed Finlandia Hall. Photo Göran Schildt.

approach. And, since he had been on the jury for the 1948 competition, he also happened to be very well versed in the project's special problems. An article he had written in 1954 for the ninetieth anniversary issue of *Hufvudstadsbladet* points up with astounding clarity how well-prepared he was to solve the problems of Helsinki's centre:

Helsinki has one peculiarity: its open central areas. The area around Töölö Bay, continuing with the railway yard, is in itself an invaluable reserve that makes it possible for the city's inner heart to grow, in contrast to most big cities. All cities grow both outward and inward. Usually there is not enough space for the latter, but Helsinki has this possibility.

To put it plainly: for the city-dweller standing on Mannerheimintie near Parliament House, the city opens up as a crater, having not only growth potential in the centre but also a face of its own with extensive views, an unusually valuable asset for a city the size of Helsinki. This face is not yet complete, however. A few landmarks exist: Töölö Bay; Mannerheimintie successfully running along a cornice; the pyramidal rise of Kallio district to Kallio Church, the city's Sacré Coeur; the Stadium and Eläintarha park, etc. But these are fragments of the impressive centre that can be achieved by erecting new public buildings around Töölö Bay while preserving and enlarging the park system.

To do this successfully is the challenge for our generation, a challenge worth almost any effort. It is here, around this problem, that we will ultimately see whether our city has enough surviving or acquired culture to leave a worthy legacy. We must remember that since the completion of Senate Square, the face of Helsinki at the time, no effective grouping of public buildings has been achieved, no unity, no real heart has been built for the modern big city.

The threat is an amorphous blend of public and commercial buildings with housing, forming a city organism reminiscent of the American Main Street town, Mr. Babbitt's petty bourgeois ideal of building complexes. Pleasant surroundings, however, can only be made by a distinct separation of functions, apart from the fact that the cultural impulse spurring man to do great deeds and create harmony between groups of people can arise only if order and the rhythm of life coincide in a limpid architectural milieu.

228. Aalto's centre plan as he presented it in 1961.
A: Rautatientori.
B: Parliament House.
C: National Museum.
D: 'Forum Triangulum'.
E: Concert Hall.
F: Opera.
G: Töölö Bay.
H: The new Avenue of Freedom.

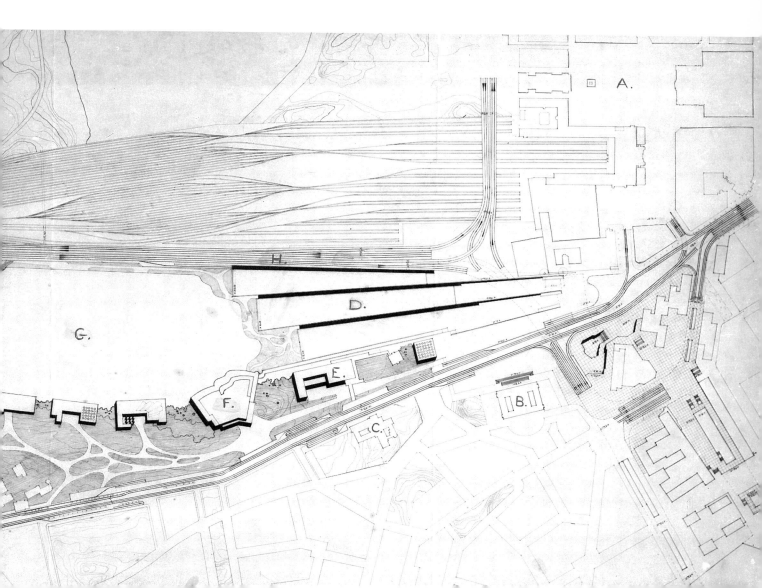

That Aalto was the right man for the job was thus undeniable. The timing also seemed favourable. He worked for over a year on the great plan with a large team of assistants. The Swedish traffic experts Bo Hertzman-Ericson and P.O. Klevemark, whom he had consulted for the Drottningstorget project in Gothenburg, helped him to find both elegant and effective solutions to the highly complex technical basis of his plan, consisting of grade-separated incoming, outgoing, and transit motor and pedestrian traffic.

An enormous model of the whole plan was built and placed on display in the City Hall's auditorium. On March 22, 1961, together with City Council chair-

229. Model of the centre of Helsinki exhibited at the City Hall's assembly hall. From Vapaudenkatu at the left, the series of cultural buildings on the opposite shore of Töölö Bay looms like a mirage of Venice. Photo: Ingervo.

230. Aalto presents the centre model to President and Mrs. Kekkonen, curator of the Ateneum Art Museum Aune Lindström, publisher Heikki Reenpää, and others. Photo: Lehtikuva.

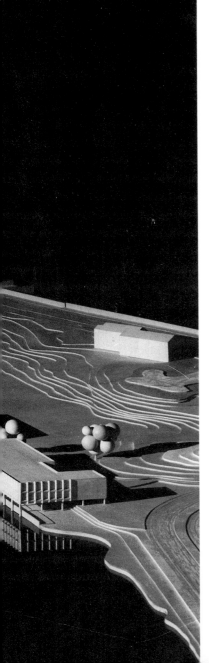

man Teuvo Aura and Lord Mayor Lauri Aho, chairman of the centre plan committee, Aalto presented the model to President Kekkonen, Speaker of Parliament Fagerholm, Prime Minister Sukselainen, and a distinguished gathering of invited guests.

There is some justification for saying that this was the culmination of Aalto's architectural career. He was livelier, wittier, and more elegant than ever. All those who attended experienced it as a historic occasion. The reaction was overwhelming. The newspapers' admiration knew no bounds. Everyone had been given more than they had ever dreamed of: Finland got a Forum

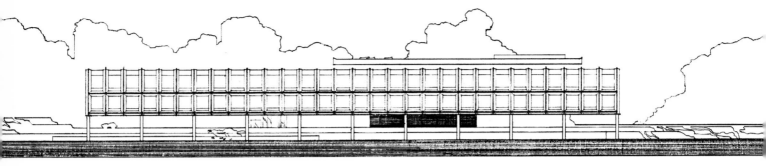

Triangulum (later known as Terassitori, or Terrace Square), opening its arms to embrace the whole country; the arts received a series of buildings rising from the waters of Töölö Bay like the palaces lining the Canal Grande in Venice; the railways had a new goods station out in Pasila to compensate for the area taken over by the centre plan; motorists had a striking new street, Vapaudenkatu, following the railway embankment, as well as parking for thousands of cars under the deck of the triangular forum; and nature lovers had a greenbelt of parks extending from Marshal Mannerheim's equestrian statue all the way to the deep forests inland. When the plan was discussed in the City Council, it turned out that none of the parties, left, right, or centre, had any objections. On October 25, 1961, the City Council unanimously approved Aalto's plan as a basis for further development by the various municipal boards and planning offices.

This set the rats loose to gnaw at the plan's foundation. The boards first targeted the monumental buildings for criticism. Aalto had placed some ten of them in a row, including a building for the Academy of Finland, a concert hall, an opera or theatre, the main city library, a city museum, and a central art museum, together forming a comprehensive cultural centre. But perhaps their bayside placing was not such a good idea? Would they not encroach on the central park, and give rise to annoying traffic problems? Aalto had expressly stated that Töölö Bay should not become "a false idyll, a Karelian starflower in the midst of the city". He thought it particularly important here that culture should be integrated with nature, man with the landscape, an attitude that was foreign to Nordic wilderness romantics.

The following target of attack was the Terrace Square, which many thought too dreary, as it did not correspond to the conventional idea of a square as an outdoor space enclosed by facades. As we already know, Aalto saw the centre of Helsinki as a kind of crater landscape. He pointed out when presenting his plan that he was aiming at "the opposite of the enclosed square, a space in which the city structure itself dominates the form". Terrace Square resembles Venice's Piazzetta, wide open to the quays, churches, and palaces surrounding the lagoon.

231. Aalto included a magnificent white marble Museum of Architecture on Töölö Bay in his plan for the new centre of Helsinki.

The most dangerous opposition, however, began to brew in the City Traffic Planning Division. Aalto had already clashed with this body by categorically condemning a plan made by the division experts for another important intersection in the city centre, the one bounded by the President's Palace, the Main Guard, and the Katajanokka canal. Experts advocated filling in the canal and building a 'traffic machine' on two levels with curving roadways, which would have completely spoiled the milieu according to Aalto. His victory in this controversy, backed by newspaper debate and foreign experts, was probably at the root of the stubborn campaign that the city traffic planners now mounted to discredit his centre plan. Their highly critical comments, and the amendments proposed by the newly established committee for the future metro, did not dampen the City Council's enthusiasm, however; in November 1966 it directed that Aalto's plan should be implemented in full, including the monumental buildings along Töölö Bay. The City Planning Office was expressly ordered to start developing the plan. The matter seemed closed, and the newspapers proclaimed on their front pages: "Helsinki To Have New Face For Centuries".

What happened? After three years of toil, the City Planning Office presented three alternatives for the centre. The first two followed Aalto's plan, but in a way intended to demonstrate its total unsuitability. The third alternative, drawn up by a city official by the name of Kalevi Hietanen, Aalto's hitherto unnamed

232. The Hietanen group's alternative plan for the centre of Helsinki. Railway Station on the right, Töölö Bay in the upper left-hand corner. Helsingin Sanomat, November 14, 1969.

principal adversary, was now splashed over all the front pages. Hietanen had removed the buildings lining the bay, replacing them with a 'multipurpose aggregate' on the site of Terrace Square. The bus station, which Aalto had placed on the edges of the Kamppi area, was now on a deck above the railway platforms, also providing parking for 2,000 cars. The arguments in favour of the project were dictated partly by economic considerations and partly by traffic-planning needs. The model for the Hietanen project resembled a gigantic factory area rather than a city centre, no disadvantage in the eyes of the newly awakened radicals. The headlines now read: "Aalto Plan Scrapped" and "Terrace Square Has No Function". On the inside pages, however, a sober observer such as Pekka Tarkka, cultural editor of *Helsingin Sanomat*, could still defy the tidal wave of the young revolt (November 9, 1969):

The opportunity opened up by Aalto's plan is architecturally unique. In some ways it is old-fashioned, magnificently National Romantic, and individualistic. Its organic emphasis is rooted in the creative individual, not the functional community. If carried out, however, it would be a work of art that all could call their own.

I want to experience the centre of Helsinki not only as a functional environment but as environmental art, as part of Aalto's grand image of Finland. I want to experience the fan of Terrace Square, opening out towards Finland, toward Tuusula, Päijänne, Rovaniemi. I want to come in by train or by car through the second city of Pasila, glide from the north towards the country's heart, and merge dynamically with the space and spaciousness that can be achieved with Aalto's plan.

This attitude to the architectural environment was naturally difficult to reconcile with the Marxist theology being preached more and more loudly at the time. A debate on the centre plan, arranged in February 1970 by the Society of Architecture for all interested parties, was illuminating. The main defender of Aalto's plan was Professor Ola Hansson, who stressed its strong grip on the spatial sequence Terrace Square–Töölö Bay: *One might say that the townscape around the strange empty space of the goods station in the heart of the city has been given a real identity for the first time, a face of its own, making it an important part of the nucleus of the capital region.* According to a summary of the proceedings in *Helsingin Sanomat* the next day, *Hietanen had no trouble in refuting this aesthetic formalism.* Deputy Mayor Alanen suggested that the term 'monumental centre' should not be used. *Monumentality cannot be an end. The question is how to meet real needs.*

A group of young radicals headed by the leftist student Asko Salokorpi agreed. He attacked both Aalto and Hietanen for being "lackeys of wealthy car owners". He expressed surprise at Aalto's use of the phrase "a new centre for democratic Finland", when his plan was so obviously undemocratic. The least one could ask was that the cultural buildings should be placed in the city outskirts, where the working classes lived.

The city fathers refused to be intimidated by either their own obstinate, technology-obsessed officials or by the arguments of the young revolutionaries. They asked Aalto to work out a new centre plan combining the merits of the first with the valid considerations advanced by critics. Aalto obediently sat down to

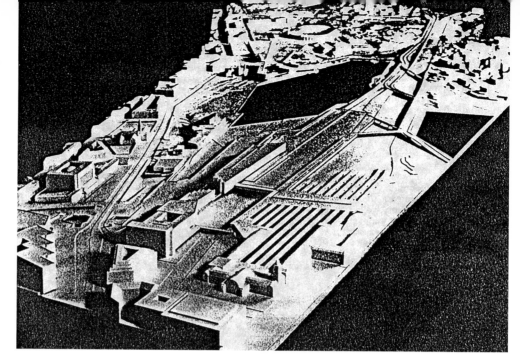

233. Aalto's reworked centre plan from 1973, with a traffic area next to the Railway Station and a watered-down Terrace Square flanked by the cultural buildings moved from the bay shore.

work again, for he was basically a man of reconciliation and balanced synthesis. His second plan, presented in early 1973, did away with the monumental buildings on the bay ("They can always be built later, when the climate of opinion has shifted", he confided to me). As we shall see in the next chapter, propitious circumstances had already permitted him to carry out a fragment of his plan – the concert and congress building that later came to be known as the Finlandia Hall. He now reserved a plot at the north end of the bay for the future opera house. He retained Terrace Square in somewhat reduced format, with a supporting length of buildings along its east side. He also introduced new motifs, including a 'traffic square' next to the railway station, where long-distance coach lines, railway, and metro would meet – obviously a concession to Hietanen's ideas. The plan was well-balanced, but there was no help for the fact that some of the brilliance of the original was gone.

For all the City Council's and Aalto's valiant efforts, however, the plan ran into ever stronger opposition. Soon the newly organized environmentalists joined the fray. They looked on cars not as the storm troops of capitalism but as dangerous sources of atmospheric poisons. They also disliked the idea of Vapaudenkatu spoiling the greenbelt along the eastern shore of Töölö Bay. Why build a new access road to the centre at all? Kaj Nyman, chairman of the Society for Social Planning, declared dogmatically (in *Helsingin Sanomat*, September 29, 1978) that new arteries such as Vapaudenkatu could only increase the pressure of traffic on the centre. According to this reasoning, any improvement in traffic communications was thus obviously harmful. The environmentalists did not go so far as to suggest a complete ban on automobiles in the centre, but in 1976 they did succeed in pushing through a City Council

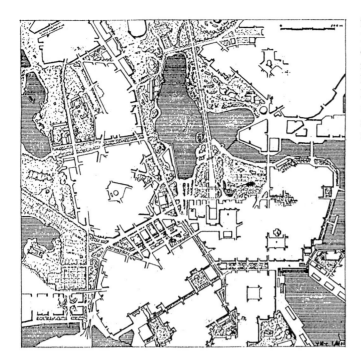

234. Vilhelm Helander's 1976 proposal for the new city centre stems from nature romanticism: Töölö Bay is enlarged beyond the Finlandia Hall, and rail traffic is cut down to allow an enormous park to engulf the whole city centre.

decision that Vapaudenkatu should not be built. The whole foundation of Aalto's plan was thereby undermined. A spate of new plans appeared. There was talk of the desirability of cleaning up the water of Töölö Bay so that a children's beach could be placed where Vapaudenkatu was to have been built. Other proposals were based on enlarging the bay far beyond Finlandia Hall, leaving small islets in the lake thus formed, while the railway embankment should be narrowed to the width of one or two tracks in order to link the west side of the tracks with the Kaisaniemi area into an enormous park. The fact that Helsinki is a relatively small city surrounded by open sea on three sides and already having a significant proportion of parkland obviously cannot extinguish the longing for a Karelian starflower in the urban core as well.

The pendulum had thus suddenly swung from the City Planning Office's brutally technical and utilitarian attitude to the romantic antitechnological approach of the environmentalists. Both attitudes were foreign to Aalto. He sought a workable balance between tamed nature, civilized man, and serviceable technology.

Surprisingly enough, the centre of Helsinki still functions, although very few of the changes listed as urgent and inevitable thirty years ago have been made. The streets that lead to the centre are just as congested, parking is still inadequate, the bus terminal stands on its old site, the goods yard disfigures the Parliament House surroundings, and the shores of Töölö Bay are as marshy and polluted as ever. Only Aalto's Finlandia Hall and the opera, on the site he selected in 1972, have been built.

Theoretically, Aalto's grandiose plan could still be implemented. Clearly, however, it will never happen. The explanation is simple: the third prerequisite discussed at the beginning of this chapter – the propitious historical moment – has been lost. Was it the postponement of the appropriation for moving the goods station that led to such fateful consequences? What would have happened if the 'young revolt' had come only one or two years later? Or did an intrinsic weakness in our democratic decision-making process make implementation impossible, as Professor Osmo Lappo has suggested in an interview (*Helsingin Sanomat,* February 1, 1981): *Carl Ludwig Engel was able to build Senate Square because the Czar gave him full powers to do so. Aalto was the last man who could have achieved something similar, but there was no longer any Czar. Democratic control diminishes the risk of mistakes, but also prevents good overall solutions. Today we can only make jigsaw puzzles.*

One thing is certain: nothing grieved Aalto as deeply as the scuttling of his magnificent, and initially so promising, plan for Helsinki's new centre.

The Two Sides of Fame

Fame, it is well known, is a drug to which one reacts quite strongly to begin with, but which calls for ever-increasing doses once one is accustomed to it. Fame inevitably had an effect on Aalto's life.

The list of the official honours he received takes up three single-spaced sheets. It does not include all that many of the ordinary crosses or commander's orders such as those given to common mortals like ministers, ambassadors, and industrialists. It is full of honorary doctorates from universities on three continents, honorary memberships in various academies and cultural organizations, and numerous gold medals and plaques. To be sure, Aalto was vain enough to be pleased every time he was notified of a new mark of recognition, but with time he naturally became inured. He probably took the greatest pleasure in his early international accolades, such as the honorary membership in the Royal Institute of British Architects he was awarded in 1937 and the honorary doctorate he received from Princeton ten years later.

The drawback of such recognition was that he had to give speeches or lectures at the award ceremonies, and travelling took up valuable time. In his younger days he did not mind the strain, but over the years it became bothersome. Increasingly, he was honoured *in absentia;* sometimes he just did not take the trouble to accept.

Honours that he declined, almost without exception, were invitations to address various kinds of seminars – or symposia, as they are often called today. After 1947, not even the CIAM meetings tempted him, let alone events such as the architects' world congress in Havana in 1963 or Farah Diba's 1974 architecture symposium in Teheran. Of course it was flattering to be invited to take part in solving spectacular international architectural problems such as, in 1961, how to save the Temple of Abu Simbel in Nubia, or, the following year, how to save fast-sinking Venice, but Aalto did not go for such paid holiday trips.

He also turned down all requests to become a guest professor at various universities. Wurster's invitation to Berkeley has already been mentioned. Aalto also received friendly inquiries from Cornell University and from the universities of Johannesburg, Manitoba, New South Wales, and Ahmedabad. He corresponded for many years with Oskar Kokoschka, who tried to recruit him as a summer instructor at his *Schule des Sehens* (School of Sight) in Salzburg.

235. Receiving honours was an increasingly frequent part of the aging Aalto's life. His sixtieth birthday in 1958.

236. Aalto and donor
Sonning's widow at the
Sonning Prize award cere-
monies in Copenhagen,
1962.

At a loss for an excuse, Aalto explained lightly that he could not possibly leave
Finland during the crayfish season. Taking this literally, Kokoschka replied
with an indignant protest. Late in life Aalto received an offer from Herman
Spiegel, dean of Yale's department of architecture, of the Shepherd Davenport
Visiting Professorship, "the best architectural chair the United States can
offer", with all teaching duties left completely open, but even this he did not
consider accepting.

As for the fame brought by invitations to exhibit, we may wonder at his
fastidiousness. When the Smithsonian Institution's National Collection of Fine
Arts tried to arrange a major Aalto exhibition in 1952, he refused, pleading the
demands of his workload. *I have on my desk building assignments of more than two
million cubic metres: this is no time for PR activity.*

The recurrent element in all of Aalto's responses was lack of time – his
unwillingness to waste days that could be used for creative work. He was, in fact,
so obsessed with his need or desire to create that anything that might hinder his
work aroused distaste. Thus it is all the more remarkable that he always gave
unstintingly of his time to friends. Both foreign and Finnish friends were made
warmly welcome to visit him and to take up as much of his time as they liked.
Aalto detested the idea of subordinating himself to duty or the clock, but he
needed other people to include in the constant, vital improvisation of his
creative life.

But let us return to the effect of his growing fame upon him. To put the issue
in perspective, a special characteristic of Finnish society must be mentioned.
During the immediate postwar years, Finland was still a country that felt the
need for great men and therefore created them. In the 19th century the
nation's growth had been the work of a handful of individuals such as

237. Aalto's role as a national hero was accentuated after his death. He was honured with a postage stamp in 1976, and today his portrait adorns the fifty-mark banknote.

Runeberg, Lönnrot, and Snellman, who were active on the cultural scene. The country had gained a certain international renown through athletes like Paavo Nurmi and men of the arts such as Sibelius. It had been piloted through serious political crises by men like Mannerheim and Kekkonen. Finland demanded that Aalto should take his place within this tradition; born actor that he was, he complied with panache.

Aalto's abandonment of his prewar role as a disciple of Aku Nyberg, the cheeky, ingenious rascal, took place gradually; his new persona fortunately never entirely effaced his old self. Society's increasing demands and the honours showered on him, not least the title of academician, slowly gave rise to a new Aalto – the revered great man, the standard-bearer of Finland's international cultural renown.

This transformation is perhaps best illustrated by an episode from his eventful life. The scene: his old school town, Jyväskylä, where he has recently built the new university and is beginning to be regarded as the town's most famous son. Late at night, together with one of his assistants, he walks – or, to be more precise, staggers – out into the street from the Jyväshovi Hotel and gets into his car. Driving under the influence, however, is a particularly serious offence in the disciplined North. A policeman who has been watching takes the gentlemen to the police station – both the younger man sitting at the wheel and the older man who is an accessory to the fact. There the chief of police receives them. But what happens? As soon as the chief has taken in the situation, he turns to his subordinate and, pointing at the door, yells: "How dare you come here with Academician Aalto? Get out!"

It is, then, understandable that initially Aalto had some difficulty in judging the limits to a great man's freedom in Finland, which is, after all, a democratic country. I have already touched on his annoyance at the tax authorities' unwillingness to grant him a greater margin for "expenses for earning income" than was allowed for ordinary citizens. In 1959 he had another instructive clash with the authorities.

The scene on this occasion: the customs control at Helsinki airport. A distinguished gentleman, noticeably stimulated by the refreshments served on the flight, and his elegant but painfully embarrassed young wife have been stopped for having with them a case of excellent French wine, which they claim to have received as a gift from Parisian friends. The gentleman refuses to pay duty on the wine, as on a previous occasion customs had carelessly broken the bottles on which he had paid duty. In the course of the argument the customs officer behaves rudely to the young lady, which so incenses her husband that he gives the officer a light slap on the face with the glove in his hand. Such "violent obstruction of an official" and "contempt for the law" naturally cannot go unpunished. A prolonged lawsuit ensues and leads to a heavy fine.

The behaviour Aalto exhibited in the 1950s is not entirely incomprehensible. It was rooted in part in the attitudes of his father, a miller's son to whom belonging to the class to which he had risen through his own efforts was so important that he gave his son this challenging advice when leaving school: "Alvar, always remember you're a gentleman!" However bohemian the young Aalto's behaviour might have been in the 1920s and 1930s, there was never anything proletarian about it. In the 1940s, he met a man who brought out a completely new side of his character: Frank Lloyd Wright.

My claim is of course unprovable, based as it is solely on what I know of the two men's contacts and on the stories about Wright that Aalto loved to dish up. I was therefore delighted to discover in conversation with Aalto's Swiss friend Karl Fleig that he shared my opinion. We both remembered a remark of Aalto's: *When I saw the arrogance with which Wright talked about architecture, I thought: perhaps this is the best way to make the general public think about these questions!* It also seems reasonable to repeat here the observation made in discussing Aalto's relation-

238. A well-turned-out Frank Lloyd Wright at the 1945 lunch with Aalto.

239. A dapper Aalto in 1956. Photo: Göran Schildt.

ship with Sven Markelius (*The Decisive Years*, pp. 52–53): Wright, who did not perceptibly influence Aalto as an architect, affected him all the more through his personality.

A conspicuous part of Wright's persona was his elegant clothing, the custom-made wide-brimmed hats and perfectly fitted suits which, together with his provocative upper-class attitudes, left America's vulgar self-made millionaires far behind. Aalto was not to be bested where clothing or deportment were concerned. I have heard stories of how, in the 1940s, he would intentionally arrive late at Helsinki airport, so that the transatlantic flight would have to wait for him and he could walk up to the plane with measured steps before the impatient eyes of his fellow travellers. Olof Hammarström, his assistant in the Boston dormitory project, noted with astonishment how, as they would cross the bridge from Aalto's rooms on the Boston side of the Charles River to MIT on the other side, Aalto would shake off his comradely demeanour in the middle of the bridge and turn into the lion he was at the school.

In the 1950s the category of hotel Aalto stayed in changed. In Stockholm he had previously stayed at the Eden or the Reisen; now it was always the Grand Hotel. In Paris he abandoned the Hôtel des Saints Pères on the Left Bank, an artists' haunt, for the Hôtel Crillon on the Place de la Concorde. In London he stayed at the Savoy, in Zurich at the Eden au Lac, in Copenhagen at the

Angleterre, in New York at the Plaza. He started ordering custom-made felt hats with extra-wide brims from the Bossi company in Milan, hand-stitched shoes from Venice. His court tailor was A.W. Bauer, the royal purveyor in Stockholm. And he reached the height of snobbery when he ordered one white and one dark dinner jacket from the most expensive tailor on the Champs Elysées, requesting that they be delivered to the porter of the Crillon, who then added the price to the hotel bill.

In this biography, I have frequently spoken of Aalto as an actor. This characterization is not intended to belittle him; on the contrary, it is a mark of admiration. Aalto had the true actor's ability never to confuse himself with his roles, not only to be conscious of the difference himself but to make it clear to the audience as well. One of the miracles of the theatre is the possibility of collusion on this point between a great actor and his audience. Aalto thought of his roles as exciting and entertaining tricks to amuse the public. The spectators felt that he was a friend and a companion because never once did he attempt to force his ideas on them; rather, he enticed them into taking part in his games.

It may well be that Aalto's appearance in the Wrightian role of hero was not as amusing in Finland as it was in the United States. It is also possible that the new generation of architects did not know him well enough to appreciate his style. We find a significant difference in the understanding of his ways shown by the older architects who had worked as assistants at his office, such as Revell, Ervi, Cedercreutz, Paatela, Luoma, Mänttäri, Leppänen, and Slangus, and that shown by the younger architects who became active members of SAFA after Aalto's chairmanship.

Aalto left his leadership position in SAFA in 1958, evidently at the right moment. Latent opposition to him had emerged within the association, partly because of a natural need for independence and opposition to authority among the young, partly because of the difficulty of turning his doctrine of intuitive synthesis and the merging of rational and subconscious needs into a pedagogically workable method.

The young architects needed hard-and-fast, schematic ideas, theories to resist or embrace. They therefore sought a counterbalance to the skeptical, ambiguous, elusive Aalto. They found one in Aulis Blomstedt, Aalto's old friend and colleague. Blomstedt, a very gifted architect with a lively appreciation of Aalto, was also intellectually receptive to the kinds of speculative theories cultivated by the De Stijl school. His penchant for pure geometry and technological clarity prompted him to introduce a modular system reminiscent of Le Corbusier's and to adopt the all-embracing geometric grid system with which Mies van der Rohe had worked.

Blomstedt succeeded the old Neo-Classicist J.S. Sirén as professor of architecture at the Helsinki University of Technology in 1959. Another theoretician, Aarno Ruusuvuori, had been teaching there since 1952 and had adopted the Bauhaus principles of the 1930s as the basis of his instruction. Thus the intellectual focus of Finnish architectural debate moved from architectural practice to the seminars of the University of Technology. A new movement called Structuralism, the members of which consciously sought to distance themselves from Aalto, began to take shape.

Its leaders were not the basically aesthetically oriented Blomstedt or the wise, conciliatory Ruusuvuori, but two 'angry young men', Kirmo Mikkola and Juhani Pallasmaa. Mikkola was a talented disciple of the Russian Constructivist movement of the '20s, which had combined Marxist idealism with the call for distinct, constructive form. For Mikkola, Aalto was a deplorable individualist, if not an example of "the superman's exhibitionism". In his opinion, Aalto's marvellous monumental buildings represented an elitist culture unrelated to the needs of "the people", an unhealthy attempt to assert the superiority of the artist. Pallasmaa was also an advocate of Constructivism, objectivism, and "the culture of the people", values that he did not find in Aalto.

The opposition grew slowly but relentlessly during the 1960s, significantly raising the temperature of architectural debate. Polemical writings and articles abounded. A very independent and artistically gifted young architect by the name of Reima Pietilä actually had the nerve to defend Aalto and to ask in what way geometrical Constructivism was more radical than an organic idiom.

The radicals did not succeed in conquering SAFA – as Mikkola narrowly lost a 1969 bid for the chairmanship – but they soon took control of the Museum

240. Two leaders of the architectural section of the young revolt of the 1960s: Kirmo Mikkola and Juhani Pallasmaa.

of Finnish Architecture. At the University of Technology, Aalto was a nonentity until his death; not a single slide of his works could be found in the archives. From the present-day perspective, this polarization seems incomprehensible, based, if on anything, on a deliberate misinterpretation of Aalto. It was his dominating personality and not his work that was resented. This interpretation is supported by the fact that both Mikkola and Pallasmaa became enthusiastic admirers of Aalto's work after his death. They published books about him and appeared at innumerable exhibitions and symposia in Finland and abroad as exegetes of Aalto's ideas.

But let us return to the turbulent 1960s. Aalto agreed in 1967 that the comprehensive retrospective exhibition that had aroused such admiration in Florence two years before should be repeated at the Art Museum of the Ateneum in Helsinki. On this occasion, the first crack in his undisputed dominance appeared in the form of a basically harmless episode. The night before the opening, tired and ill, he was putting the finishing touches to the arrangements. Suddenly two young men stormed into the Ateneum, their pockets full of beer cans, and started to assail him with obscure arguments. They were Mikkola and Pallasmaa, who had been sitting in a pub and had been overcome by the urge to finally confront the old tyrant. Otherwise the exhibition went well. The press lavished its praise on Aalto then, and did so again the following year, when he turned 70.

Curiously, it was an Aalto exhibition in Stockholm in 1969 that sparked a debate on Aalto in Finland that, in fact, toppled him from his pedestal. The Swedish journalists, who had no inhibitions and who had scented the international 'cultural revolution', came to Helsinki to interview the master and view his latest works before the Stockholm opening. In a double-spread article in *Dagens Nyheter* (April 13, 1969), Rebecka Tarschys wrote of Aalto's "betrayal of his earlier fine ideas", his new "flashy buildings" and "orgies of volumetric expressionism". In *Svenska Dagbladet* (April 17, 1969), Åsa Wall reported on "the myth, the genius, the superman, the diva, the charmer" who "subdues people into silently admiring his tricks". Kristian Romare of Swedish television saw Enso-Gutzeit's new marble palace as proof that Aalto had become a servile accomplice of big business – overlooking the trifling point that this particular business was state-owned.

This gave the domestic hounds all the encouragement they needed to join in the hunt. On the occasion of Helsinki's sesquicentennial as the capital, the city had decided to carry out the part of Aalto's centre plan that involved the concert and congress building now known as the Finlandia Hall. The cornerstone was laid in spring 1969, and the building was ready for consecration in December 1971. The event was no triumph for Aalto: in fact, it provided his detractors with an opportunity to air their grievances. I was present at the celebration, at which sparkling wine was served to a large crowd of invited guests, including many from abroad – but Aalto was absent, bedridden with pneumonia. The young radicals were openly contemptuous: they considered

241. Students demonstration against high culture and elite architecture, Helsinki 1970.

the whole building a political and cultural scandal. I myself was berated by Mikkola for being "Aalto's lackey".

This time the newspapers did not mince words. A columnist in *Helsingin Sanomat* wrote sarcastically that *Aalto was not good enough for the city when he was doing his best work, warm, friendly, humane houses. He had to go draw them elsewhere. Only when he managed to pull himself up to his present marble senility did the commissions start coming from the City of Helsinki.*

Suomen Kuvalehti magazine (No. 1, 1972) took exception to the violation of democracy evinced in the fact that the foyer had wall-to-wall carpeting and the caretaker's residence did not. Other publications joined in with two main complaints: the building had been too expensive (10 million) and its acoustics were flawed. *The main floor is for the deaf, for there you hear nothing, and the balcony is for the blind, for there you see nothing.* In the City Council, the populist politician Jörn Donner asked: *Can we find a better example of the morbid elitism with which so-called art culture is managed in Helsinki than the Finlandia Hall? It could just as well have been designed by the chief architect of Nazi Germany, Albert Speer. We could have built ten cultural centres in Helsinki, with youth clubs, libraries, sports facilities, and dance floors, for the same money.*

Foreign critics were divided. Sweden's *Aftonbladet* wrote (December 7, 1971): *It is a national boast of a house, created by an architect's power. A jukebox for high culture. It appears just at a time when cultural policy is reporting quite different needs: investment in the culture of the people, a policy of democratic decentralization for culture in rural areas and suburbs . . .* The writer professed outrage at the serving of unlimited quantities of champagne and whiskey to the elite crowd at the inauguration! The Hamburg newspaper Die Zeit was also critical: *Alvar Aalto loves expensive and beautiful materials, but the white Carrara marble and black Finnish granite of the facades are about as attractive as a starched shirt under a tailcoat: statuesque, cold, even ostentatious.*

The *New York Times* took a different tack. Ada Louise Huxtable praised the Finlandia Hall and compared it favourably with I.M. Pei's newly completed Kennedy Memorial Library in Boston, which she had criticized. And Alfred Roth wrote in *Neue Zürcher Zeitung: This work marks the high point of what Alvar Aalto has created so far.*

Roth was right to the extent that in the Finlandia Hall Aalto truly succeeded in creating a unique synthesis of characteristics that had been scattered through his previous work. The spatial flow of the foyer, with its wide staircase and undulating gallery front, makes it perhaps the most effective of his many 'indoor exteriors', and the main auditorium, with its balconies hovering like clouds against the blue background of the side walls, is the most tightly knit non-geometrical space conceivable.

The storm surrounding the Finlandia Hall, which had the misfortune of being completed just as the 'cultural revolution' reached its height in Finland, also affected other Aalto designs. The Enso-Gutzeit headquarters, next to the Katajanokka piers in Helsinki, was attacked with particular ferocity. It had been

242. The Finlandia Hall's main auditorium.

243. Henrik Tikkanen's homage to the new Enso-Gutzeit building.

Täckelset av byggnadsställningar har fallit och en skönhet i carraramarmor speglar sin ännu en aning omornade fasad i Södra hamnens vatten. Marmorn är vit som måsarnas vingar och det förefaller som om materialet självt av gammal vana skulle ha rest sig i smäckra kolonner mot taket som ser ut att sväva fritt ovanför byggnaden. Men samtidigt som huset är fulländat i sin egen form förenar det sig harmoniskt med hela sin omgivning Man tänker inte på gammalt och nytt, bara på att det är vackert.

Henrik.

244. The Enso-Gutzeit building in Helsinki, Aalto's most fiercely criticized design. Photo: Mäkinen.

245. Lahti Church was not 'popular' enough for the social utopians of the 1970s.

greeted with enthusiasm when it was completed in 1961. *Hufvudstadsbladet*'s Henrik Tikkanen, later a famous cartoonist and columnist, had celebrated it with an attractive landscape drawing and the words: *One does not think of old and new, just of its beauty . . . While the building is complete in its own right, it also blends entirely with the surroundings.* But by 1969, as we already know, it was a *lackey's service to vile big business,* and in 1981 author Arto Paasilinna challenged his readers in the magazine Apu to *blow up the Enso-Gutzeit building with TNT, because it is so abominably ugly and particularly because it hides the beautiful Uspenski Cathedral. The author of this monster is Alvar Aalto, whom no one dared oppose at the time. Its demolition would be the deed of the decade.*

Aalto had won a competition to design the new main church for the city of Lahti back in 1950, but until 1969 the time was not ripe for construction, which took place on a completely new site and with a partly revised building programme. The revised design by Aalto, however, ran into unexpected opposition from the vigilant progressivists who had managed to infiltrate even the national church board, which rejected the Aalto plan as being out-of-date. The pulpit was too dominating and thus 'authoritarian', the congregation did not have equal access to the altar railing, and the fixed pews were not consistent with the kind of 'multipurpose church' required in modern times. The people of Lahti, however, proved unreceptive to dictates from the capital, and wanted a good, old-fashioned cathedral, which Aalto's design could reasonably be said to be. After much debate and various bureaucratic twists, the Ministry of Education approved the controversial church in 1973, and it was built to Aalto's plan.

Another of Aalto's plans, the Lehtinen Art Museum on Kuusisaari island, had already been undermined by the defenders of 'the people' in 1968. Aalto's old friend, industrialist William Lehtinen, who headed the Enso-Gutzeit company until his retirement, wished to donate his villa and land on the island, along with his considerable fortune, to the city of Helsinki for use as a museum of modern art, something like the Louisiana museum near Copenhagen. In 1965 Aalto designed a beautiful building for this purpose. The time, however, was not right for such private capitalist initiatives. The bureaucrats' pettiness regarding road lines, building permits, and so forth, so incensed the old industrialist that he gave up the idea of a museum and bought a castle and vineyards in Tuscany instead. Helsinki still lacks a modern art museum and thus has no suitable facilities for any extensive exhibitions of modern art.

To summarize, let me quote a statement published October 18, 1973 in the left-wing newspaper *Kansan Uutiset,* which gives vent to resentment more freely but also more candidly than the more balanced papers: *The aging Alvar Aalto knows how to spoil, rant, and lug his "cubes", his boxy houses, to every street corner. Cannot this great man find peace at last, or what is the short circuit that makes the Helsinki city authorities approve such marble eyesores as the one on Katajanokka's shore?* Again it was the Enso-Gutzeit building that was singled out.

Thus persistent efforts were made to put Aalto in the dock during these years. This was partly because his complex, skeptical intellect was out of tune with the dogmatic simplification and short-sighted fanaticism on which the path of Mao was based, but his exposed position was also partly due to the isolation brought upon him by excessive fame. The extroverted conversationalist who could find something to talk about with anybody and was happy only when he was in pleasant company had slowly been left alone on the floodlit stage. At the office he was still the familiar "boss", though even there the distance was growing, but among colleagues he was increasingly the chosen one whom no one could feel equal to, no matter how collegial Aalto's behaviour was.

In a way, Aalto could not be touched by the criticism to which he was subjected, because it was so obviously unjustified. To reproach him for aestheticism and for making art for art's sake was absurd, so uncompromisingly had he pursued social justice all his life. His distrust of Mies van der Rohe's Constructivism, which had so easily been accepted by the technological and capitalist interests in the United States, was a poor reason for branding him a reactionary. The young people who attacked him would have done better to take him as their model rather than Blomstedt, who took little interest in social concerns. Blomstedt did have one outstanding merit, however: he was the antithesis of Aalto, and that was enough.

The error or blindness was so obvious that Aalto's writer friends could not remain silent. Foreign critics, in particular, had difficulty in understanding the aggression directed at him. When William Marlin, editor of the U.S. journal *Architectural Forum,* visited Finland in 1974 and discovered what was going on, he declared:

However much he may be criticized today, those who criticize him would do well to remember that they are barely able to hold a candle to him in terms of legacy and long-range significance. Just as our Frank Lloyd Wright was much more than an architect – a moral force, a social force, and a unifying force – so is Alvar Aalto, culturally as well as socially.

We Finnish friends also threw all our insufficient weight into the struggle. Between 1965 and 1975, I wrote a dozen long articles about Aalto for Swedish and Finnish newspapers. He himself was silent, but he did make an indirect rejoinder. He allowed me to compile a selection of the articles, lectures, and interviews that he had spawned during his long career. This book, to which he gave the disparaging title *Sketches,* came out in 1973 and showed irrefutably how consistently he had fought throughout his life for a socially responsible, humane architecture.

The misinterpretations could not be swept away instantly, however. More than a decade was needed to dissipate the ill will, and Aalto never witnessed the conversion of his adversaries. His last years were embittered by hostility, and he became solitary, even misanthropic. The once frequent lectures and formal addresses were now rare highlights; he hardly ever attended meetings or cultural events. He even stopped reading the daily newspapers at about this time. His wife told me: *When he came out of his bedroom in the morning he would only ask: Who's been killed today? Naturally, whenever he went abroad, he would buy all the papers he could get hold of –* Neue Zürcher Zeitung, Le Monde, *the* New York Times *– to find out what was going on in the world. The trouble with the Finnish papers was that they so often contained humiliating comments about him.*

He never talked to anyone about his problems, but it was obvious that he brooded. Had his hubris aroused an angry nemesis, had he brought adversity down on his own head? He commented indirectly on his plight two or three years before he died, as I shall try to show in the next and last chapter.

The Last Years

The shadow that fell upon Aalto's last years was not caused solely by the opposition his work encountered. More inexorable menaces also crept ever closer: old age, illness, and the black gate toward which he had never dared direct his gaze. Aalto had a fearful attitude toward death, stemming perhaps from the childhood trauma caused by the brutal way in which his mother was torn away from him. He never spoke of the inevitable; he tried to live as if it did not exist. He went to Switzerland every year to visit his personal physician, Professor Wilhelm Löffler, whose treatment consisted of assuring him that he had the soul of a seventeen-year-old in the body of a fifty-year-old, and that he should go on with the lifestyle to which he was accustomed.

Unfortunately, reality did not quite match the benevolent professor's diagnosis. Aalto had always had a tendency to catch colds, bronchitis, even pneumonia, and these illnesses returned with increasing frequency, especially in wintertime. He dislocated his right shoulder more and more often and needed medical attention for it. He suffered increasingly from problems with balance, which malicious tongues took for symptoms of intoxication. His insomnia also got worse. He kept a stack of favourite books on his nightstand, reading and rereading them at night, but he would get sleepy by 6 p.m. and go to bed. In his last years he only felt really well after he had completed his two or three-hour stint at the office and had sat down with his first glass of wine in the cosy *taverna*, for a conversation with some friend called in for the purpose. Then he was again the same old Alvar, full of amusing stories, curious about the world, sly, touchingly affectionate. But the interval that elapsed before he went to bed grew ever shorter.

One of the depressing things about aging is that messages of the deaths of close friends become increasingly frequent. It was bad enough when old Eliel Saarinen died in 1950, but it was downright macabre when his son Eero, Alvar's friend and younger colleague, followed him, eleven years later. The deaths of Henry van de Velde in 1958 and of Frank Lloyd Wright the following year were painful personal losses for Aalto, and so was Le Corbusier's in 1965, but they were all far ahead of him in age. Harder blows were the loss of his old friend Sigfried Giedion in 1968 and of the faithful Wurster five years later. When Professor Löffler himself, Aalto's guarantee of eternal life, had the bad taste to let him down in 1972, he felt truly abandoned.

SÄHKÖSANOMA
TELEGRAM

Lähettämisestä — För avs.
RP _____ w _____
Yhteensä — Summa

Vast.ott. nimim.
Mottaget av sign.

Edell. läh. nimim.
Vidaresänts av sign.

LÄHETETTY — AVSÄNT
Minne — Vart   New York
Pvm. — Dat.   10. 4-57.
Klo — Kl.   16.00

Luokka — Klass   Lähtötoimipaikka — Avgångsanstalt   No — Nr   Sanaluku — Ordantal   Jättöaika inlämn. tid Klo Kl.   Virkahuom. — Tjänsteanm.

Maksunalaiset virkamerk.
Avgiftsbelagda tjänsteanm.   Vastaanottaja ja osoite — Adressat och adress   Osoitetoimipaikka — Adressanstalt

LT
JOSEPH HAZEN   ARCHITECTURAL FORUM

Teksti ja allekirjoitus —. Text och underskrift

A FINE AND GOOD MAN HAS PASSED ON HE WAS A GENIUS
NOT ONLY OF THE BUILDING ART OF AMERICA BUT ALSO IN
HIS LIFE AND ART IN GENERAL AND HAS IN HIS CREATIONS
SHOWD A PASSION FOR HUMANITY STOP HIS FORMS IN ART
WILL SURELY RETAIN THEIR GREATNESS MORE THAN HUNDRED
YEARS AHEAD STOP PERSONALLY I HAVE LOST A REAL FRIEND

ALVAR AALTO

EI SÄHKÖTETÄ
AVTELEGRAFERAS ICKE   Lähettäjän nimi ja osoite — Avsändarens namn och adress

246. Aalto's telegram on the death of Frank Lloyd Wright in 1959, sent for publication in *Architectural Forum*.

In desperation, he clung to his work. After all, creating new buildings and solving architectural problems represented the true continuity in his life. The results of his efforts, built of stone, brick, concrete, and, yes, even wood, were more durable than the fragile human body: they lent him a comforting kind of immortality. The frailer he became, the more enthusiastically he took up new projects.

Aalto's correspondence during his last years reveals the most unexpected plans. He ordered the programme for the Centre Pompidou competition in Paris. In 1967 and 1968 he corresponded with a Swiss man living in Hawaii who owned large tracts of land on the island and asked Aalto to help him build a luxury villa town. He negotiated with his old MIT pupil and furniture agent Harry Weese, who now had a large and successful architectural practice in Chicago. He hoped to collaborate with Weese in carrying out a series of commissions that had been offered him in the United States. One was a Scandinavian Cultural Center in Wisconsin, another "one house close to New York, but outside Manhattan", another a job near Vancouver in Canada. Aalto would be responsible for the main sketches, and "some partner between my friends in America, of whom you are the number one" would do the details. Weese responded enthusiastically, but nothing ever came of their collaboration. Aalto also hoped to work with Jean-Jacques Baruël in Denmark on the design of a bank palace for Hamburg, commissioned by a Count Schaffgotsch – but, inopportunely, the Count went bankrupt.

The work that enticed Aalto most, however, was a concert hall the size of the

Finlandia Hall, for Jerusalem. The initiative stemmed from Golda Meir's circle; Meir herself wrote to ask him to come to Israel for discussions. The Jerusalem concert hall project became a fata morgana for him, a goal that always seemed in reach but stubbornly eluded his grasp. On two occasions he was all set to go, his flight booked and suitcase packed, but his health said no. Fever, fatigue, vertigo were obstacles that he would not allow for. He went back to the office as soon as he could stand; he was constantly starting new projects.

I remember Aalto in this period as a sort of King Lear. He had grown old and walked with stumbling steps. He had been stripped of his royalty; two of his beloved daughters had betrayed him and treated him with disrespect, but he still had his Cordelia and his belief in the values he had fought for. It was a painful transformation, but King Lear became a wiser and more moving figure in his humiliation than he had been in his days of glory.

A little episode from Aalto's late years, a portrait sketch in words by Sweden's most sensitive journalist of all time, Jolo (Jan-Olof Olsson), illustrates what I mean. The occasion was the opening of the Aalborg Art Museum in 1972. As I mentioned in the chapter on Aalto's contacts with Denmark, he won the competition to design this building in 1958. It took fourteen years before all the committees reached agreement, funding was arranged, and construction was completed. During that time, the new idea of a culture of the people as opposed to the culture of the capitalist elite had gained a foothold in Denmark as elsewhere. Just before the inauguration, architect Svend Erik Møller wrote in

247. Aalto during the preparations for the 1969 exhibition at Stockholm's Museum of Modern Art, sitting in front of a model of the controversial centre plan. Photo: Nyberg.

248. Aalto greets Denmark's Queen Dowager Ingrid at the inauguration of the Aalborg museum, 1972. Photo: René.

the newspaper *Politiken* (June 8, 1972): *The building is remarkably obsolete, out of step with the times, as if it were not suited to a society in transition. It is too fine, almost sophisticated, aristocratic.* And in the *Berlingske Tidende*, his colleague Henrik Sten Møller commented: *One might think this was the imposing head office of a bank. Oh this purity, indicating that it has nothing to do with real, sordid life. Here speaks the entrenched older generation.*

Trouble similar to that Aalto had met at home could thus be expected at the ceremony. Jolo reports (*Dagens Nyheter,* June 13, 1972): *A more beautiful museum Copenhagen will not have in a generation, certainly not Denmark, perhaps not Scandinavia. Of course the inauguration came at a time when museums are being*

questioned. On the grassy slope outside, young people demonstrated against the high cost.
He continues:

Alvar Aalto's international fame almost overshadows the man – one no more expects to see Sibelius going around in an overcoat, stick in hand, while the world plays the Finlandia *than to find Aalto in company on an ordinary Thursday. He is accompanied by his wife-cum-colleague, who steers him through the crowd. He looks sad, worried, even a little angry. He makes a magnificent speech, beautiful words spoken in a deep, rasping voice. He speaks of the "balance" that characterizes Denmark, but pronouncing the word in the French way, bul-awnce . . . It sounds wonderful the way he says it. He also says that there is "a divergent equality" in Denmark. One must admit that this is well put.*

A Finnish report rounds off the scene (*Arkkitehtiuutiset*, no. 13–14, 1972): *His speech was greeted with a veritable storm of applause, culminating in a standing ovation.*

As I related at the beginning of this biography, the old Aalto felt the need to write a 'spiritual will', a summing up of his life's experience. It was never written, but he did dictate a few fragments to his secretary. One such was the story of *The White Table,* his father's working table, on which the varied planning requirements that the surveyor had to take into account were synthesized in a single creative act. This story showed the basis of his own work. He also dictated the following fragment, which he called *The Human Factor:*

249. One of Aalto's last designs: Göran Schildt's Villa Skeppet in Ekenäs. Photo: Berengo Gardin.

Nowadays "the human factor" is cited only in connection with accidents, such as when an exhausted engine driver falls asleep in a critical situation. Investigations of accidents always assume two alternatives: either the human factor or technical failure is to blame.

But the human factor is not as simple as it sounds. It is one of the world's oldest ideas, at least in principle. Ancient religions that take us back thousands of years always made allowance for man's special tendency to err. The idea is certainly inherent in the Christian religion (and I say this without being a philosopher or a theologian). Of course religions do not speak of human error in its modern technical meaning but call it human weakness or even sin, one of the basic problems of human life. In other words, the modern "human factor" is a childish variant of the great tragedy of the human race.

Nowadays we use computations and prognoses in an effort to make absolutely accurate calculations even about the future. But it is impossible for such systems, if that is what we must call them, to be free of the margin of human error, since it always follows people, however they live. The 'accurate' calculations contain just as much human error as earlier planning methods based on faith and emotion.

It is thus as important as ever today to take the human factor into account. True, no exact percentage can be given of the human error in all present-day plans, but it is not likely to be any lower or higher than before. We must therefore be extremely cautious. Rational calculations are no more reliable than faith or dreams. What we can do is try with careful analysis to avoid being hurt by human error. We must not be blinded by short-sightedness.

There is no easy answer to how to suppress the human factor, since it is obviously an inescapable constant. Technical error is more easily eliminated, although this takes time, but in the end it always involves isolated problems that can be solved case by case. The human factor, however, can never be neutralized; it is an eternal problem that cannot be changed by tackling its consequences.

We can go beyond this observation by returning to our comparison with ancient religions. Note that they never really tried to eliminate human error; in fact, they treated it as a constant and only sought to keep it under control. It is part of the ideology of most religious systems that this error should give rise to something positive in exchange, rather as a good gardener turns even the weaknesses of his seedlings to his benefit.

One might say that the human factor has always been a part of architecture. In a deeper sense, it has even been indispensable to make it possible for buildings to fully express the richness and positive values of life. Thus the attempt to eliminate the human factor from planning is a sign of helplessness, a prayer for advance pardon. People wish to replace the knowledge of life's uncertainty with absolute certainty and some kind of truth, but the result is that the same margin of error that was inherent in emotional calculations is transferred to rational calculations. The hope to eliminate the human factor remains an illusion.

Aalto's description of the human factor, like all statements based on truly profound reflection, is enigmatic and lends itself to various interpretations. For me it is natural to see it against the background of rationalism, nature, and man discussed earlier in this biography. If this is correct, we can say that the human factor is what distinguishes us from the larger context that is often called nature. Man alone among all living things, with his capacity for symbolic thought, has achieved the ability to form ideas about nature, which are necessarily simplistic and incomplete. Thus both the breaking free that gives man the power to change the circumstances of his life and the misfortunes brought by inevitable relapses into dependence are specifically human.

The aspect of industrialism that Aalto opposed was its tendency to isolate goals, to ignore the whole picture and the main objective, which must be man's well-being. This short-sightedness, this abandonment to the temptations of the moment or to egotistical motives that run counter to the interests of the community, is closely related to what religions call "sin". Nature cannot commit a sin, animals do not sin, storms and earthquakes are innocent though destructive; only man has received this dubious gift that causes so much suffering, but can, if all goes well, also be a source of progress.

Aalto thought that we cannot avoid this fate, which is part and parcel of human life, but he believed that it could be counterbalanced by the right kind of acceptance. He saw modern man's belief that human existence can be rationally controlled as a dangerous form of hubris which would be punished inexorably. Nature is not bound by simple rational and mechanical causality, as scientists up to the present day have believed: everything is much more chaotic and complicated than we are able to comprehend.

Therefore: watch out. Be rational, but do not put your faith in rationalism. Distrust all theoretical systems, sustain your contact with nature, learn from practical experience, always be prepared for new difficulties. This was Aalto's advice for dealing with the human factor.

Once upon a time, when the word "sin" still had meaning, there were virtuous people who succeeded in minimizing their sins, and even saints who were absolutely sinless. Aalto, too, thought there are people who are more successful than others at keeping the human tendency to err in check. These include, first and foremost, artists, whose task, according to Aalto, is to provide a counterbalance to the simplifications that threaten common men. Their intuition gives them the ability to help their fellow men understand the complexity of life and thus to bring it under control.

This description is not altogether easy to apply to artists who adhere to various kinds of formal or philosophical simplifications, but it fits Aalto well. In his buildings and plans, he truly sought to fuse the whole spectrum of positive factors into a comprehensively satisfying architecture.

If this was the wisdom of the old Aalto, we may ask whether it was optimistic or pessimistic. The answer depends on the premise of the question. If one wishes to believe that mankind has made tremendous progress in our days and will continue to do so, it is naturally depressing to find Aalto saying that even though our technical discoveries, the spread of democracy, and the widely improved standard of living have solved many difficult problems and redressed many wrongs, these very solutions, through the effect of the human factor, have given rise to new, perhaps even more serious problems. Yet looking back at history, one may also find that the human condition and society have occasionally and in certain places been more humane than they seem today. A relative equilibrium is thus not out of the question – and this is basically an optimistic assessment of our chances.

It was an ordinary day in 1976. As usual, Aalto had gone after lunch to his office at Tiilimäki to take a look at the work in progress and to talk with his assistants about any problems that had arisen. He would spend the late morning home at Riihitie, sketching undisturbed in his beautiful pyjamas, and in the afternoon he would visit the office. He was busy as always, not working as intensely as before, but still with his life ahead. *It's enough to have talent for half an hour a day, for many don't have any even for one minute,* he would say.

The office had shrunk. There were far fewer designers at the desks than even one year before. The congress wing of the Finlandia Hall and the Rovaniemi Theatre had just been completed. The last redesign of the Essen Opera had been sent to Germany. The only continuing major project was Lahti Church; the other work was renovations and enlargements – the Technical Research Centre of Finland in Otaniemi, Jyväskylä University, and the endless serial story of the Paimio Sanatorium. He would thus have to get new major projects going – the city centre of Jyväskylä, Reykjavik University, or the concert hall in Jerusalem . . .

But on this ordinary day his future was taken away from him. When the burning pain around his heart started, he immediately felt that this was no temporary disorder. "Call an ambulance", was all he managed to gasp out. Meilahti Hospital is close to Munkkiniemi. There the leading Finnish heart specialist took charge, and immediately had him placed in intensive care in one of the terrifying machines that can keep one's heart and breathing going almost indefinitely.

The crisis passed, and after two weeks it seemed as though he might survive. When I visited him in hospital, the frightening machines had been moved into the corner of the room. Alvar lay in bed, freed from his fetters but very weak. "This is a lousy hotel", he grumbled and refused to discuss his illness. I got the impression that he seriously thought he was in a hotel abroad, as he had been so many times during his long life. We talked about spring, which was on the way, and of the possibility that he should go to incomparable Venice to recuperate. "I'm sure you'd like a glass of wine", he said and rang the bell. A nurse came in with two glasses of dark red liquid. "Cheers", said Alvar, "this is no great vintage, but for lack of anything better . . ."

I began to wonder: did he really take the hospital's insipid juice for wine? That is how it always was with him, one never knew whether he was joking or serious. The ability to transsubstantiate reality, to turn water into wine, is something he had always possessed.

Of course his friends hoped that he would recover from the heart attack, though we wondered how his pride would accommodate the humiliations and dependence on the help of others that prolonged illness brings. Was not this a role that was beyond his scope? Could he ever agree to stop working, to see

250. Alvar with Elissa in
his last years. Photo: Adam
Woolfitt.

his limit? Fortunately he was spared this ultimate test. Aalto died on May 11, 1976, and was interred in Hietaniemi graveyard, where his first wife Aino already lay buried, along with his architecture teacher Usko Nyström and his colleagues Ahto Virtanen and Uno Ullberg, whose tombstones he had designed. There lie many other acquaintances and friends, artists, learned men, and simple souls, keeping him company.

That is good; he never did want to be alone.

INDEX